365 Ways
to Cook Hamburger
and Other
Ground Meats

Rick Rodgers

A JOHN BOSWELL ASSOCIATES BOOK

HarperPaperbacks
A Division of HarperCollins*Publishers*

HarperPaperbacks *A Division of* HarperCollins*Publishers*
10 East 53rd Street, New York, N.Y. 10022

A hardcover edition of this book was published in 1992 by HarperCollins*Publishers*.

Series editor: Susan Wyler
Cover design and illustrations by Richard Rossiter
Text design by Nigel Rollings
Index by Maro Riofrancos

First HarperPaperbacks printing: August 1994

Printed in the United States of America

HarperPaperbacks and colophon are trademarks of HarperCollins*Publishers*

10 9 8 7 6 5 4 3 2 1

ATTENTION: ORGANIZATIONS AND CORPORATIONS

Contents

and cholesterol with healthy fresh vegetables. These garden greats include Warm Chicken and Basil Salad Bangkok, Szechuan Green Beans and Pork, Hill Country Four-Bean Bake, and Cabbage Rolls with Sauerkraut.

Introduction:
Making the Most of Ground Meat

Ground meats are a staple of the traditional American diet. They form the main ingredient of some of our country's favorite, most enduring recipes. What would All-American home cooking be without steaming slices of meatloaf, slathered with gravy ladled over a heap of mashed potatoes? How many grandmothers have lovingly served up their old-country versions of cabbage rolls stuffed with ground beef, veal, or pork? How many church socials and potluck dinner buffets have been graced by time-honored casseroles laced with ground meats? And where would the backyard barbecue be without sizzling, juicy burgers? *365 Ways to Cook Hamburger and Other Ground Meats* celebrates these American classics and offers many exciting new ideas for using flavorful, economical, versatile ground meats.

Shopping for ground meat used to mean one thing: hamburger. Indeed, ground beef still accounts for 45 percent of all the beef sold in the United States. But America's love affair with new flavors and a healthy, vital interest in good nutrition has given rise to a variety of ground meats never available before. Today's supermarket meat case boasts a huge variety of ground meats: at least three different kinds of beef, ground turkey, and ground chicken—the new, lighter ground meats— ground pork, ground veal, ground lamb, and meatloaf mixtures. Not to speak of a dizzying array of sausages. It's not just hamburger anymore.

The recipes in this book have been influenced by cooking from all over the world. Practically every cuisine has its own classic ground meat dish, from the complexities of Italian lasagne, French pâté, and Russian filled dumplings to the simplicity of American meatloaf and chili. Of course, ground meat's budget price and stretchability help boost its popularity. In most recipes, the cook gets at least four servings from a single pound of ground meat, and there's virtually no waste. Because ground meat is so adaptable, it can be seasoned with all kinds of herbs and spices, disguised, dressed up, and packaged in pastry or combined with all kinds of vegetables, beans, pasta, and whole grains. Because the meat is ground, many of these recipes are faster than comparable dishes made with large cuts of meat, and little attention is needed during the cooking process. Unlike other economical cuts, ground meats can be cooked quickly without marinating, trimming, or pounding at home.

With all the new ground meats available, the

temptation to the cook is simply to substitute one meat for
another, to use ground turkey in place of ground meat,
for example. Sometimes this works and sometimes it
doesn't. Using the right ground meat for the right recipe
is essential. Understanding how ground meats are
labeled, and what their different characteristics are in
terms of lean-to-fat ratio, texture, moisture, cooking time
and temperature, and so on will help you to make substi-
tutions wisely.

Recent improvements in labeling of ground
meats make it easier for consumers to choose the right
product for their dietary and culinary needs. The lean-to-
fat ratio, marked right on the label, shows the proportion
of lean meat to fat. In fact, this percentage has become so
popular that in many stores it has replaced traditional
labeling. Since round of beef, for example, averages about
15 percent fat, instead of being labeled as "ground
round," the package might read "ground beef—not less
than 85% lean." Sometimes both terms are used. Instead
of having to guess the relative fat content of each cut of
meat, the consumer can shop with confidence. These
lean-to-fat ratio guidelines are set by the USDA. Because
the poultry industry does not yet have established guidelines, it is necessary to read the individual manufacturers'
label for fat content when purchasing ground turkey or
ground chicken. It can vary significantly from brand to
brand.

There are cooking tricks that will help you
remove unwanted fat from ground meats. Many recipes
call for cooking the meat with aromatic vegetables in a
skillet before adding the mixture to the other ingredients.
Added fat is rarely needed; the mixture will cook in its
own juices, and in a few minutes the meat will be seared
so that it has lost its pink color, and the vegetables softened. When pre-cooking ground meat in this fashion,
never cook it until browned, or it will be dry, tough, and
tasteless. After this initial cooking, drain off all excess fat
before continuing with the recipe either by pouring the
fat out of the skillet, holding back the ingredients with a
large spoon and tilting the pan, or by draining the meat
mixture in a large strainer. Then the meat is seasoned. If
the herbs and spices are added in the beginning, they'll be
discarded with the fat.

While from a nutritional point of view many of
us are cutting down on saturated fat in our diets, it is a
fact of life that fat adds flavor and moisture to meat. As
the fat content drops, meat becomes less juicy and more
compact. This lost moisture can be replaced, however,
with the addition of flavorful ingredients, such as
ketchup, mustard, Worcestershire sauce, soy sauce, and,

of course, broth or milk. Texture can be improved by adding binders like oatmeal, bread crumbs, cracker crumbs, or stuffing mix crumbs. It is largely the difference in fat content that must be considered when you substitute one meat for another, as well as the temperature to which it must be cooked. Beef can be eaten rare, for example, while pork, turkey, and chicken must be cooked through with no trace of pink.

Following are descriptions of the different ground meats used in this book:

Ground Sirloin (Averages not less than 90 percent lean): While ground sirloin is appealing because of its low fat content, it is pricey and tends to be dry and crumbly. Use ground sirloin in recipes that contain vegetables and liquid, such as casseroles and pasta sauces to add moisture and flavor, but not calories.

Ground Round (Averages not less than 85 percent lean): This is my favorite all-purpose ground beef. It is juicy, flavorful, and moderately priced. Because it holds it shape well after cooking, ground round makes great meatloaves, fabulous burgers, and excellent meatballs. Always pour off any excess fat that may collect during cooking.

Ground Chuck (Averages not less than 80 percent lean): Ground chuck is perfect for recipes that call for the meat to be skillet-cooked before adding to other ingredients, such as casseroles and Mexican meat fillings for tacos, enchiladas, and burritos. I always drain off the fat from the skillet after searing meat. Unless you use a lot of binders like bread crumbs in your meat mixture, chuck won't hold its shape in meatloaves or meatballs as well as ground round.

Hamburger: This term is rarely used on labels anymore, although many people use the word casually to refer to any ground beef. Ground sirloin, ground round, and ground chuck are nothing but ground beef and the fat that is naturally found on the meat. Technically, hamburger is ground meat blended with additional fat, seasonings, and flavorings. These additives can supply up to 30% of the hamburger's weight. In fact, notice that hamburger is not marked "70% lean," in keeping with the other lean-to-fat ratios. The USDA says that meat products with over 25 percent fat cannot have the word *lean* on the label.

Ground Turkey: Many cooks are turning to ground turkey as a low-fat substitute for ground beef in many of their favorite recipes. The average fat content in top brands of ground turkey is as low as 7 percent. It is important to read the nutritional labels, though, because cheaper brands, especially frozen ground turkey packed in tubes, can reach as high as 15 percent fat, the same as ground chuck.

If you buy your ground turkey freshly prepared from a butcher, ask him for the fat content, or at least the cut he grinds up. White breast meat yields ground turkey with a lower fat content—and higher price tag—than dark meat. Many times a butcher will add some fat and skin for necessary moisture.

Ground turkey is exceptionally versatile, and it has a well-rounded flavor and firm texture. But because of its low fat content, it must be cooked properly, or it may dry out. Ground turkey is most successful in recipes that have liquid added, such as chilis and other stews, pasta sauces, and meatloaves. With a little care—and a little added moisture—ground turkey can make a great burger.

Unlike hamburger, ground turkey should be cooked over medium, rather than high or medium-high, heat to retain as many juices as possible. Never cook ground turkey less than medium-well done, however. The meat should be white, rather than pink, straight through to the center.

Ground Chicken: After the success of ground turkey, many poultry producers now offer ground chicken, which averages 10 percent fat. Its delicate flavor and tender texture are more subtle than ground turkey, but it takes well to strong seasonings, like Mexican and Mediterranean. It will remind you of ground veal, for which it can substitute. Like ground turkey, it works best in recipes with flavorful liquids added and moderate cooking temperatures. Never cook ground chicken less than medium-well done.

Ground Pork: There's an old farmhouse saying, "You can cook all of the pig except the 'oink.' " It certainly is a versatile ground meat, and mixes well with beef and veal to create many delectable dishes. If you want to control the amount of fat in your ground pork, ask the butcher to grind trimmed Boston or butt roast. I use ground pork to make homemade breakfast sausage patties, avoiding the preservatives, and excess sodium and fat of many commercial brands.

Meatloaf Blend: A combination of beef, pork, and veal makes a first-class meatloaf, and many butchers sell a 2-pound package of these meats in their proper proportions. Beef, the predominant flavor, makes up about 1 pound. Veal, lending its binding qualities, and pork, contributing moisture and flavor, are added in equal amounts of about ½ pound each. The butcher is also allowed to include binders like oatmeal or bread crumbs, if he wishes.

Ground Veal: There is no lean-to-fat ratio for ground veal, ground lamb, or ground pork, but they cannot be more than 30 percent fat, nor include any fillers or seasonings. Ground veal makes firm, juicy dishes, and it is a delicately flavored meat that can accept lots of seasoning. I like to mix it with heartier meats like beef and pork. It is a must for many pâtés, terrines, and meatloaves, as veal's natural gelatin content firms up the meat mixture, making it easier to slice. If your butcher doesn't have ground veal, ask him to grind a boneless veal shoulder roast or veal stew. Or grind it yourself in a food processor at home.

Ground Lamb: Ground lamb is readily available at meat markets with a Middle Eastern or Indian clientele. If your supermarket doesn't carry it, have the butcher grind trimmed boneless leg of lamb or lamb shoulder. It's important that the strong-tasting outside fat be well trimmed and discarded before grinding. Lean ground lamb can be used just like ground beef, with ground sirloin the closest substitute.

Don't worry too much about color changes in your ground beef or ground lamb. Unprocessed beef is normally deep purple in color. When ground and exposed to oxygen, it turns red, and eventually will take on a brownish tinge. This color change is called "bloom," and it is the reason why the outside of a block of ground beef (exposed to air) can be brownish, but the inside remains red. If your ground beef is light brown, it is a natural color change, and it is still good to eat. However, ground poultry should always be an appetizing pinkish color, with no hint of brown. Ground pork and ground veal are both relatively pale, and should appear pink; they are much more highly perishable than beef and should be cooked within a day of purchase.

Ground meat is highly perishable, and will only keep for 1 to 2 days in the coldest part of your refrigerator. Be sure to notice the "sell-by" date on the package. Buy only as much ground meat as you need for that period, and don't remove the plastic overwrap until you're ready to use the meat. (If it is wrapped in butcher paper, remove the paper and wrap tightly in plastic wrap.)

If you wish to freeze your ground meat, wrap it first in plastic wrap, then in aluminum foil. With an indelible pen, write what kind of meat it is, and the date. Ground meat keeps well in the freezer for up to 3 months.

Defrost frozen ground meat in the refrigerator, never at room temperature. It can take almost 24 hours to defrost completely, so I take it out of the freezer the night before the evening I plan to cook it. Ground meat can be successfully defrosted in the microwave. First remove the aluminum foil wrapping. For a pound of ground meat microwave on Medium-Low for 3 minutes, turn it over, and microwave for another 2 to 3 minutes, until defrosted. (Or follow Defrost instructions on your model.) If the outside edges of the meat start to cook, remove that portion and continue microwaving the remaining frozen meat until softened. Do not refreeze defrosted ground meat.

Chapter 1

Appetizers and Hors d'Oeuvres

Ground meats can be used creatively to produce an enticing array of first courses, appetizers, and pass-around hors d'oeuvres. And it may amaze you to see how many dozens of bite-size morsels just a pound of ground meat can produce.

There are hot hors d'oeuvres, such as Baked Turkey Balls with Zesty Cranberry Sauce, Five-Alarm Nachos, and Baked Italian Mushrooms with Ground Pork and Cheese Caps, and cold buffet dishes, such as Chicken and Chicken Liver Terrine. Many of these treats—Pork and Shrimp Steamed Dumplings, Chinese Pot Stickers, Fried Won Tons with Orange-Mustard Dipping Sauce, to name just a few— were inspired by my favorite Chinese dim sum, pop-in-your-mouth snacks. They are easy to prepare with ready-made egg roll and won ton wrappers, widely available in the produce, refrigerated, or frozen food section of most supermarkets.

Many of these recipes are perfect for entertaining, because they can be made well ahead. In fact, in the case of pâtés and terrines, they *must* be prepared in advance to allow them to mellow overnight. Chafing Dish Cocktail Meatballs can be baked in batches the day before, cooled, and refrigerated, then reheated in their sauce just before the party begins.

For a dinner party, several of these recipes can be arranged together on plates for a first course that's sure to be a conversation piece.

When planning your party menus, be sure to take a look at Chapter 13, It's a Wrap: Savory Pastries, on page 221, as well. Many of these savory pastries, such as the Spicy Lamb Samosas, can be made ahead, frozen, and baked at the last minute, for carefree entertaining.

1 FIVE-ALARM NACHOS

Prep: 5 minutes   Cook: 5 to 8 minutes   Serves: 4 to 6

Of course, it's the amount of pickled peppers sprinkled on top of the nachos that makes the number of alarms, so set your own pace.

1 cup Mexican Meat Filling, (page 212)	½ cup tomato salsa
6 ounces tortilla chips (½ a 12-ounce bag)	¼ cup sour cream Sliced pickled jalapeño peppers
1 cup shredded sharp Cheddar cheese	

1. Preheat oven to 400°. In a medium saucepan, cook meat filling over medium-low heat, stirring often, until hot. Spread half of tortilla chips over bottom of a 10-inch glass pie plate. Spoon ½ cup meat filling over tortilla chips and sprinkle on ½ cup cheese. Repeat with remaining chips, meat filling, and cheese.

2. Bake until cheese is melted, 5 to 8 minutes. Spoon dollops of salsa and sour cream over top and garnish with jalapeño slices. Serve immediately.

NOTE: *Nachos can also be cooked in a microwave. Microwave on High 1 minute, until cheese is melted.*

---

2 PORK AND SHRIMP STEAMED DUMPLINGS

Prep: 25 minutes   Cook: 12 minutes   Makes: 20 dumplings

½ pound medium shrimp, shelled and deveined	¼ teaspoon salt
½ pound ground pork	⅛ teaspoon pepper
1½ tablespoons soy sauce	¼ cup frozen peas, thawed
1 tablespoon dry sherry	20 round won ton or gyoza wrappers
1 teaspoon Asian sesame oil	Soy sauce, for dipping
¼ teaspoon sugar	

1. In a food processor, pulse shrimp until very finely chopped. Add ground pork, soy sauce, sherry, sesame oil, sugar, salt, and pepper; process until smooth. Transfer to a small bowl and stir in peas.

2. Place 1 tablespoon filling in center of 1 won ton wrapper and brush edges with cold water. Bring edges of wrapper up and pleat 4 or 5 times to form a little cup. Do not cover top of filling. Pinch dumpling slightly in middle to form a "waist" and tap on work surface to form a bottom. Transfer to a cornstarch-dusted baking sheet. Repeat procedure with remaining wrappers and filling.

3. Arrange a lightly oiled steaming rack in the bottom of a large saucepan or flameproof casserole. Add enough water to reach 1 inch below rack and bring to a full boil over high heat. Add dumplings to steamer, cover, reduce heat to medium-low, and steam until dumplings are cooked through, about 12 minutes. Serve warm with a small dish of soy sauce for dipping.

---

3 CURRIED CHICKEN SPRING ROLLS WITH PINEAPPLE DIP

Prep: 30 minutes   Cook: 27 minutes   Makes: About 50 spring rolls

This is a popular recipe I used when I was catering. It was inspired by a dish from Los Angeles's La Petite Chaya restaurant.

1 tablespoon butter	1 tablespoon curry powder
¼ cup vegetable oil	1 tablespoon flour
2 medium Granny Smith apples, peeled, cored, and finely chopped	½ cup heavy cream or evaporated milk
1 medium onion, finely chopped	50 won ton skins
2 garlic cloves, minced	1 cup pineapple or apricot preserves
2 teaspoons minced fresh ginger	1 tablespoon rice or cider vinegar
1 pound ground chicken	2 teaspoons soy sauce

1. Preheat oven to 375°. In a large skillet, melt butter in 2 tablespoons oil over medium heat. Add apples, onion, garlic, and ginger and cook, stirring often, until onion is softened, about 3 minutes. Add ground chicken and cook, stirring often to break up lumps of meat, until chicken loses its pink color, about 5 minutes. Drain off excess liquid. Sprinkle on curry powder and flour and cook, stirring, 1 minute. Add heavy cream and bring to a boil, stirring, until thickened, about 1 minute. Remove from heat and let filling cool completely.

2. Brush a large baking sheet with some of remaining oil. Place a won ton skin on a work surface, with the points at 12, 3, 6, and 9 o'clock. Place about 1½ teaspoons filling in center of skin. Fold in points at 3 and 9 o'clock, then roll up to form a cylinder. Place spring roll seam side down on baking sheet. Repeat procedure with remaining filling and skins. Brush spring rolls with remaining oil.

3. Bake spring rolls, turning once, until crisp and brown, about 15 minutes.

4. Meanwhile, in a small nonreactive saucepan, combine pineapple preserves, vinegar, and soy sauce. Bring to a simmer over medium heat and cook, stirring constantly, until smooth and melted, about 2 minutes. Serve spring rolls with pineapple sauce for dipping.

PORK-STUFFED MUSHROOMS CHINOISE
Prep: 10 minutes   Cook: 12 to 15 minutes   Serves: 6 to 8

24	large mushrooms (about ¾ pound total)
½	pound ground pork
1	scallion, minced
1½	teaspoons grated fresh ginger
1	garlic clove, minced
2	tablespoons soy sauce

2	tablespoons dry sherry
1	teaspoon cornstarch
1	egg white, lightly beaten
¼	teaspoon sugar
⅛	teaspoon crushed hot red pepper
½	cup beef broth
¼	cup chopped parsley

1. Remove stems from mushrooms and save for another use. In a medium bowl, combine ground pork, scallion, ginger, garlic, 1 tablespoon each soy sauce and sherry, cornstarch, egg white, sugar, and hot pepper.

2. Using a spoon, stuff mushrooms with ground pork mixture. Dip spoon in cold water and use to smooth top of stuffing in each mushroom into a dome.

3. In a 12-inch skillet, arrange mushrooms, stuffed sides up. Add beef broth and remaining 1 tablespoon each soy sauce and sherry. Bring liquid to a simmer over low heat, cover, and simmer until stuffing is cooked through and shows no trace of pink, 10 to 12 minutes. Transfer to serving plates, garnish with parsley, and drizzle pan juices over mushrooms.

5   GRAPE LEAVES WITH LAMB AND RICE FILLING
Prep: 30 minutes   Cook: 1 hour 5 minutes   Makes: About 3 dozen

1	(16-ounce) jar prepared grape leaves, drained
¾	cup long-grain white rice
¼	cup pine nuts (pignoli)
1	pound ground lamb
1	medium onion, finely chopped

3	medium scallions, chopped
1	teaspoon dried mint
¼	cup currants or raisins
3	tablespoons lemon juice
¾	teaspoon salt
¼	teaspoon pepper
2	tablespoons olive oil

1. In a large saucepan of boiling water, cook grape leaves for 1 minute. Drain, rinse well under cold water, and drain again. Sort through leaves, choosing largest for stuffing; reserve smaller leaves separately.

2. In a medium saucepan of lighlty salted boiling water, cook rice until just tender, about 10 minutes. Drain, rinse under cold water, and drain well.

3. In a dry medium skillet, toast pine nuts over medium heat, stirring often, until lightly browned, about 2 minutes. Transfer to a plate and reserve. In same skillet, cook ground lamb, onion, and scallions over medium-high heat, stirring often to break up meat, until lamb loses its pink color, about 5 minutes. Off heat, stir in rice, toasted pine nuts, mint, currants, 1 tablespoon lemon juice, salt, and pepper.

4. Line bottom of a 5- to 6-quart Dutch oven with about 10 of the smaller grape leaves. Place a large grape leave, veined side up, on a flat work surface. Place about 1 tablespoon lamb-rice filling in center of leaf, fold in sides, and roll up to form a cylinder. Repeat procedure with remaining leaves and filling. Arrange grape leaves, seam side down, packed closely together, in layers in prepared pan, separating layers with a few remaining small leaves. In a measuring cup, combine 1 cup water, remaining 2 tablespoons lemon juice and olive oil; pour over grape leaves.

5. Bring to a boil over medium heat, reduce heat to low, cover tightly, and simmer until liquid is almost completely absorbed, about 45 minutes. Let cool to room temperature before serving.

---

6   CHICKEN AND CHICKEN LIVER TERRINE
Prep: 20 minutes   Cook: 1 hour 50 minutes   Chill: Overnight
Serves: 6 to 8

2 tablespoons butter	½ cup heavy cream
1 medium onion, finely chopped	¼ cup brandy
3 shallots or scallions, minced	¼ cup packed parsley leaves
2 pounds ground chicken	2 eggs
1 pound chicken livers, trimmed	2½ teaspoons salt
1 cup fresh bread crumbs	½ teaspoon pepper
	½ teaspoon ground ginger
	¼ teaspoon ground allspice

1. Preheat oven to 350°. In a large skillet, melt butter. Add onion and shallots and cook over medium heat, stirring often, until onions are softened, about 5 minutes.

2. In a food processor, combine ground chicken, ¾ pound chicken livers, bread crumbs, cream, brandy, parsley, eggs, salt, pepper, ginger, and allspice. Puree until smooth, about 1 minute. Add onion and shallots and process 10 seconds.

3. Transfer half of chicken puree to a lightly oiled 9 x 5 x 3-inch loaf pan. Arrange remaining chicken livers on top and cover with remaining chicken puree. Cover tightly with foil and place in a baking pan large enough to hold loaf pan.

4. Place baking pan in oven and add enough boiling water to pan to reach 1 inch up sides of loaf pan. Bake until a meat thermometer inserted in center of loaf (through foil) reads 160°, about 1¾ hours. Remove loaf pan from baking pan and let cool completely with foil still in place.

5. Place loaf pan on a baking sheet. Place another loaf pan of same size filled with heavy cans on top of terrine to weight it down. Refrigerate overnight. Before serving, remove foil. Cut into slices directly from loaf pan, or unmold and wipe away congealed fat before slicing.

7 PORK AND SAUERKRAUT COCKTAIL NIBBLES

Prep: 20 minutes   Cook: 20 minutes   Makes: About 40 meatballs

For best results, use fresh packaged or bottled sauerkraut from the refrigerated deli section, and avoid canned varieties.

¾ cup saltine cracker crumbs	1 pound sauerkraut, rinsed
4 eggs	and chopped
2 tablespoons spicy brown	1 pound ground pork
mustard	2 cups finely crumbled fresh
1½ teaspoons caraway seeds	bread crumbs
½ teaspoon salt	4 tablespoons butter, melted
¼ teaspoon pepper	

1. Preheat oven to 375°. In a medium bowl, mix cracker crumbs, 2 eggs, mustard, caraway seeds, salt, and pepper until well blended. Add sauerkraut and pork and knead in bowl with hands until mixed. Using about 1 tablespoon for each, form into meatballs.

2. In a medium bowl, beat remaining 2 eggs until foamy. Place bread crumbs on a plate. One at a time, dip meatballs in eggs, then roll in bread crumbs to coat. Place on a lightly greased baking sheet.

3. Drizzle melted butter over meatballs. Bake, turning once, until golden brown, about 20 minutes. Serve warm with toothpicks.

---

8 BAKED ITALIAN MUSHROOMS WITH GROUND PORK AND CHEESE CAPS

Prep: 30 minutes   Stand: 20 minutes   Cook: 30 minutes
Serves: 6 to 8

1 ounce dried mushrooms,	½ pound ground pork
preferably porcini	½ teaspoon Italian seasoning
1 cup boiling water	½ teaspoon salt
24 large mushrooms (about	¼ teaspoon fennel seed,
12 ounces)	crushed
⅓ cup fresh bread crumbs	⅛ teaspoon crushed hot red
¼ cup milk	pepper
2 tablespoons olive oil	2 ounces Italian fontina or
¼ cup minced onion	mozzarella cheese, thinly
2 garlic cloves, minced	sliced

1. In a small bowl, soak dried mushrooms in boiling water until softened, about 20 minutes. Lift out soaked mushrooms and strain liquid through paper towel–lined sieve; reserve soaking liquid. Rinse soaked mushrooms well under cold running water to remove any hidden grit. Chop coarsely.

2. Preheat oven to 350°. Remove stems from fresh mushrooms and chop one half of stems. Discard remaining stems or save for another use. In a medium bowl, combine bread crumbs and milk. Set aside.

3. In a large skillet, heat oil. Add onion and cook over medium heat, stirring often, until softened, 2 to 3 minutes. Add garlic, chopped mushroom stems, soaked mushrooms, and reserved mushroom soaking liquid. Increase heat to high and boil until liquid has entirely evaporated, 7 to 9 minutes. Stir mushroom mixture into soaked bread crumbs.

4. Add ground pork, Italian seasoning, salt, fennel, and hot pepper and knead to mix well. Using a spoon, stuff mushrooms with ground pork mixture. Dip spoon in cold water and use to smooth top of stuffing in each mushroom into a dome.

5. Cut cheese into 24 squares to fit tops of stuffed mushrooms. Arrange mushrooms in a lighlty oiled 9 x 13-inch baking dish. Bake until cheese is melted and golden brown, 15 to 20 minutes. Transfer mushrooms to individual plates, drizzle juices over tops, and serve hot.

---

9 PORK AND RICE STICK DIM SUM
Prep: 20 minutes   Cook: 15 minutes   Makes: About 18 meatballs

Don't confuse rice sticks *(mai fun)* with bean threads *(sai fun)*, as they look alike. Rice sticks are sometimes labeled "long rice" or "rice vermicelli."

4 ounces rice sticks	**2¼ teaspoons hot chili oil**
1 pound ground pork	**¼ teaspoon sugar**
1 teaspoon minced fresh ginger	**½ cup flour**
2 garlic cloves, minced	**2 eggs**
¼ cup plus 2 tablespoons soy sauce	**Vegetable oil, for deep-frying**
½ teaspoon salt	**2 tablespoons rice vinegar**

1. In a large saucepan of boiling salted water, cook rice sticks until tender, about 3 minutes. Drain well, rinse under cold water, and drain again. Coarsely chop rice noodles and place on a plate.

2. In a medium bowl, combine ground pork, ginger, garlic, 2 tablespoons soy sauce, salt, ¼ teaspoon hot oil, and sugar. Using about 1 tablespoon for each, form mixture into meatballs.

3. Place flour on a plate. In a small bowl, beat eggs well. Dredge meatballs in flour and shake off excess. Dip meatballs in beaten eggs, then roll in rice noodles, pressing noodles to adhere. Transfer meatballs to a wax paper–lined baking sheet.

4. Preheat oven to 200°. Fill a deep-fryer halfway with vegetable oil and heat to 375°. In batches, without crowding, deep-fry meatballs until golden brown, about 5 minutes. With a slotted spoon, transfer cooked meatballs to a paper towel–lined baking sheet and keep warm in oven. (Reheat oil to 375° before deep-frying each batch.)

5. In a small bowl, stir together remaining ¼ cup soy sauce, rice vinegar, and remaining 2 teaspoons hot oil. Serve as a dipping sauce for warm meatballs.

10 MEATBALLS BARCELONA
Prep: 15 minutes   Cook: 20 minutes   Makes: About 32 meatballs

1 cup fresh bread crumbs	½ pound ground pork
1 egg	¼ pound smoked ham, finely
2 garlic cloves, minced	chopped
1 teaspoon paprika	32 pimiento-stuffed olives
¾ teaspoon salt	2 tablespoons olive oil
⅛ teaspoon pepper	½ cup dry white wine
½ pound ground round (85% lean)	

1. In a medium bowl, combine bread crumbs, egg, garlic, paprika, salt, and pepper. Add ground round, ground pork, and ham; mix well.

2. Using about 1 tablespoon of meat mixture for each, form into meatballs. Flatten a meatball slightly, place an olive in center, and reroll into a ball, completely enclosing olive. Repeat procedure with remaining meatballs and olives.

3. In a large skillet, heat olive oil. Add meatballs and cook over medium-high heat, turning often, until browned all over.

4. Add wine and bring to a boil. Reduce heat to low, partially cover, and simmer until meatballs are cooked through, about 10 minutes. Serve hot, warm, or at room temperature.

11 BEEF AND EGGPLANT LOAF
Prep: 10 minutes   Cook: 2¾ hours   Chill: 4 hours   Serves: 6 to 8

The cooking time here is mostly unattended, so don't let the long estimate deter you from creating this excellent terrine.

1 medium eggplant (about 1 pound)	½ teaspoon pepper
1½ cups fresh bread crumbs	1 pound ground round (85% lean)
½ cup grated Parmesan cheese	1 pound lean ground lamb
⅓ cup dry red wine	1 (4-ounce) jar roasted red
2 eggs	peppers, drained and
2 teaspoons Italian seasoning	rinsed
2 teaspoons salt	

1. Preheat oven to 475°. Place eggplant on a lightly oiled baking sheet. Bake, turning once, until eggplant is very tender and skin is darkened, about 45 minutes. Let cool. Halve eggplant, scoop out cooked insides, and coarsely chop; discard eggplant skin.

2. In a large bowl, combine bread crumbs, grated cheese, wine, eggs, Italian seasoning, salt, and pepper. Blend well. Add chopped eggplant, ground round, and ground lamb. Knead with your hands until mixed.

3. Reduce oven temperatures to 350°. Transfer half of meat-eggplant mixture to a lightly oiled 9 x 5 x 3-inch loaf pan. Arrange roasted peppers in a single layer over meat mixture, then cover with remaining meat mixture. Cover tightly with foil and place on a baking sheet.

4. Bake until a meat thermometer inserted in center of loaf (through foil) reads 160°, about 2 hours. Let cool completely.

5. Pour off juices, unmold, wrap completely in foil, and refrigerate at least 4 hours, or overnight. Cut into slices to serve.

---

12 FRIED WON TONS WITH ORANGE-MUSTARD DIPPING SAUCE

Prep: 25 minutes   Cook: 5 minutes   Makes: 40 won tons

1 **pound ground pork**	¼ **teaspoon salt**
1 **tablespoon minced fresh**	¼ **teaspoon pepper**
ginger	40 **won ton wrappers**
1 **scallion, minced**	**Vegetable oil, for frying**
1 **tablespoon soy sauce**	**Orange-Mustard Dipping**
1 **tablespoon dry sherry**	**Sauce (recipe follows)**
½ **teaspoon sugar**	

1. In a medium bowl, combine ground pork, ginger, scallion, soy sauce, sherry, sugar, salt, and pepper. Blend well.

2. Brush edges of 1 won ton wrapper with cold water. Place 1 teaspoon of filling in center of wrapper. Fold one corner of wrapper over to opposite corner, enclosing filling in a triangle shape. Press edges of wrapper to seal filling. Transfer won ton to a cornstarch-dusted baking sheet. Repeat procedure with remaining wrappers and filling.

3. In a large skillet, pour enough oil to reach 1 inch up sides of skillet. Heat oil until hot but not smoking. (An electric skillet set at 375° works best.) In batches, fry won tons until golden brown, about 1 minute. Transfer won tons to paper towels to drain. Serve with warm Orange-Mustard Dipping Sauce.

ORANGE-MUSTARD DIPPING SAUCE
Makes about 1 cup

1 **cup orange marmalade**	1 **tablespoon rice or white**
1 **tablespoon prepared**	**vinegar**
Chinese or Dijon mustard	2 **teaspoons soy sauce**

In a small saucepan, cook marmalade, mustard, vinegar, and soy sauce over low heat, stirring, until melted and smooth, 1 to 2 minutes.

13 BAKED TURKEY BALLS WITH ZESTY CRANBERRY SAUCE

Prep: 20 minutes   Cook: 25 minutes   Makes: About 64 meatballs

1 large onion, minced	2½ pounds ground turkey
2 cups dry herb-seasoned stuffing mix, crushed	1 (16-ounce) can jellied cranberry sauce
2 eggs	3 tablespoons ketchup
Grated zest of 2 limes	2 tablespoons honey
2 teaspoons salt	2 tablespoons lime juice
½ teaspoon pepper	

1. Preheat oven to 350°. In a large bowl, combine onion, stuffing crumbs, eggs, lime zest, salt, and pepper. Add ground turkey and mix well.

2. Using about 1 tablespoon for each, form into meatballs and place on lightly oiled baking sheets.

3. Bake, turning once, until browned and cooked through, about 20 minutes.

4. Meanwhile, in a medium nonreactive saucepan, combine cranberry sauce, ketchup, honey, and lime juice. Bring to a simmer over medium heat and cook, stirring constantly, until smooth and melted, about 2 minutes. Serve meatballs with warm cranberry sauce for dipping.

14 PHILIPPINE CHICKEN AND VEGETABLE ROLLS

Prep: 30 minutes   Cook: 10 minutes   Makes: 14 rolls

Practically every Asian cuisine seems to have a variation on the egg roll theme. Try these flavorful appetizers, served with an unusual sweet garlic dipping sauce.

½ cup distilled white vinegar	1 small onion, thinly sliced
2 tablespoons sugar	½ medium head of Chinese (napa) cabbage, shredded (4 cups)
4 garlic cloves, minced	
¼ teaspoon crushed hot red pepper	2 tablespoons soy sauce
2 tablespoons vegetable oil	1 teaspoon salt
¾ pound ground pork or ground chicken	¼ teaspoon pepper
2 celery ribs, sliced ⅛ inch thick	14 egg roll sheets, 6½ inches square
1 medium carrot, grated	Vegetable oil, for deep-frying

1. In a small nonreactive saucepan, combine vinegar, sugar, 2 minced garlic cloves, and hot pepper. Bring to a simmer over low heat, stirring constantly to dissolve sugar. Pour garlic sauce into a small bowl and let cool completely.

2. In a wok or large skillet, heat 1 tablespoon oil over high heat until hot. Add ground pork and stir-fry over medium-high heat until meat is no longer pink, about 2 minutes.

3. Add celery, carrot, onion, and remaining garlic to wok. Stir-fry vegetables, gradually adding a handful of cabbage at a time, until all cabbage has been added and wilts, about 3 minutes. Add soy sauce, salt, and pepper and stir-fry 1 minute. Drain mixture in a colander, discarding juices; let cool completely.

4. Place 1 egg roll sheet on a flat surface, with points at 12, 3, 6, and 9 o'clock. Place about 2 tablespoons cooled filling in center of egg roll sheet. Fold in points at 3 and 9 o'clock, then roll up sheet to form a cylinder, moistening top point with a little water to adhere. Repeat procedure with remaining sheets and filling.

5. Preheat oven to 200°. Line a baking sheet with paper towels. In a wok or large skillet, heat 1 inch of vegetable oil until very hot but not smoking, 350°. Deep-fry rolls in batches, turning once, until golden brown, about 2 minutes per batch. With a slotted spoon, transfer fried rolls to prepared baking sheets to drain and keep warm in oven. Serve with sweet garlic sauce for dipping.

---

15 CHINESE POT STICKERS
Prep: 25 minutes   Cook: 12 minutes   Makes: 24 dumplings

½ pound ground pork
¾ cup finely chopped Chinese (napa) cabbage
1 scallion, minced
2 teaspoons minced fresh ginger
1 garlic clove, minced
1 tablespoon soy sauce
1 tablespoon dry sherry

¼ teaspoon salt
24 round won ton or gyoza wrappers
2 tablespoons vegetable oil
1 cup reduced-sodium chicken broth
Soy sauce, rice vinegar, and hot chili oil

1. In a medium bowl, mix ground pork, cabbage, scallion, ginger, garlic, soy sauce, sherry, and salt.

2. Place 1 tablespoon of filling in center of 1 wrapper; brush edges of wrapper with cold water. Bring edges of wrapper up to meet in center above filling; pinch and pleat closed. Transfer to a cornstarch-dusted baking sheet, standing up on plump filled side. Repeat procedure with remaining wrappers and filling.

3. In a large nonstick skillet, heat oil until hot but not smoking. Add dumplings, reduce heat to medium, and cook until undersides are browned, about 2 minutes. Increase heat to medium-high, add broth, and cover tightly. Boil until liquid has almost completely evaporated, about 8 minutes. Remove cover and cook until liquid is evaporated and dumplings are sizzling, about 2 minutes. Serve immediately, letting guests choose their own proportions of soy sauce, vinegar, and hot oil for dipping.

16 PEARL BALLS

Prep: 15 minutes   Stand: 3 hours   Cook: 30 minutes
Makes: About 22 meatballs

⅔ cup long-grain white rice (*not* converted)	1 tablespoon dry sherry
1 pound ground pork	1 teaspoon Asian sesame oil
½ cup water chestnuts, finely chopped	1 teaspoon minced ginger
1 scallion, minced	½ teaspoon sugar
¼ cup soy sauce	¼ teaspoon salt
	¼ teaspoon pepper

1. In a small bowl, combine rice and enough cold water to cover rice by 1 inch. Let stand 3 hours. Drain well and place rice on a plate.

2. In a medium bowl, combine ground pork, water chestnuts, scallion, 1 tablespoon soy sauce, sherry, sesame oil, ginger, sugar, salt, and pepper.

3. Using about 1 tablespoon of meat mixture for each, roll into small meatballs. Roll meatballs in rice to coat.

4. Place a steamer rack in a large saucepan. Add enough water to come ½ inch below steamer. Place meatballs in a single layer in steamer and bring to a boil over high heat. Reduce heat to low and steam for 30 minutes, or until rice is tender and meatballs are cooked through. Serve pearl balls with remaining 3 tablespoons soy sauce for dipping.

17 HERBED PATE VERTE

Prep: 15 minutes   Freeze: 30 minutes   Cook: 1½ hours
Chill: Overnight   Serves: 6 to 8

¼ pound fatback or other firm white pork fat, cubed	¼ cup Madeira or brandy
12 slices of bacon	¼ cup chopped parsley
2 tablespoons butter	2 eggs
1 medium onion, finely chopped	2 teaspoons salt
1 garlic clove, minced	½ teaspoon thyme
1 (10-ounce) package frozen chopped spinach, thawed and squeezed dry	¼ teaspoon ground allspice
	¼ teaspoon pepper
¾ cup fresh bread crumbs	Pinch of ground cloves
	1 pound ground veal
	1 pound ground pork
	2 bay leaves

1. Preheat oven to 350°. Place fat on a baking sheet and freeze until partially frozen, about 30 minutes. In a food processor, process fat until pureed; set aside.

2. Place bacon in a large saucepan and add cold water to cover. Bring to a boil over medium heat and cook 5 minutes. Drain, rinse under cold water, and drain again. Line bottom and sides of a 9 x 5 x 3-inch loaf pan with 6 bacon slices.

3. In a large skillet, melt butter over medium heat. Add onion and garlic and cook, stirring often, until onion is softened, about 5 minutes. Add spinach and cook, stirring often, until spinach is dry, about 2 minutes. Transfer mixture to a large bowl.

4. Add bread crumbs, Madeira, parsley, eggs, salt, thyme, allspice, pepper, and cloves to bowl. Mix until blended. Add pureed fat and ground veal and pork and mix to blend well. Spoon pâté mixture into bacon-lined pan. Place bay leaves and remaining bacon strips on top, trimming if necessary. Cover tightly with foil and place in a baking pan large enough to hold loaf pan.

5. Place baking pan in oven and add enough boiling water to reach 1 inch up sides of loaf pan. Bake until a meat thermometer inserted in center of pâté (through foil) reads 160°, about 1¼ hours. Remove loaf pan from baking pan and let cool completely, still covered with foil.

6. Place loaf pan on a baking sheet. Place another loaf pan of same size filled with heavy cans on top of pâté to weight it down. Refrigerate overnight. Before serving, remove foil and bay leaves. To serve, cut into slices directly from loaf pan, or unmold and wipe away any congealed juices before slicing.

---

18 TURKEY PATE PROVENCALE
Prep: 20 minutes   Cook: 1¼ hours   Chill: 4 hours   Serves: 6 to 8

1 medium onion, finely chopped	1½ teaspoons salt
2 garlic cloves, minced	1 teaspoon herbes de Provence (see Note)
1 cup fresh bread crumbs	½ teaspoon pepper
½ cup chopped black olives	1½ pounds ground turkey
¼ cup milk	½ pound ground pork
2 eggs	
Grated zest of 1 small orange	
¼ cup chopped fresh basil or 1 teaspoon dried basil mixed with ¼ cup chopped parsley	

1. Preheat oven to 350°. In a medium bowl, combine onion, garlic, bread crumbs, chopped olives, milk, eggs, orange zest, basil, salt, herbes de Provence, and pepper. Add ground turkey and ground pork and mix well. Transfer to a lightly oiled 9 x 5 x 3-inch loaf pan. Cover tightly with foil.

2. Bake until a meat thermometer inserted in center of loaf (through foil) reads 160°, about 1¼ hours. Let cool completely.

3. Pour off juices, unmold pâté, wrap completely in foil, and refrigerate at least 4 hours, or overnight. Cut into slices to serve.

NOTE: *Herbes de Provence is a mixture of dried thyme, basil, fennel seed, rosemary, marjoram, and lavender available at many supermarkets and specialty stores. If it's not available, mix ¼ teaspoon each of thyme, basil, rosemary, and marjoram with a pinch of ground fennel.*

19   BAKED PORK AND CRAB SPHERES

Prep: 15 minutes   Cook: 20 minutes   Makes: About 28

½ cup minced carrots
½ cup minced celery
½ pound ground pork
½ pound crabmeat, coarsely
       chopped
1 scallion, minced
1 tablespoon minced fresh
       ginger
1 garlic clove, minced
2 tablespoons dried bread
       crumbs

1 tablespoon soy sauce
1 teaspoon Asian sesame oil
1 teaspoon cornstarch
½ teaspoon salt
¼ teaspoon pepper
   Duck sauce and hot
       prepared Chinese
       mustard, for dipping

1. Preheat oven to 375°. In a medium saucepan of boiling salted water, cook carrots and celery until crisp-tender, about 1 minute. Drain, rinse under cold water, and drain again.

2. In a medium bowl, combine ground pork, crabmeat, carrots and celery, scallion, ginger, garlic, bread crumbs, soy sauce, sesame oil, cornstarch, salt, and pepper. Using about 1 tablespoon for each, form into meatballs and transfer to a lightly greased baking sheet.

3. Bake meatballs, turning once, 20 to 25 minutes, or until browned and cooked through. Serve warm with duck sauce and hot mustard for dipping.

20   CHINATOWN PORK AND SHRIMP EGG ROLLS

Prep: 30 minutes   Cook: 10 minutes   Makes: 14 egg rolls

To be sure they don't get oil-logged, keep your oil temperature constant. An electric skillet is a great way to assure good deep-frying results.

2 tablespoons soy sauce
2 tablespoons dry sherry
½ teaspoon sugar
½ teaspoon salt
2 teaspoons cornstarch
2 tablespoons beef broth
3 tablespoons vegetable oil
½ pound peeled and deveined
       medium shrimp (thawed
       and well drained, if
       frozen), chopped
3 celery ribs, sliced ⅛ inch
       thick
1 small onion, sliced

5 ounces fresh mushrooms,
       sliced
½ cup sliced water chestnuts,
       drained
1 cup fresh bean sprouts
       (about 4 ounces)
½ pound ground pork or
       ground chicken
14 egg roll sheets, 6½ inches
       square
   Vegetable oil, for deep-
       frying
   Chinese mustard and/or
       duck sauce, for dipping

1. In a small bowl, combine soy sauce, sherry, sugar, and salt. In another bowl, dissolve cornstarch in broth. Set both bowls aside.

2. In a wok or large skillet, heat 2 tablespoons oil over high heat until hot. Add shrimp and stir-fry just until shrimp turn pink, about 45 seconds. Remove with a slotted spoon to a plate.

3. Add celery, onion, mushrooms, and water chestnuts to wok and stir-fry until onion is softened, about 2 minutes. Add bean sprouts and stir-fry until heated through, 1 minute. Remove to plate with shrimp.

4. Heat remaining 1 tablespoon oil in same wok until hot. Add ground pork and stir-fry until meat is no longer pink, about 2 minutes. Return shrimp and vegetables to wok. Add soy sauce mixture and stir-fry for 1 minute. Add cornstarch mixture and cook until liquid is almost completely evaporated. Let filling cool completely.

5. Place 1 egg roll sheet on a flat surface, with points at 12, 3, 6, and 9 o'clock. Place about 2 tablespoons cooled filling in center of egg roll sheet. Fold in points at 3 and 9 o'clock, then roll up sheet to form a cylinder, moistening top point with a little water to adhere. Repeat procedure with remaining sheets and filling.

6. Preheat oven to 200°. Line a baking sheet with paper towels. In a wok or large skillet, heat 1 inch vegetable oil until very hot but not smoking, 350°. Deep-fry egg rolls in batches, turning once, until golden brown, about 2 minutes per batch. With a slotted spoon, transfer fried egg rolls to prepared baking sheets to drain and keep warm in oven. Serve with Chinese mustard and/or duck sauce for dipping.

---

21 CHAFING DISH COCKTAIL MEATBALLS

Prep: 15 minutes   Cook: 12 to 15 minutes   Makes: About 4 dozen

¾ cup saltine cracker crumbs	1 small onion, minced
1 egg	1 small red bell pepper, minced
1 (15-ounce) bottle chili sauce	
Grated zest of 1 medium lemon	¾ cup grape jelly
	3 tablespoons lemon juice
1½ teaspoons garlic salt	¼ teaspoon crushed hot red pepper
¼ teaspoon pepper	
2 pounds ground round (85% lean)	

1. Preheat oven to 375°. In a large bowl, combine cracker crumbs, egg, 3 tablespoons chili sauce, lemon zest, garlic salt, and pepper. Stir with a fork until mixed. Add ground round, onion, and minced red pepper and mix until blended. Using about 1 teaspoon of mixture for each, form into small meatballs. Arrange meatballs in a single layer on a baking sheet.

2. Bake until lightly browned and cooked through, 12 to 15 minutes. Drain off excess fat.

3. Meanwhile, in a medium nonreactive saucepan, combine grape jelly, remaining chili sauce, lemon juice, and hot pepper. Cook over medium heat, stirring often, until jelly melts and sauce is simmering. In a chafing dish, combine meatballs and sauce. Serve warm with toothpicks.

Chapter 2

Hearty Soups and Chowders

Nothing brightens up a chilly, gray day like a big, steaming hot bowl of soup. Served with a green salad and a loaf of crusty bread, a chunky soup becomes a meal in a pot. For dinner parties, soup is a great beginning, because it almost invariably can be made in advance, and only requires a quick reheating just before the meal. And kids seem to love foods they can eat with a spoon.

Using meat in your soup means you're going to get an abundance of deep flavor in every spoonful. Choosing ground meat rather than a large cut or lots of bones not only means lack of waste and economy, but the flavor will be drawn into the broth in a fraction of the time. Making soup from scratch is easy these days, with excellent convenience products, such as the reduced-sodium chicken broth that is now available in supermarkets across the country.

Variety abounds in this chapter, from the delicate creamed Velvety Corn and Chicken Soup to the substantial Alpine Leek, Potato, and Turkey Soup, perfect for after-ski revival. There are Asian specialties, such as Hot and Sour Soup Saigon and Won Ton Soup, and well-loved ethnic heritage recipes done with a slight twist, such as Sweet-and-Sour Borscht with Dilled Meatballs and Grandma's Chicken Soup with Chicken Matzoh Balls. Hearty pea and bean soups—Lamb and Lentil Soup Casbah and Split Pea Soup with Bacon Meatballs, for example—have not been neglected. Most of these recipes make plenty, so you can serve some now and freeze the rest for a day when you're too busy to cook.

22　FOUR LILIES SIRLOIN SOUP

Prep: 15 minutes　Cook: 1 hour 10 minutes　Serves: 6

Garlic, onion, scallions, and leeks are all aromatic members of the lily family. Long simmering reduces their aggressiveness significantly and melds their flavors into a lovely golden soup.

3　tablespoons butter	6½　cups beef stock or canned
2　large onions, sliced	broth
2　large leeks (white and	½　cup dry white wine
tender green) well	1　bay leaf
cleaned and chopped	1　teaspoon salt
4　garlic cloves, minced	½　teaspoon pepper
1　pound ground sirloin	2　scallions, chopped
(90% lean)	
¼　cup flour	

1. In a large saucepan or Dutch oven, melt butter. Add onions, leeks, and garlic. Cover and cook over low heat, stirring often, until onions are very soft and golden brown, 15 to 20 minutes.

2. Add ground sirloin, increase heat to medium, and cook, stirring often to break up lumps of meat, until beef loses its pink color, about 5 minutes.

3. Sprinkle in flour and cook, stirring constantly, 1 minute. Stir in stock, wine, bay leaf, salt, and pepper. Bring to a boil over high heat, skimming to remove fat and foam from surface. Reduce heat to low and simmer 45 minutes. Remove bay leaf and serve in individual bowls, garnished with chopped scallions.

23　ESCAROLE AND MEATBALL SOUP

Prep: 20 minutes　Cook: 30 minutes　Serves: 6 to 8

1　large head escarole (about	¼　cup grated Parmesan cheese
1¼ pounds)	¼　cup fresh bread crumbs
2　quarts chicken stock or	2　tablespoons chopped
reduced-sodium canned	parsley
broth	1　garlic clove, minced
½　teaspoon pepper	½　teaspoon salt
1　pound ground sirloin (90%	2　eggs, well beaten
lean) or ground round	
(85% lean)	

1. Cut escarole crosswise into 1-inch-wide strips, discarding thick stem ends. Plunge escarole into a sink or large bowl filled with cold water and swirl to remove hidden sand and dirt. Let stand in water 5 minutes. Lift escarole from water, and transfer to a large colander to drain.

2. In a large saucepan or Dutch oven, cook escarole with ½ cup water over medium heat, covered, stirring occasionally, until wilted, 5 to 7 minutes. Drain, rinse under cold water, and drain again. Coarsely chop escarole.

3. In same pot, combine chicken stock, escarole, and ¼ teaspoon pepper. Bring to a boil over high heat, reduce heat to low, and simmer for 10 minutes.

4. Meanwhile, in a medium bowl, combine ground sirloin, Parmesan cheese, bread crumbs, parsley, garlic, salt, and remaining ¼ teaspoon pepper. Knead with your hands in bowl until well blended. Using about 2 teaspoons for each, form meat mixture into small meatballs, dropping as formed into simmering soup. Partially cover and simmer until meatballs are cooked through, 10 to 12 minutes.

5. Stirring soup, slowly pour in beaten eggs. Simmer until eggs have set into ribbons, about 2 minutes.

---

24 SWEET-AND-SOUR BORSCHT WITH DILLED MEATBALLS

Prep: 20 minutes   Cook: 1 hour 10 minutes   Serves: 6

2 tablespoons vegetable oil	½ small head of cabbage, thinly sliced (about 8 ounces)
1 medium onion, chopped	
2 medium carrots, chopped	
2 garlic cloves, minced	1 egg
2 (13¾-ounce) cans beef broth	1 scallion, minced
1 (14-ounce) can Italian peeled tomatoes, with their juice	1 tablespoon chopped fresh dill or 1½ teaspoons dried
¼ cup red wine vinegar	1 pound ground round (85% lean) or ground sirloin (90% lean)
4 teaspoons brown sugar	
1¾ teaspoons salt	
½ teaspoon pepper	Sour cream (optional)
4 medium beets, well scrubbed, cut into ½-inch cubes	

1. In a 6-quart saucepan or flameproof casserole, heat oil over medium heat. Add onion, carrots, and garlic. Cover and cook, stirring occasionally, until onion is softened, about 5 minutes. Add beef broth, tomatoes with their juice, vinegar, brown sugar, 1 teaspoon salt, ¼ teaspoon pepper, and 1½ cups water. Increase heat to high and bring to a boil. Add beets, reduce heat to low, and simmer, partially covered, until beets are almost tender, 40 to 45 minutes. Add cabbage and cook, partially covered, 10 minutes.

2. Meanwhile, in a medium bowl, combine egg, scallion, dill, and remaining ¾ teaspoon salt and ¼ teaspoon pepper. Beat with a fork until mixed. Add ground round and mix until blended.

3. Using 1 tablespoon of meat mixture for each, form 16 meatballs, dropping each meatball as formed into simmering soup. Cover soup and cook until meatballs are just cooked through, about 10 minutes. Serve soup immediately, garnished with sour cream, if desired.

25   ORIENTAL MEATBALL SOUP
Prep: 10 minutes   Cook: 25 to 30 minutes   Serves: 6 to 8

1   pound ground pork
1   egg, lightly beaten
3   scallions—1 minced,
      2 sliced
2   garlic cloves—1 minced,
      1 crushed
2   teaspoons minced fresh
      ginger plus 3 slices fresh
      ginger

1   tablespoon soy sauce
1   teaspoon Asian sesame oil
¾   teaspoon salt
¼   teaspoon pepper
2   quarts chicken stock or
      reduced-sodium canned
      broth
1   (16-ounce) frozen package
      mixed Oriental
      vegetables

1. In a medium bowl, combine ground pork, egg, minced scallion, minced garlic, minced ginger, soy sauce, sesame oil, salt, and pepper. Blend well. Set meat mixture aside.

2. In a large Dutch oven or soup kettle, bring chicken stock, sliced ginger, and crushed garlic to a boil over medium heat. Reduce heat to low, partially cover, and simmer 15 minutes. Using a slotted spoon, remove ginger slices and garlic from stock and discard.

3. Add frozen vegetables to soup and return to a boil. Drop heaping tea-spoonfuls of meat mixture into soup and simmer until meatballs are cooked through, 10 to 15 minutes. Serve hot, garnished with sliced scallions.

---

26   SPLIT PEA SOUP WITH BACON MEATBALLS
Prep: 15 minutes   Stand: 1 hour   Cook: 1¼ hours   Serves: 6 to 8

1   pound dried split peas
4   strips bacon, cut into 1-inch
      pieces
1   medium onion, chopped
1   medium carrot, chopped
1   celery rib, chopped
1   quart chicken stock or
      reduced-sodium canned
      broth

2   medium red potatoes, cut
      into ½-inch cubes
1½   teaspoons salt
1   teaspoon marjoram
1   bay leaf
¾   teaspoon pepper
1   pound lean ground pork
1   egg, lightly beaten
1   teaspoon sage

1. In a large saucepan, bring split peas and 1 quart water to a boil over high heat; cook 2 minutes. Remove from heat, cover tightly, and let stand 1 hour. Drain, reserving soaking liquid.

2. In a large soup kettle or Dutch oven, cook bacon over medium heat until crisp, about 4 minutes. Using a slotted spoon, transfer bacon to paper towels to drain, leaving fat in pot.

3. Add onion, carrot, and celery to bacon fat in pot. Cook over medium heat, stirring often, until onion is lightly browned, about 6 minutes. Add soaked peas with reserved soaking liquid, chicken stock, potatoes, and 2 cups water. Bring to a boil over medium-high heat, skimming often. Add ¾ teaspoon salt, marjoram, bay leaf, and ½ teaspoon pepper. Reduce heat to low and simmer until peas are tender, about 45 minutes.

4. Meanwhile, crumble cooked bacon. In a medium bowl, combine ground pork, bacon, egg, sage, remaining ¾ teaspoon salt, and ¼ teaspoon pepper. Using about 1 tablespoon for each, form meat mixture into meatballs, dropping as formed into simmering soup. Simmer until meatballs are cooked through with no trace of pink in center, 12 to 15 minutes.

---

27 HUNGARIAN PORK, EGGPLANT, AND PEPPER SOUP

Prep: 15 minutes Stand: 30 minutes Cook: 1 hour 35 minutes
Serves: 8 to 12

If you wish to make this soup even more substantial, include ½ pound red potatoes, cubed, to simmer along with the vegetables, or add 1½ cups elbow macaroni after 1 hour of cooking.

1 medium eggplant (about 1 pound)	3 tablespoons paprika, preferably sweet Hungarian
2 teaspoons salt	
6 slices of bacon, chopped	1 (35-ounce) can Italian peeled tomatoes, with their juice
1 large onion, chopped	
2 medium Italian frying peppers or green bell peppers, chopped	2 (13¾-ounce) cans beef broth
	1 teaspoon savory
	1 teaspoon celery salt
1 pound ground pork or ground round (85% lean)	½ teaspoon pepper
	Sour cream or plain low-fat yogurt
2 garlic cloves, minced	

1. Cut eggplant into 1-inch cubes. In a colander, toss eggplant cubes and salt; let stand at least 30 minutes. Rinse well under cold running water, drain, and pat cubes dry with paper towels.

2. In a large nonreactive saucepan or Dutch oven, cook bacon over medium-high heat until crisp, about 4 minutes. With a slotted spoon, transfer bacon to paper towels to drain. Pour off all but 2 tablespoons bacon fat.

3. Reduce heat to medium. Add onion, peppers, and eggplant cubes. Cover and cook, stirring occasionally, until vegetables are softened, about 10 minutes. Increase heat to medium-high. Add ground pork and garlic. Cook, stirring often, until pork loses all pink color, about 5 minutes. Add paprika and cook, stirring, 1 minute.

4. Stir in tomatoes with their juice, beef broth, savory, celery salt, and pepper. Bring to a boil over high heat, breaking up tomatoes in pot with a spoon. Reduce heat to low and simmer, partially covered, 1 hour 15 minutes. Top each serving of soup with a dollop of sour cream or yogurt.

28 HOT AND SOUR SOUP SAIGON
Prep: 15 minutes   Cook: 15 minutes   Serves: 6

½ pound ground pork
2 garlic cloves, minced
2 shallots, thinly sliced, or
    3 tablespoons minced
    red onion
1 (8-ounce) can sliced bamboo
    shoots, drained
6 cups chicken stock or
    reduced-sodium canned
    broth
¼ cup fresh lime juice
3 tablespoons Asian fish sauce
    (see Note)

1 tablespoon sugar
½ to 1 fresh jalapeño or other
    chile pepper, thinly sliced
    into rounds
½ pound peeled and deveined
    medium shrimp
1 cup fresh bean sprouts
2 scallions, chopped
¼ chopped fresh cilantro or
    mint

1. In a large saucepan or Dutch oven, cook ground pork and garlic over medium-high heat, stirring often to break up lumps of meat, until pork loses its pink color, about 5 minutes. Drain off excess fat. Add shallots and bamboo shoots and cook, stirring often, until shallots are softened, about 2 minutes.

2. Add chicken stock, lime juice, fish sauce, sugar, and sliced chile. Bring to a boil, reduce heat to low, and simmer 5 minutes. Add shrimp and cook just until shrimp turn pink, about 1 minute. Serve in soup bowls, topped with bean sprouts, scallions, and cilantro.

NOTE: *Fish sauce is available in Asian markets and in many supermarkets. It is called nuoc mam in Vietnam, nam pla in Thailand, and pastis in Indonesia. If unavailable, substitute a mixture of 1 tablespoon each soy sauce, Worcestershire sauce, and water.*

29 BLACK BEAN SOUP WITH SHERRY AND LEMON
Prep: 15 minutes   Stand: 1 hour   Cook: 2½ hours   Serves: 6 to 8

1 pound dried black beans,
    rinsed and picked over
2 tablespoons olive oil
1 large onion, chopped
1 medium carrot, chopped
1 medium celery rib, chopped
1 medium green bell pepper,
    chopped
1 pound ground pork

2 (13¾-ounce) cans beef broth
3 tablespoons tomato paste
1 teaspoon oregano
1 bay leaf
¼ teaspoon pepper
½ cup dry sherry
2 tablespoons lemon juice
1 teaspoon salt
    Sour cream, for garnish

1. Place black beans and enough cold water to cover by 2 inches in a large saucepan. Bring to a boil over high heat, then cook for 2 minutes. Remove from heat, cover, and let stand 1 hour. Drain, rinse well with cold water, and drain again.

2. In a large soup kettle or Dutch oven, heat olive oil. Add onion, carrot, celery, and bell pepper. Cover and cook over medium heat, stirring often, until softened, 10 to 12 minutes. Add ground pork and cook, stirring often to break up meat, until pork loses its pink color, about 5 minutes. Tilt pot and spoon off excess fat.

3. Add drained beans, beef broth, tomato paste, oregano, bay leaf, pepper, and 2 cups water. Bring to a simmer over medium heat, stirring often. Reduce heat to low and simmer, stirring often, 1½ hours. Add sherry and cook until beans are tender, 40 to 50 minutes. Discard bay leaf. Stir in lemon juice and salt. Top each serving with a dollop of sour cream.

---

30 AVGOLEMONO SOUP WITH TURKEY DUMPLINGS
Prep: 15 minutes   Cook: 53 minutes   Serves: 6 to 8

1 tablespoon butter	¼ cup fresh bread crumbs
1 medium onion, chopped	1 egg
1 medium carrot, chopped	1½ teaspoons oregano
1 celery rib, chopped	¾ teaspoon salt
1 medium leek (white part only), chopped	½ teaspoon pepper
	1 pound ground turkey
7 cups chicken stock or reduced-sodium canned broth	3 egg yolks
	¼ cup fresh lemon juice
1 bay leaf	2 tablespoons chopped parsley
¼ cup converted rice	

1. In a large saucepan or Dutch oven, melt butter over low heat. Add onion, carrot, celery, and leek. Cover and cook, stirring often, until onion is softened, about 10 minutes.

2. Add chicken stock and bay leaf. Increase heat to high and bring to a boil. Reduce heat to low and simmer 20 minutes, or until vegetables are almost tender.

3. Meanwhile, in a small saucepan of boiling salted water, cook rice until tender, about 12 minutes. Drain, rinse well under cold water, and drain again.

4. In a medium bowl, combine bread crumbs, egg, oregano, salt, and ¼ teaspoon pepper. Add ground turkey and rice; mix well. Drop tablespoons of turkey mixture into simmering soup and simmer until dumplings are cooked through, 8 to 10 minutes.

5. In a small bowl, whisk together egg yolks, lemon juice, and remaining ¼ teaspoon pepper. Gradually whisk about 1 cup of hot soup into egg yolk mixture. Stir egg yolk mixture into simmering soup and cook until soup is slightly thickened, about 1 minute. Do not let soup boil. Garnish with chopped parsley and serve immediately.

31   CURRIED CHICKEN AND APPLE SOUP
Prep: 15 minutes   Cook: 42 minutes   Serves: 6

1 **pound ground chicken**	2 **garlic cloves, minced**
1 **large onion, chopped**	4 **teaspoons curry powder**
2 **medium Granny Smith apples, peeled, cored, and chopped**	¼ **cup flour**
	6 **cups chicken stock or reduced-sodium canned broth**
1 **medium carrot, chopped**	⅓ **cup converted rice**
1 **celery rib, chopped**	¼ **cup evaporated milk**
1 **tablespoon minced fresh ginger**	

1. In a large saucepan or Dutch oven, cook ground chicken, onion, apples, carrot, celery, ginger, and garlic over medium heat, stirring often to break up meat, until chicken has lost its pink color, 8 to 10 minutes. Drain off excess liquid.

2. Add curry and cook, stirring, 1 minute. Add flour and cook, stirring often, 2 minutes without letting flour brown. Stir in chicken broth and bring to a boil, skimming off any foam or fat that rises to the surface. Reduce heat to low and simmer 15 minutes.

3. Meanwhile, in a medium saucepan of boiling water, cook rice just until tender, about 12 minutes. Drain, rinse under cold water, and drain again. Stir evaporated milk and rice into simmering soup. Cook just until heated through, about 2 minutes.

---

32   TURKEY POTATO CHOWDER
Prep: 10 minutes   Cook: 53 minutes   Serves: 6 to 8

1 **pound ground turkey**	1 **large russet potato, cut into ¾-inch cubes**
1 **medium onion, chopped**	1 **bay leaf**
1 **celery rib, chopped**	½ **teaspoon salt**
1 **medium red bell pepper, chopped**	¼ **teaspoon pepper**
6 **cups chicken stock or reduced-sodium canned broth**	½ **cup heavy cream**
	¼ **cup chopped parsley**

1. In a large saucepan or Dutch oven, cook ground turkey, onion, celery, and bell pepper over medium heat, stirring often to break up lumps of meat, until turkey loses its pink color, about 5 minutes.

2. Add chicken stock, potato, bay leaf, salt, and pepper. Bring to a boil over high heat. Reduce heat to low and simmer, stirring occasionally, 45 minutes.

3. Stir in heavy cream and cook just until heated through, about 3 minutes. Stir in chopped parsley. Remove bay leaf and serve.

33 ALPINE LEEK, POTATO, AND TURKEY SOUP

Prep: 20 minutes   Cook: 45 minutes   Serves: 6 to 8

1 tablespoon butter	1 teaspoon tarragon
1 tablespoon vegetable oil	1½ teaspoons salt
3 medium leeks (white part only), well rinsed and coarsely chopped	¼ teaspoon white pepper
	1 egg white
	1 small garlic clove, crushed through a press
2 medium onions, finely chopped	¼ cup chopped parsley
4 large russet potatoes (about 2 pounds), peeled and sliced ½ inch thick	½ teaspoon basil
	⅛ teaspoon cayenne
	¾ pound ground turkey
6 cups chicken stock or reduced-sodium canned broth	Vegetable cooking spray
	½ cup low-fat milk

1. In a large saucepan or flameproof casserole, melt butter in oil. Add leeks and 1 chopped onion and cook over medium heat, stirring often, until onion is softened, about 5 minutes. Add potatoes, cover, and cook, stirring occasionally, until they lose their raw look, 6 to 8 minutes. Add chicken stock, tarragon, 1 teaspoon salt, and pepper. Bring to a boil, reduce heat to low, and simmer until potatoes are tender, about 15 minutes. Strain soup through a sieve set over a large bowl; reserve broth and potato-leek mixture separately.

2. In a medium bowl, beat egg white with a fork until foamy. Add garlic, 2 tablespoons parsley, basil, remaining ½ teaspoon salt, and cayenne. Mix well. Add ground turkey and mix until well blended. Using about 2 teaspoons of meat mixture for each, form into 20 small meatballs.

3. Spray a large nonstick skillet with vegetable cooking spray. Add meatballs and cook over medium heat, turning often, until browned all over, about 8 minutes. Add ⅓ cup reserved broth and cook until broth is evaporated and meatballs are cooked through, about 5 minutes.

4. In a food processor, puree cooked potatoes and leeks with 1 cup reserved broth. Return puree and remaining reserved broth to saucepan. Add milk and meatballs and cook over low heat until heated through, about 5 minutes. Serve garnished with remaining parsley.

34 LAMB AND LENTIL SOUP CASBAH
Prep: 15 minutes   Cook: 50 minutes   Serves: 6 to 8

1½ pounds ground lamb
2 medium onions, chopped
2 medium carrots, chopped
2 medium celery ribs, chopped
2 garlic cloves, minced
1 pound dried lentils, rinsed and picked over
1 (14-ounce) can Italian peeled tomatoes, drained and coarsely chopped

¼ cup tomato paste
1 teaspoon turmeric
1 teaspoon ground cumin
½ teaspoon cinnamon
¼ teaspoon salt
¼ teaspoon cayenne
6 cups beef stock or canned broth
3 tablespoons lemon juice
2 tablespoons chopped fresh mint or parsley

1. In a large nonreactive Dutch oven, cook ground lamb, onions, carrots, celery, and garlic over medium-high heat, stirring often to break up lumps of meat, until lamb loses its pink color, about 6 minutes. Drain off excess fat.

2. Add lentils, tomatoes, tomato paste, turmeric, cumin, cinnamon, salt, cayenne, and beef stock. Bring to a boil. Reduce heat to low and simmer, partially covered, until lentils are tender, about 45 minutes. Stir in lemon juice and serve each portion sprinkled with mint.

35 WON TON SOUP
Prep: 30 minutes   Cook: 10 minutes   Serves: 6 to 8

½ pound ground pork
3 scallions—1 minced, 2 chopped
1 tablespoon plus 1½ teaspoons soy sauce
1 tablespoon plus 1½ teaspoons dry sherry
1 teaspoon minced fresh ginger

¼ teaspoon sugar
32 won ton wrappers
2 quarts chicken stock or reduced-sodium canned broth
1 cup fresh or thawed frozen peas

1. In a medium bowl, combine ground pork, minced scallion, 1½ teaspoons each soy sauce and dry sherry, ginger, and sugar.

2. Place 1 won ton wrapper on a flat work surface with points at 12, 3, 6, and 9 o'clock. Moisten edges of wrapper with water. Place about 1 teaspoon filling in center of wrapper. Fold up wrapper from 6 to 12 o'clock, enclosing filling, with points at top. Press edges to seal. Bring 3 and 9 o'clock points together to meet, dab with water, and press to seal. Transfer filled won ton to a wax paper–lined baking sheet. Repeat procedure with remaining wrappers and filling.

3. In a large pot of boiling water, cook won tons until filling is cooked through, about 2 minutes. With a slotted spoon, transfer cooked won tons to a wax paper–lined baking sheet.

4. In a large saucepan or Dutch oven, bring chicken stock, chopped scallions, peas, and remaining 1 tablespoon each soy sauce and sherry to a boil over high heat. Reduce heat to low. Add cooked won tons to simmering soup and cook just until heated through, about 2 minutes.

---

36 MEXICAN MEATBALL SOUP
Prep: 15 minutes   Cook: 1½ hours   Serves: 6

In Mexico, many soups are made as substantial as stews with chunks of vegetables and meat, and this *sopa* is no exception.

2 tablespoons olive oil	½ teaspoon ground cumin
1 large onion, chopped	¼ teaspoon pepper
2 medium carrots, chopped	1 cup cooked fresh corn
2 medium zucchini, chopped	kernels or thawed frozen
2 garlic cloves, minced	½ cup converted rice
1 jalapeño pepper, seeded and	1 egg
minced, or 2 tablespoons	2 tablespoons chopped
canned chopped green	cilantro or parsley
chiles	2½ teaspoons chili powder
2 (13¾-ounce) cans beef broth	1 teaspoon salt
1 (14-ounce) can Italian peeled	1 pound ground round
tomatoes, coarsely	(85% lean)
chopped, juice reserved	½ pound ground pork (or
1 teaspoon marjoram	additional beef)

1. In a large nonreactive saucepan or Dutch oven, heat olive oil. Add onion, carrots, zucchini, garlic, and jalapeño pepper. Cover and cook over medium heat, stirring often, until vegetables are softened, 8 to 10 minutes.

2. Add beef broth, tomatoes with their juice, marjoram, cumin, pepper, and 2 cups water. Bring to a simmer, reduce heat to low, and simmer 1 hour. Stir in corn.

3. Meanwhile, in a medium saucepan of lightly salted boiling water, cook rice 5 minutes. Drain, rinse under cold water, and drain again.

4. In a medium bowl, stir together rice, egg, cilantro, chili powder, and salt with a fork until well blended. Add ground round and ground pork and mix well.

5. Using about 1 tablespoon for each, roll mixture between palms into meatballs, dropping as formed into simmering soup. Increase heat to high and return soup to a simmer. Reduce heat to low, partially cover, and simmer, stirring gently to submerge as many meatballs as possible, until meatballs are cooked through with no trace of pink in center, 15 to 20 minutes.

37   VELVETY CORN AND CHICKEN SOUP
Prep: 15 minutes   Cook: 30 minutes   Serves: 4

2 egg whites
1¼ pounds ground chicken
2 tablespoons vegetable oil
1 scallion, minced
2 teaspoons minced fresh
   ginger
2 (17-ounce) cans creamed
   corn

3 cups reduced-sodium
   chicken broth
2 tablespoons soy sauce
1 tablespoon dry sherry
1 tablespoon cornstarch

1. In a medium bowl, beat egg whites with an electric mixer until they form stiff peaks. Add ground chicken and stir until combined. (Egg whites will deflate.)

2. In a large saucepan or Dutch oven, heat oil over medium-high heat. Add scallion and ginger and stir-fry until fragrant, about 30 seconds. Add chicken mixture and stir-fry until chicken has lost its pink color, about 3 minutes.

3. Stir in creamed corn, chicken broth, soy sauce, and sherry. Reduce heat to low and simmer 20 minutes.

4. In a small bowl, dissolve cornstarch in 2 tablespoons water. Stir cornstarch mixture into simmering soup and cook until thickened, about 3 minutes.

38   TUSCAN BEEF AND SPINACH SOUP
Prep: 15 minutes   Cook: 49 minutes   Serves: 6 to 8

1 tablespoon olive oil
1 pound ground sirloin
   (90% lean)
1 medium onion, chopped
2 garlic cloves, minced
6 cups beef stock or canned
   broth
1 (28-ounce) can Italian peeled
   tomatoes, with their juice
1 (10-ounce) package frozen
   chopped spinach, thawed
   and squeezed dry

1 teaspoon basil
½ teaspoon salt
¼ teaspoon pepper
½ cup elbow macaroni
1 (16-ounce) can cannellini
   beans, drained and rinsed
Grated Parmesan cheese

1. In a 5-quart Dutch oven, heat olive oil. Add ground sirloin, onion, and garlic and cook over medium-high heat, stirring often to break up lumps of meat, until beef loses its pink color, about 5 minutes.

2. Add tomatoes with their juice, spinach, basil, salt, and pepper; stir to break up tomatoes with a large spoon. Bring to a boil, reduce heat to low, and simmer 30 minutes.

3. Meanwhile, in a medium saucepan of boiling salted water, cook macaroni until just tender, about 9 minutes. Drain well.

4. Add drained cannelini beans and macaroni to soup. Simmer 5 minutes. Pass a bowl of grated Parmesan cheese on the side.

39 TORTILLA SOUP WITH CHICKEN
Prep: 20 minutes   Cook: 45 minutes   Serves: 6 to 8

About 1/3 cup vegetable oil
12 corn tortillas, torn into 1-inch-wide strips
1 tablespoon olive oil
1 pound ground chicken or ground turkey
1 (14-ounce) can Italian peeled tomatoes, with their juice
1 medium onion, chopped
2 garlic cloves, minced
1 jalapeño pepper, seeded and minced, or 2 tablespoons canned chopped green chiles

6 cups chicken stock or reduced-sodium canned broth
1½ teaspoons marjoram
½ teaspoon salt
¼ teaspoon sugar
¼ teaspoon crushed hot red pepper

1. In a large skillet, heat 2 tablespoons vegetable oil over medium-high heat until very hot but not smoking. In batches, cook tortilla strips, turning often, until crisp and browned, about 20 seconds. (Use additional oil for each batch, as necessary.) Transfer to paper towels to drain, then transfer to a bowl.

2. In a large nonreactive saucepan or Dutch oven, heat olive oil. Add ground chicken and cook over medium heat, stirring often to break up lumps of meat, until chicken loses its pink color, about 5 minutes. Drain off excess liquid.

3. In a blender or food processor, puree tomatoes with their juice, onion, garlic, and jalapeño pepper. Increase heat to high, pour tomato mixture into Dutch oven and cook, stirring often, for 5 minutes, or until slightly reduced.

4. Add chicken stock, marjoram, salt, sugar, and hot pepper. Bring to a boil, reduce heat to low, and simmer 30 minutes. For each serving, place a small handful of tortilla strips in bottom of each soup bowl. Ladle on soup and serve hot.

40 GRANDMA'S CHICKEN SOUP WITH CHICKEN MATZOH BALLS

Prep: 20 minutes   Cook: 1¼ hours   Serves: 6 to 8

2 tablespoons butter
2 medium onions, chopped
2 medium carrots, cut into
   ½-inch-thick rounds
2 celery ribs, cut into ½-inch-
   thick pieces
2 quarts chicken stock or
   reduced-sodium canned
   broth

1 bay leaf
1 cup matzoh meal
¼ cup chopped parsley
2 eggs
2 tablespoons club soda
1¼ teaspoons salt
¼ teaspoon pepper
1 pound ground chicken

1. In a 5- to 6-quart soup kettle or Dutch oven, melt butter over medium heat. Add onions, carrots, and celery. Cover and cook, stirring occasionally, until vegetables are softened, about 10 minutes. Add chicken stock and bay leaf. Bring to a boil, reduce heat to low, and simmer 45 minutes.

2. Meanwhile, in a medium bowl, combine matzoh meal, 2 tablespoons chopped parsley, eggs, club soda, salt, and pepper; mix well. Add ground chicken and blend well. Using about 2 tablespoons of chicken mixture for each, form into large meatballs.

3. Lower meatballs, one at a time, into a large saucepan of boiling, salted water. Simmer over medium heat until a meatball shows no sign of pink when prodded in the center with the tip of a sharp knife, about 15 minutes. Drain into a colander and rinse under cold running water.

4. Add meatballs to the simmering soup and cook until heated through, about 5 minutes. Sprinkle with remaining 2 tablespoons parsley.

Chapter 3

Chili and Other Stews on the Range

In the last few years, as America's tastebuds have become more accustomed to spicy food, chili, a humble little stew from the Lone Star State, has reached cult status. I remember when the only chili you could get was from a can. Now there are chili cook-offs, chili restaurants, and chili cookbooks, all singing the praises of this Tex-Mex specialty.

(A note on the proper spelling of the word. While editorial styles vary, in this book *Chile* with a capital "C" is the South American country. The hot little fresh green and dried red things with seeds are *chile* peppers, with a small "c." If it's meaty and served in a bowl, it is *chili*, with a small "i" on the end.)

It seems that there is a different chili recipe for every household in Texas, not to mention every other state in the Union. I've managed to pick out a few of my favorites, and deciding between them is largely a matter of personal preference. Do you like your chili with beans? Then choose Extra-Spicy Italian Chili with Cannelini Beans. If you prefer yours without beans, then cook up Red's Secret Ingredient Chili. Some chilis are made with ground beef, some with ground pork, and some with a mixture of beef, pork, and veal. There are even a couple of chilis made with ground lamb. On the lighter side, Chicken Chili with Cornbread Ribbon Topping and Turkey Chili Mole offer lower-cholesterol versions with no sacrifice of taste.

As far as fixings go, chili can be topped with shredded Cheddar cheese, Monterey Jack, goat cheese, or grated Parmesan cheese. Sliced black olives, pickled jalapeño peppers, tortilla chips, chopped sweet onions or scallions, and sour cream or plain low-fat yogurt can all be set out in separate bowls. Let everyone help themselves; it's half the fun.

Riding shotgun with the chilis in this chapter are some more rib-sticking stews, like Fulton County Brunswick Stew, made with ground turkey and thickened with mashed potatoes, and Chicken and Rice Gumbo. With any of these stews, be sure to serve plenty of bread to sop up every last bit of savory sauce.

41   CHILI CON QUESO CON CARNE
Prep: 10 minutes   Cook: 10 minutes   Serves: 8

Here's a beefed-up version of the popular hot dip.

1 **pound ground round (85% lean)**	1 **tablespoon flour**
1 **medium onion, chopped**	¾ **cup milk**
1 **to 2 jalapeño peppers, seeded and minced, or 3 tablespoons canned chopped green chiles**	2 **cups shredded Cheddar cheese (8 ounces)**
1 **garlic clove, minced**	2 **cups shredded Monterey Jack cheese (8 ounces)**
	Tortilla chips and/or assorted fresh vegetables

1. In a large skillet, cook ground round, onion, jalapeño peppers, and garlic over medium-high heat, stirring often to break up lumps of meat, until beef loses its pink color, about 5 minutes. Sprinkle on flour and cook, stirring, for 1 minute. Stir in milk and bring to a boil, stirring until thickened. Reduce heat to low and simmer, stirring often, 3 minutes.

2. Gradually stir in cheese until melted. Transfer to a heatproof serving bowl. Serve on a warming plate or in a fondue pot, with tortilla chips or vegetables for dipping.

42   FIESTA CHILI
Prep: 20 minutes   Cook: 2 hours   Serves: 6 to 8

1 **pound ground round (85% lean)**	4 **garlic cloves, minced**
1 **pound ground pork**	⅓ **cup chili powder**
1 **pound ground veal**	1 **teaspoon oregano**
2 **large onions, chopped**	1 **teaspoon marjoram**
1 **large russet potato, peeled and cut into 1-inch chunks**	1 **teaspoon ground cumin**
	1 **(28-ounce) can tomato puree**
1 **large red bell pepper, seeded and chopped**	2 **cups beef broth**
2 **medium carrots, chopped**	2 **teaspoons salt**
2 **medium celery ribs, chopped**	½ **teaspoon crushed hot red pepper**
2 **jalapeño peppers, seeded and minced, or 3 tablespoons canned chopped green chiles**	2 **(16-ounce) cans black beans, drained and rinsed**
	Sour cream, chopped onion, shredded Cheddar cheese, tortilla chips

1. In a 6-quart Dutch oven, cook ground round, ground pork, ground veal, onions, potato, bell pepper, carrots, celery, jalapeño peppers, and garlic over medium-high heat, stirring often to break up lumps, until meat loses its pink color, about 10 minutes. Drain off excess fat.

2. Add chili powder, oregano, marjoram, and cumin. Cook, stirring, 1 minute. Stir in tomato puree, beef broth, salt, and hot pepper. Bring to a boil, reduce heat to low, and simmer, stirring often, until chili is thickened, about 1¾ hours.

3. Add black beans and simmer, stirring often, 5 minutes. Remove from heat and let stand 5 minutes; then skim excess fat from surface. Serve in bowls and let everyone choose their own fixings.

---

43 RED'S SECRET INGREDIENT CHILI
Prep: 15 minutes   Cook: 2 hours   Serves: 8 to 12

The secret ingredient is a tall bottle of beer. While just about any brand will do, use a Mexican dark beer, if you can find it.

2 pounds ground round
   (85% lean)
1 pound ground pork
2 medium onions, chopped
1 large red bell pepper,
   chopped
4 garlic cloves, minced
3 fresh jalapeño peppers,
   seeded and minced, or
   ¼ to ½ teaspoon crushed
   hot red pepper
¼ cup chili powder
1 (28-ounce) can Italian peeled
   tomatoes, cut up, juices
   reserved

1 (12-ounce) bottle beer
1 (6-ounce) can tomato paste
2 teaspoons salt
1½ teaspoons cumin
1½ teaspoons oregano
2 bay leaves
¼ cup yellow cornmeal
   Sour cream, pickled
   jalapeño pepper slices,
   shredded Cheddar
   cheese, chopped onions

1. In a 6-quart Dutch oven, cook ground round, ground pork, onions, bell pepper, garlic, and jalapeño peppers over medium-high heat, stirring often to break up lumps of meat, until meat loses its pink color, about 8 minutes. Add chili powder and cook, stirring, 1 minute.

2. Stir in tomatoes with their juice, beer, tomato paste, salt, cumin, oregano, and bay leaves. Bring to a simmer, stirring often. Reduce heat to low and simmer, uncovered, stirring occasionally, until chili is slightly thickened, about 1¾ hours.

3. In a small bowl, stir together cornmeal and ½ cup chili until smooth. Stir cornmeal mixture into chili and cook until thickened, about 5 minutes.

4. Place sour cream, pickled jalapeños, Cheddar cheese, and onions in separate dishes. Serve chili in bowls and encourage guests to choose their own garnishes.

44   PORCUPINE MEATBALL CHILI
Prep: 15 minutes   Cook: 1 hour   Serves: 4

Pop some cornbread into the oven to serve with this rib-sticking fare. It's a mild, fun-to-eat chili that isn't too spicy, so the youngest members of the family will enjoy it, too.

1 medium onion, chopped	1 egg
1 medium green bell pepper, chopped	½ cup fresh bread crumbs
2 tablespoons olive oil	¾ teaspoon salt
2 garlic cloves, minced	⅛ teaspoon pepper
1 tablespoon plus 1½ teaspoons chili powder	1 pound ground round (85% lean)
1 (14-ounce) can Italian peeled tomatoes, with their juice	⅓ cup rice
1 cup tomato sauce	1 (16-ounce) can kidney beans, drained

1. Measure out ¼ cup each of chopped onion and bell pepper and mince with a sharp knife. Place minced vegetables in a medium bowl and set aside.

2. Heat oil in a large skillet. Add remaining chopped onion and bell pepper and cook over medium heat, stirring often, until onion is softened, about 4 minutes. Add garlic and 1 tablespoon chili powder and cook, stirring, 1 minute. Stir in tomatoes with their juice and tomato sauce, breaking up tomatoes in skillet with a spoon. Bring to a boil, reduce heat to low, and simmer 5 minutes.

3. Meanwhile, add egg, bread crumbs, remaining 1½ teaspoons chili powder, salt, and pepper to minced vegetables in bowl. Mix with a fork until well combined. Add ground round and rice and knead with your hands until mixed. Using a heaping tablespoon for each, roll meat mixture between palms to form meatballs, dropping each as formed into simmering sauce.

4. Cover tightly and simmer over low heat, stirring occasionally to avoid scorching, until rice in meatballs is tender and sauce is thickened, about 50 minutes. Gently stir in beans, cover, and cook until heated through, about 3 minutes. Serve hot in individual bowls.

45 LONE STAR CORN CHIP-CHILI PIE
Prep: 5 minutes   Cook: 20 minutes   Serves: 4 to 6

3 cups corn chips
1 cup shredded Cheddar
   cheese
1 small onion, chopped

3 cups leftover chili (your
   favorite, but try Red's
   Secret Ingredient Chili,
   page 39)

1. Preheat oven to 375°. Spread half of corn chips in a 2-quart casserole. Sprinkle with ½ cup of Cheddar cheese and onion. Cover with chili. Top with remaining chips and sprinkle with remaining cheese.

2. Bake until heated through and cheese is melted, about 20 minutes.

46 QUICK BEEFY GUMBO
Prep: 5 minutes   Cook: 30 minutes   Serves: 6

If you can't find filé powder, add 1 (10-ounce) package frozen okra, thawed, to the gumbo with the stewed tomatoes and broth. Either filé powder or okra will thicken up your gumbo nicely, but don't use both in the same recipe.

1 tablespoon olive oil
½ pound beef kielbasa,
   andouille, or other
   smoked sausage, sliced
   ½ inch thick
1 pound ground round
   (85% lean)
2 tablespoons flour
½ teaspoon thyme
½ teaspoon basil

½ teaspoon salt
¼ teaspoon crushed hot red
   pepper
2 (15-ounce) cans stewed
   tomatoes, with their juice
1 (13¾-ounce) can beef broth
3 tablespoons long-grain
   white rice
1 teaspoon filé powder

1. In a 5- to 6-quart Dutch oven, heat olive oil. Add sliced sausage and cook over medium-high heat, turning often, until browned, about 4 minutes. Using a slotted spoon, transfer sausage to a plate and set aside, leaving fat in pan.

2. Add ground round to pot and cook over medium-high heat, stirring often to break up lumps of meat, until beef loses its pink color, about 5 minutes. Tilt pan and spoon off all but 2 tablespoons fat.

3. Sprinkle in flour, thyme, basil, salt, and hot pepper. Cook over medium-high heat, stirring, until flour is lightly browned, about 3 minutes. Add stewed tomatoes with their juice and beef broth. Bring to a simmer. Stir in rice. Reduce heat to medium-low and simmer until rice is tender, about 15 minutes.

4. Remove from heat and stir in filé powder. Cover and let stand 5 minutes, to allow filé powder to thicken soup. Do not cook soup after adding filé powder, or it will turn stringy.

47   CHICKEN CHILI WITH CORNBREAD RIBBON TOPPING

Prep: 10 minutes   Cook: 30 minutes   Serves: 4 to 6

1½ pounds ground chicken or
    ground turkey
1 small onion, chopped
1 small green bell pepper,
    chopped
1 jalapeño pepper, seeded and
    minced
1 garlic clove, minced
1 cup tomato sauce

1 cup corn kernels, fresh,
    canned, or thawed frozen
2 teaspoons chili powder
½ teaspoon ground cumin
½ teaspoon salt
1 (11.5-ounce) package
    refrigerated cornbread
    twists

1. Preheat oven to 350°. In a large ovenproof skillet or flameproof casserole, cook ground chicken, onion, bell pepper, jalapeño pepper, and garlic over medium heat, stirring often to break up lumps, until chicken loses its pink color, about 5 minutes. Drain off excess liquid.

2. Stir in tomato sauce, corn, chili powder, cumin and salt. Reduce heat to low and simmer, stirring often, until thickened, about 10 minutes. Remove skillet from heat.

3. Unroll cornbread twist dough and separate into strips. Arrange cornbread strips in rows over chili, trimming strips as necessary.

4. Bake until strips are golden brown, 12 to 15 minutes. Serve directly from skillet.

48   MOROCCAN MEATBALL STEW

Prep: 20 minutes   Cook: 45 minutes   Serves: 4 to 6

1 pound ground round
    (85% lean) or lean ground
    lamb
1 small onion, minced, plus
    2 medium onions,
    chopped
2 tablespoons chopped fresh
    cilantro or parsley
1½ teaspoons ground cumin
½ teaspoon paprika
½ teaspoon ground allspice
¾ teaspoon salt

⅜ teaspoon cayenne
1 tablespoon butter
1 tablespoon vegetable oil
2 medium carrots, chopped
2 garlic cloves, minced
1 (35-ounce) can Italian peeled
    tomatoes, drained
½ cup chopped parsley
2 tablespoons lemon juice
½ teaspoon ground cinnamon
    Hot cooked couscous

1. In a medium bowl, combine ground round, minced onion, cilantro, ½ teaspoon cumin, ¼ teaspoon paprika, allspice, ½ teaspoon salt, and ⅛ teaspoon cayenne. Knead with your hands until well blended. Using about 1 tablespoon meat mixture for each, form into meatballs.

2. In a large skillet, melt butter in oil over medium-high heat until hot but not smoking. Add meatballs and cook, turning often, until browned all over, about 8 minutes. Remove meatballs to a plate. Pour off all but 2 tablespoons fat.

3. Add chopped onions and carrots to skillet. Cook, stirring often, until onions are lightly browned, about 5 minutes. Add garlic and cook, stirring, 30 seconds. Add tomatoes, parsley, lemon juice, cinnamon, remaining 1 teaspoon cumin, and ¼ teaspoon each paprika, salt, and cayenne. Bring to a simmer, breaking up tomatoes in skillet with a spoon. Reduce heat to low and cook, partially covered and stirring often, 15 minutes.

4. Return meatballs to skillet and cook, partially covered and stirring occasionally, until sauce is thickened, about 15 minutes. Serve with hot couscous.

---

49 EXTRA-SPICY ITALIAN CHILI WITH CANNELINI BEANS

Prep: 15 minutes   Cook: 55 minutes   Serves: 6 to 8

1½ pounds hot Italian sausage, casings removed	¾ cup beef broth
1½ pounds ground chuck (80% lean)	½ teaspoon salt
2 medium onions, chopped	¼ teaspoon crushed hot red pepper
1 medium green bell pepper, chopped	1 (19-ounce) can cannelini beans, rinsed and drained (or use pink beans)
2 garlic cloves, minced	Sour cream, chopped
2 tablespoons chili powder	peperoncini (Italian
1 teaspoon oregano	pickled peppers), grated
½ teaspoon ground cumin	Parmesan cheese
1 bay leaf	
1 (14-ounce) can Italian tomatoes, drained	

1. Crumble sausage into a 5-quart Dutch oven set over medium-high heat. Add ground chuck, onions, bell pepper, and garlic. Cook, stirring often to break up meat, until beef loses its pink color, about 5 minutes. Add chili powder, oregano, cumin, and bay leaf. Cook 1 minute, stirring often. Stir in tomatoes, beef broth, salt, and hot pepper. Bring to a simmer, breaking up tomatoes in pot with a spoon. Reduce heat to low and simmer, stirring often, until chili is thickened, about 45 minutes.

2. Stir in cannelini beans and cook until beans are heated through, about 5 minutes. Serve immediately with sour cream, peperoncini, and Parmesan cheese, if desired.

50 TURKEY CHILI MOLE
Prep: 20 minutes   Cook: 1 hour   Serves: 4 to 6

2 pounds ground turkey
2 medium onions, chopped
2 garlic cloves, minced
1 fresh jalapeño pepper,
   seeded and minced, or
   2 tablespoons canned
   chopped green chiles
2 tablespoons chili powder
¼ teaspoon cinnamon
¼ teaspoon ground coriander
1 (15-ounce) can Italian peeled
   tomatoes, coarsely
   chopped, juices reserved

1 cup chicken broth
1 teaspoon salt
⅓ cup raisins
⅓ cup finely chopped
   blanched almonds
1 ounce unsweetened
   chocolate, chopped
2 tablespoons yellow
   cornmeal

1. In a 5- to 6-quart Dutch oven, cook ground turkey, onions, garlic, and jalapeño pepper over medium heat, stirring often, until turkey loses its pink color, about 5 minutes.

2. Add chili powder, cinnamon, and coriander. Cook, stirring, 30 seconds. Stir in tomatoes with their juice, chicken broth, salt, raisins, and almonds. Bring to a boil, reduce heat to low, and simmer, stirring occasionally, until chili is slightly thickened, about 50 minutes.

3. Stir in chocolate and cornmeal and cook, stirring often, until thickened, about 5 minutes.

51 IRISH MEATBALL STEW
Prep: 20 minutes   Cook: 40 minutes   Serves: 4 to 6

2 medium red potatoes (about
   ¾ pound), cut into 1-inch
   cubes
1 cup fresh bread crumbs
2 eggs
1 teaspoon savory
1½ teaspoons salt
½ teaspoon pepper
2 pounds lean ground lamb or
   ground round (85% lean)
2 tablespoons vegetable oil

1 large onion, chopped
2 medium carrots, cut into
   ½-inch-thick rounds
1 medium celery rib, sliced
   ½ inch thick
1 tablespoon flour
1 (13¾-ounce) can beef broth
½ cup dry white wine
2 tablespoons chopped
   parsley

1. In a medium saucepan of boiling salted water, cook potatoes until almost tender when pierced with tip of a small sharp knife, about 10 minutes. Drain and reserve.

2. In a medium bowl, combine bread crumbs, eggs, savory, salt, and ¼ teaspoon pepper. Add ground lamb and mix well. Using about 1 tablespoon for each, form into 24 meatballs.

3. In a large skillet, heat oil. Add meatballs and cook over medium-high heat, turning often, until browned all over, 8 to 10 minutes. Using a slotted spoon, transfer to paper towels to drain. Pour off all but 1 tablespoon fat from skillet.

4. Add onion, carrots, and celery to skillet and cook, stirring often, until onions are lightly browned, about 4 minutes. Add potatoes and toss to mix. Sprinkle flour over vegetables and cook, stirring, 1 minute.

5. Add beef broth, wine, and remaining ¼ teaspoon pepper. Bring to a boil. Return meatballs to skillet, stirring to submerge as much as possible into liquid. Reduce heat to low, cover, and simmer, until potatoes are tender and meatballs are cooked through, about 15 minutes. Serve, garnished with chopped parsley.

---

52 NAPA VALLEY LAMB AND ZINFANDEL CHILI

Prep: 15 minutes   Cook: 1¼ hours   Serves: 6 to 8

Two heads of garlic? Long simmering renders them tender and mild, a perfect counterpoint to the hearty flavors of lamb and red wine.

2 heads of garlic, separated into cloves
3 pounds ground lamb
1 large onion, chopped
1 medium green bell pepper, chopped
1 medium red bell pepper, chopped
3 fresh jalapeño peppers, seeded and minced, or ½ teaspoon crushed hot red pepper
2 tablespoons chili powder
1 teaspoon rosemary
1 (28-ounce) can peeled tomatoes with added puree
1 cup dry red wine, preferably Zinfandel
1 teaspoon salt
¼ teaspoon pepper
¾ cup fresh bread crumbs
½ pound goat cheese, chèvre, or feta, crumbled
1 cup Mediterranean black olives, pitted and chopped

1. Peel and mince 2 cloves of garlic; set aside. In a medium saucepan of boiling water, cook remaining garlic cloves 1 minute. Drain, rinse under cold water, and drain again. Pinch garlic out of skins or peel with a small knife.

2. In a 6- to 8-quart Dutch oven, cook ground lamb, onion, green and red bell peppers, jalapeño peppers, and reserved minced garlic over medium-high heat, stirring often to break up meat, until lamb loses its pink color, about 8 minutes. Drain off excess fat. Add whole garlic cloves, chili powder, and rosemary. Cook, stirring, 30 seconds. Stir in tomatoes with puree, wine, salt, and pepper, breaking up tomatoes with a spoon. Bring to a simmer, reduce heat to low, and simmer 1 hour.

3. Tilt Dutch oven and skim off excess fat from surface of liquid. Stir in bread crumbs and cook, stirring often, until chili is thick, about 5 minutes. Serve, topped with crumbled goat cheese and olives.

53 CHICKEN AND RICE GUMBO
Prep: 15 minutes   Cook: 1 hour   Serves: 6 to 8

¼ cup vegetable oil
1 large onion, chopped
1 celery rib, chopped
1 medium red bell pepper, chopped
2 garlic cloves, minced
¼ cup flour
1½ pounds ground chicken
1 (28-ounce) can Italian peeled tomatoes, drained and coarsely cut up

6 cups chicken stock or reduced-sodium canned broth
1 (10-ounce) package frozen okra, thawed
1 teaspoon thyme
¾ teaspoon salt
½ teaspoon basil
½ teaspoon oregano
½ teaspoon crushed hot red pepper
¼ cup converted rice

1. In a 5- to 6-quart Dutch oven, heat oil over medium-high heat. Add onion, celery, bell pepper, and garlic. Cook, stirring often, 1 minute. Sprinkle on flour and cook, stirring and scraping bottom of pan often, until vegetables are softened and flour coating is golden, about 5 minutes.

2. Add ground chicken and cook, stirring often to break up lumps of meat, until chicken loses its pink color, about 5 minutes. Add tomatoes and scrape bottom of pan well with a wooden spoon. Add chicken stock and okra. Bring to a boil over high heat, skimming to remove foam and fat on surface. Season with thyme, salt, basil, oregano, and hot pepper. Reduce heat to low and simmer, stirring occasionally, 30 minutes.

3. Meanwhile, in a medium saucepan of boiling salted water, cook rice until tender, about 15 minutes. Drain, rinse well, and drain again. Stir cooked rice into simmering soup and cook until heated through, about 3 minutes.

54 FULTON COUNTY BRUNSWICK STEW
Prep: 10 minutes   Cook: 4 minutes   Serves: 4 to 6

In the old days, Brunswick stew was made with furred game, like squirrel. I like it just fine with ground turkey, thank you. This version thickens the stew with mashed potatoes, for a soul-satisfying effect. Serve with hot biscuits.

2 medium russet potatoes (about ¾ pound), peeled and cut into 1-inch pieces
1½ pounds ground turkey
1 medium onion, chopped
1 (16-ounce) can creamed corn
1 (14-ounce) can Italian peeled tomatoes, with their juice

1 (13¾-ounce) can reduced-sodium chicken broth
1 (10-ounce) package frozen lima beans, thawed
⅓ cup ketchup
2 teaspoons Worcestershire sauce
½ teaspoon pepper

1. In a large saucepan of boiling salted water, cook potatoes until tender, about 15 minutes. Drain well and mash; set aside.

2. Meanwhile, in a large Dutch oven, cook ground turkey and onion over medium heat, stirring often to break up lumps of meat, until turkey loses its pink color, about 5 minutes. Drain off excess liquid. Add creamed corn, tomatoes with their juice, chicken broth, lima beans, ketchup, Worcestershire sauce, and pepper. Stir to break up tomatoes. Bring to a boil, reduce heat to low, and simmer, stirring often, until slightly thickened, about 15 minutes.

3. Add mashed potatoes and cook, stirring often, until thickened, about 5 minutes.

---

55 CINCINNATI FIVE-WAY CHILI
Prep: 15 minutes   Cook: 1¼ hours   Serves: 4 to 6

In Cincinnati, they like their chili on top of spaghetti, further enhanced with helpings of kidney beans, cheese, raw onions, and oyster crackers.

1 pound ground round (85% lean)	½ cup beef broth
2 medium onions, chopped	1 tablespoon red wine vinegar
1 medium celery rib, chopped	½ ounce (½ square) unsweetened chocolate, grated
2 garlic cloves, minced	12 ounces spaghetti
1 tablespoon chili powder	3 tablespoons butter
1 teaspoon salt	1 (16-ounce) can kidney beans, heated
½ teaspoon cinnamon	2 cups shredded Cheddar cheese (8 ounces)
½ teaspoon ground cumin	Chopped raw onion and oyster crackers
½ teaspoon basil	
½ teaspoon oregano	
¼ teaspoon ground allspice	
¼ teaspoon pepper	
1 (28-ounce) can peeled tomatoes with added puree	

1. In a large Dutch oven, cook ground round, 1 onion, celery, and garlic, stirring often to break up lumps of meat, until beef loses its pink color, about 5 minutes. Add chili powder, salt, cinnamon, cumin, basil, oregano, allspice, and pepper. Cook, stirring, 1 minute.

2. Add tomatoes with puree, beef broth, vinegar, and chocolate; break up tomatoes with a large spoon. Bring to a boil, reduce heat to low, and simmer until thickened, about 1 hour, adding more beef broth or water if chili gets too thick.

3. Meanwhile, in a large saucepan of boiling salted water, cook spaghetti until tender but still firm, 9 to 10 minutes. Drain well. Toss in a large bowl with butter.

4. Place warm kidney beans, Cheddar cheese, raw onion, and oyster crackers in separate bowls. Serve spaghetti on plates and top with chili. Let guests choose their own toppings.

56 CRESCENT CITY RED BEANS AND RICE
Prep: 15 minutes   Stand: 1½ hours   Cook: 1 hour 10 minutes
Serves: 6 to 8

1 pound small dried red beans
  or kidney beans
1 pound ground pork
4 scallions, chopped
2 celery ribs, chopped
1 medium onion, chopped
1 medium green bell pepper,
  chopped

2 garlic cloves, chopped
1 large ham hock, about
  1 pound
½ teaspoon crushed hot red
  pepper
1 teaspoon salt
  Hot cooked rice

1. In a 5- to 6-quart soup kettle or Dutch oven, combine beans and 8 cups water. Heat to boiling over high heat and cook 2 minutes. Remove from heat, cover tightly, and let stand 1½ hours. Drain beans, reserving soaking liquid. Add water to soaking liquid, if necessary, to measure 6 cups.

2. Rinse out pot and add ground pork, scallions, celery, onion, bell pepper, and garlic to it. Cook over medium heat, stirring often to break up meat, until vegetables are softened, about 6 minutes. Add soaked beans, reserved soaking liquid, ham hock, and hot pepper. Bring to a boil over high heat, stirring often. Reduce heat to low and simmer, partially covered, until beans are tender, about 1 hour.

3. With a large spoon, crush beans against side of pot until liquid is thickened to desired consistency. Season with salt. Serve beans in individual bowls, topped with hot rice.

57 LAMB AND HOMINY CHILI
Prep: 15 minutes   Cook: 2 hours   Serves: 6

3 pounds lean ground lamb
2 medium onions, chopped
6 garlic cloves, minced
2 fresh jalapeño peppers,
  seeded and minced, or
  3 tablespoons canned
  chopped green chiles
⅓ cup chili powder
1 tablespoon oregano
1 tablespoon pepper
1 tablespoon dry mustard
2 teaspoons ground cumin

1½ teaspoons thyme
1 teaspoon ground allspice
1 teaspoon ground ginger
4 cups beef broth
1 (28-ounce) can Italian peeled
  tomatoes, drained and
  cut up
3 tablespoons yellow
  cornmeal
2 (16-ounce) cans white
  hominy, drained

1. In a 5- to 6-quart Dutch oven, cook ground lamb, onions, garlic, and jalapeño peppers over medium-high heat, stirring often to break up lumps of meat, until lamb has lost its pink color, about 10 minutes. Spoon off any excess fat.

2. Add chili powder, oregano, pepper, mustard, cumin, thyme, allspice, and ginger. Cook, stirring, 1 minute. Add beef broth and tomatoes. Bring to a boil, reduce heat to low, and simmer, partially covered, until liquid is evaporated by two-thirds, about 1¾ hours.

3. In a small bowl, stir about 1 cup of chili into cornmeal. Stir cornmeal mixture into chili. Add hominy and cook until thickened, about 5 minutes.

---

58 CHILE VERDE WITH POSOLE
Prep: 15 minutes   Cook: 2 hours   Serves: 6 to 8

3 pounds ground pork
2 medium onions, chopped
2 medium zucchini, cut into ¾-inch dice
3 garlic cloves, minced
2 jalapeño peppers, seeded and minced, or 1 (4-ounce) can chopped green chiles
3 (11-ounce) cans tomatillos (see Note), drained and rinsed

1 cup reduced-sodium chicken broth
2 teaspoons salt
½ teaspoon sugar
1 (16-ounce) can golden hominy or corn kernels, drained and rinsed
⅓ cup chopped fresh cilantro
Sour cream, for garnish

1. In a 5- to 6-quart Dutch oven, cook ground pork, onions, zucchini, garlic, and jalapeño peppers over medium-high heat, stirring often, until pork loses its pink color, about 10 minutes. Drain off excess fat.

2. Add tomatillos, chicken broth, salt, and sugar. Bring to a boil, stirring to break up tomatillos with a spoon. Reduce heat to low and simmer, partially covered, stirring occasionally, until slightly thickened, about 1¾ hours.

3. Stir in hominy and cilantro and cook until hominy is heated through, about 5 minutes. Top each portion with a dollop of sour cream.

   NOTE: *If fresh tomatillos are available, 2½ pounds can be substituted for canned. Remove husks and simmer until barely tender in salted water, about 6 minutes. Do not overcook tomatillos or they will burst.*

Chapter 4

Magnificent Meatloaf

Be it ever so humble, there's nothing like meatloaf. Everyone has their special recipe. I have one friend who swears that meatloaf must have "ketchup in and ketchup on" to reach perfection. Others insist that meatloaf has to be served with steaming mashed potatoes and piping hot brown gravy. Some families love spicy tomato sauce with theirs, particularly when the loaf is made with a sausage and meat combination.

For a moist, juicy meatloaf that slices nicely, ground round (85% lean) is my favorite. While ground sirloin (90% lean) can be used, it makes a drier, more compact loaf. Budget-minded cooks can certainly use 80% lean ground chuck, but it won't hold together as well as ground round. Don't overlook the ground turkey or ground chicken recipes I've devised especially for these wonderful new additions to the meat counter. Many butchers prepare an excellent meatloaf combination of beef, pork, and veal ready for you to add other ingredients.

I have found that even such a simple, homespun dish as meatloaf has its little secrets that make it especially delicious. Here are some tips:

Many older meatloaf recipes call for separately beaten eggs. I like to make my meatloaf a one-bowl affair. To simplify matters, I mix all of the ingredients *except the ground meat* together in a medium bowl, being sure to lightly beat the eggs. In this way, the seasonings are well blended and will be distributed more evenly throughout when the ground meat is added.

When you add the ground meat to the other ingredients, knead it lightly in the bowl with your hands, mixing just until well blended with the other ingredients. Don't overwork the meat mixture, or it will make a heavy-textured loaf. A sturdy wooden spoon is only a fair alternative to mixing with your hands.

Meatloaves almost always have a starchy binder of some kind to help hold things together. You can be creative in this department, using whatever the pantry offers. Rolled oats (either old-fashioned or quick), fresh or dried bread crumbs (seasoned or plain), corn or bran flakes, crispy rice cereal (stay away from the sugared breakfast cereals), small cooked pasta shapes like orzo or pastina, cooked or raw rice, crumbled bread stuffing mixes, crushed potato or tortilla chips can all serve well. Of course, be sure the flavor of your binder is compatible with the other ingredients. Don't skimp on the binders. They're not only important for texture, they help the look of the loaf as well. It's just one more boon that they help stretch a pound of meat so far.

Most meatloaves are baked at 350° to minimize shrinkage and loss of juices. If you are cooking against the clock, don't turn up the oven, but divide your meatloaf mixture into smaller portions and make mini-loaves.

If you like crusty meatloaves, form the meat mixture into a free-form loaf on a lightly oiled baking sheet instead of packing it into a loaf pan, so the loaf's entire surface is exposed to the oven heat. Mini free-form loaves, about 4 by 3 inches, will bake in around 30 minutes—perfect for cooking against the clock.

A molded loaf shape can be obtained by packing the meat mixture into a cold water–rinsed pan. Invert the loaf pan onto a baking sheet, then unmold. Create a molded dome shape by packing the meat mixture into a plastic wrap–lined 2-quart bowl. Let the excess plastic wrap hang over the edges of the bowl. Unmold the mixture onto the baking sheet and peel off the plastic wrap.

Ring-shaped loaves are pretty, too, and the center can be filled with vegetables, mashed potatoes, or rice. Invert a small, lightly oiled ovenproof bowl on the baking sheet and shape the meat mixture around the bowl in a ring. After the loaf is baked, carefully remove the bowl. You can also pack the meatloaf mixture into a lightly oiled ring mold and invert it onto a baking sheet. Or for a tender, crustless loaf, simply bake it in the pan and unmold it after baking.

In a hurry? Pack your meatloaf mixture into lightly oiled muffin pans. You will have mini-meatloaves in less than 30 minutes.

As a precaution against oven spills, place your meat-filled loaf pan on a baking sheet to catch any bubbling juices. Never bake your meatloaf in the lower part of the oven, or the bottom may scorch. Position the racks in the center or upper third of the oven.

Most important, *always* let your meatloaf stand for 5 to 10 minutes before slicing to let the juices settle. Pour off any accumulated fat before slicing from the loaf pan or unmolding.

59 DINER MEATLOAF WITH PAN GRAVY

Prep: 15 minutes   Cook: 1 hour 5 minutes   Serves: 4 to 6

This recipe yields not only a luscious loaf, but a wonderful gravy just waiting to be poured onto mountains of hot mashed potatoes.

1 medium onion, finely chopped	⅜ teaspoon pepper
1 small green bell pepper, finely chopped	1½ pounds ground round (85% lean)
1 egg	½ pound ground pork
¾ cup rolled oats	2 tablespoons flour
½ cup tomato sauce	2 cups beef broth
2 tablespoons steak sauce	¼ teaspoon liquid gravy seasoning
¾ teaspoon garlic salt	¼ teaspoon salt

1. Preheat oven to 375°. In a medium bowl, combine onion, bell pepper, egg, oats, tomato sauce, steak sauce, garlic salt, and ¼ teaspoon pepper. Stir with a fork to mix. Add ground round and ground pork and blend well.

2. Rinse an 8 x 4 x 2½-inch loaf pan with cold water; shake out excess water but do not dry. Pack meat mixture into rinsed pan. Invert and unmold meatloaf onto a lightly oiled baking sheet.

3. Bake until a meat thermometer inserted into center of loaf reads 160° to 165°, about 1 hour. Let stand 5 minutes. Drain off excess fat into a small bowl; measure out 2 tablespoons fat, discarding remainder. Cover meatloaf with foil to keep warm.

4. In a medium saucepan, heat reserved fat over medium heat. Sprinkle in flour and cook, whisking constantly, until flour is lightly browned, about 2 minutes. Whisk in beef broth and gravy seasoning and bring to a boil, whisking until thick and smooth. Reduce heat to medium-low and simmer, stirring often, 5 minutes. Season with salt and remaining ⅛ teaspoon pepper. Slice meatloaf and pass a sauceboat of gravy on the side.

60 MOM'S CLASSIC MEATLOAF
Prep: 10 minutes   Cook: 1 hour   Serves: 4 to 6

1 small onion, chopped
1 egg
⅔ cup rolled oats
½ cup plus 3 tablespoons ketchup
1 tablespoon Worcestershire sauce

1 teaspoon salt
¼ teaspoon pepper
1 pound ground chuck (80% lean) or ground round (85% lean)
½ pound ground pork
½ pound ground veal

1. Preheat oven to 375°. Line a baking sheet with aluminum foil. Lightly oil foil.

2. In a medium bowl, combine onion, egg, oats, ½ cup ketchup, Worcestershire sauce, salt, and pepper. Stir with a fork until mixed. Add the ground chuck, pork, and veal and blend well.

3. Rinse an 8 x 4 x 2½-inch loaf pan with cold water; shake out excess water but do not dry. Pack meat mixture into rinsed pan. Invert and unmold meat mixture onto a foil-lined baking sheet. (If you prefer a moister, softer meatloaf to a crusty one, bake meatloaf in loaf pan on a baking sheet.)

4. Bake 45 minutes. Spread remaining 3 tablespoons ketchup over top of loaf and bake until a meat thermometer inserted in center of loaf reads 160° to 165°, about 15 minutes longer. Let stand 5 minutes before slicing.

61 EASY CHEESY MEATLOAF WITH QUICK CHEESE SAUCE
Prep: 10 minutes   Cook: 1¼ hours   Serves: 4 to 6

1 small onion, chopped
1 garlic clove, minced
1 (10¾-ounce) can Cheddar cheese soup
½ cup crushed tortilla chips, preferably unsalted
½ cup tomato juice
1 egg

½ teaspoon pepper
2 pounds ground round (85% lean)
1 (3.5-ounce) can sliced ripe olives
½ cup milk
⅛ teaspoon hot pepper sauce

1. Preheat oven to 375°. In a medium bowl, combine onion, garlic, ½ cup soup, tortilla chips, tomato juice, egg, and pepper. Add ground round and olives and mix well. Transfer meat mixture to center of a 9 x 13-inch flameproof baking pan and pack firmly into a free-form 8 x 4-inch loaf.

2. Bake until a meat thermometer inserted in center of loaf reads 160°, about 1¼ hours. Let stand 5 minutes, then transfer to a platter. Drain off excess fat.

3. Place baking pan on 2 burners on top of stove. Stir together remaining soup and milk and add to pan. Bring to a simmer over medium heat, stirring up browned bits from bottom of pan. Stir in hot sauce and serve cheese sauce with sliced meatloaf.

62 MEATLOAF RING WITH CAULIFLOWER GRATIN

Prep: 20 minutes   Cook: 64 minutes   Serves: 6

Mom's Meatloaf (4 ounces)
(page 54)
1 small head cauliflower,
broken into florets (about
1 pound)

1 cup shredded Cheddar
cheese
½ cup fresh bread crumbs
½ teaspoon paprika
1 tablespoon butter

1. Preheat oven to 375°. Prepare Mom's Meatloaf through step 2, deleting 3 tablespoons ketchup for topping loaf. Pack meat mixture into a rinsed 9-inch round, 5-cup ring mold. Invert onto a round ovenproof platter or pizza pan.

2. Bake until a meat thermometer inserted in center of meat reads 150°, about 45 minutes.

3. Meanwhile, in a large saucepan of boiling salted water, cook cauliflower just until crisp-tender, about 4 minutes. Drain well.

4. Heap drained cauliflower in center of meat ring. Sprinkle cheese over cauliflower and meat. Sprinkle bread crumbs and paprika over cauliflower; dot with butter. Bake until cheese is melted and crumbs are browned, about 15 minutes.

63 SOUTHWESTERN-STYLE NACHO MEATLOAF

Prep: 10 minutes   Cook: 1 hour   Serves: 4 to 6

1 cup tomato salsa, lightly
drained
¾ cup finely crushed tortilla
chips
1 egg
1 small onion, chopped
1 garlic clove, minced
1 small fresh green chile,
seeded and minced, or
⅛ teaspoon crushed hot
red pepper

1 tablespoon chili powder
1 teaspoon salt
½ teaspoon ground cumin
1½ pounds ground chuck
(80% lean) or ground
round (85% lean)
½ cup shredded sharp
Cheddar cheese

1. Preheat oven to 375°. In a medium bowl, combine salsa, tortilla chips, egg, onion, garlic, chile, chili powder, salt, and cumin. Stir with a fork until mixed. Add the ground chuck and mix until blended.

2. Pack mixture into an 8 x 4 x 2½-inch loaf pan. Place on a baking sheet and bake, uncovered, until a meat thermometer inserted in center of loaf reads 160° to 165°, about 1 hour. Sprinkle shredded Cheddar over top of loaf and bake until cheese is melted, about 3 minutes. Let stand 5 minutes before slicing.

64   MEATLOAF AND MASHED POTATO CROQUETTES

Prep: 10 minutes   Cook: 40 minutes   Serves: 4

1 pound boiling potatoes,
   peeled and cut into 1-inch
   pieces
2 tablespoons butter
¼ cup milk
1 egg
1 tablespoon minced fresh
   chives or 1 teaspoon dried

¼ teaspoon salt
1 pound ground round
   (85% lean)
¼ cup ketchup
¾ teaspoon onion salt
¼ teaspoon pepper
¼ cup grated Parmesan cheese
1 teaspoon paprika

1. Preheat oven to 375°. In a large saucepan of boiling salted water, cook potatoes until tender, about 15 minutes. Drain well. Mash potatoes with butter, milk, egg, chives, and salt.

2. In a medium bowl, mix ground round, ketchup, onion salt, and pepper. Divide meat mixture among 8 muffin cups (about 2¾ inches in diameter and 1¼ inches deep). With your fingers, press meat mixture evenly against bottoms and sides of each cup to form shells. Fill shells with mashed potatoes. Sprinkle Parmesan cheese and paprika over tops of potatoes.

3. Bake until tops are golden brown and meat shells are cooked through, about 25 minutes.

65   CORNY MEATLOAF

Prep: 15 minutes   Cook: 1 hour   Serves: 4 to 6

1½ cups corn flakes, crushed
2 eggs
1 cup tomato sauce
1 medium onion, chopped
1 medium green bell pepper,
   chopped
1 cup corn kernels, fresh or
   thawed frozen

1½ teaspoons garlic salt
¼ teaspoon pepper
2 pounds ground round
   (85% lean)
⅓ cup ketchup

1. Preheat oven to 350°. In a large bowl, mix corn flakes, eggs, tomato sauce, onion, bell pepper, corn, garlic salt, and pepper with a fork until well mixed. Add ground round and knead with your hands until blended. Transfer to an 8 x 4 x 2½-inch loaf pan.

2. Bake until a meat thermometer inserted in center of loaf reads 160°, about 1 hour. During last 15 minutes of baking time, spread ketchup over top of loaf. Let stand 5 minutes. Drain off excess fat and slice.

66 SCANDINAVIAN MEATLOAF WITH HORSERADISH AND SCALLIONS
Prep: 15 minutes   Cook: 1 hour   Serves: 4 to 6

1⅓ cups fresh pumpernickel
    bread crumbs (about
    2 slices)
1¼ cups sour cream
  3 tablespoons prepared
    horseradish
  3 scallions, chopped

  1 egg
  1 teaspoon salt
  ½ teaspoon pepper
  2 pounds ground chuck
    (80% lean) or ground
    round (85% lean)

1. Preheat oven to 375°. In a medium bowl, combine pumpernickel crumbs, ¾ cup sour cream, horseradish, scallions, egg, salt, and pepper. Mix with a fork until blended. Add ground chuck and mix well.

2. Pack mixture into a 9 x 5 x 3-inch loaf pan. Place on a baking sheet and bake, uncovered, 50 minutes. Spread remaining ½ cup sour cream over top of loaf and bake until a meat thermometer inserted in center of loaf reads 160° to 165°, about 10 minutes. Let stand 5 minutes before slicing.

---

67 "THE REAL THING" MEATLOAF
Prep: 10 minutes   Cook: 1¼ hours   Serves: 4 to 6

Ann Landers had a similar recipe that was so popular, she had to publish it once a year. No claims were made, but it seems to have had a revitalizing effect on marriages lacking in culinary harmony.

1½ cups dried bread crumbs
  ¾ cup ketchup
  1 envelope dry onion soup
    mix
  ½ cup hot water
  2 eggs
  1 teaspoon Worcestershire
    sauce

  1 pound ground round (85%
    lean)
  ½ pound ground pork
  ½ pound ground veal
  4 strips of bacon
  1 cup tomato sauce

1. Preheat oven to 350°. In a large bowl, mix bread crumbs, ketchup, onion soup mix, and hot water. Stir in eggs and Worcestershire sauce. Add ground round, ground pork, and ground veal and knead with your hands until well blended.

2. In a 10 x 7-inch baking pan, form meat mixture into a 9 x 5-inch free-form loaf. Top loaf with bacon slices. Pour tomato sauce over loaf, smoothing top to allow sauce to run down sides.

3. Bake until a meat thermometer inserted in center of loaf reads 165°, about 1¼ hours. Let stand 5 minutes before cutting into slices to serve.

68   GARDEN PATCH MEATLOAF
Prep: 15 minutes   Cook: 1 hour 18 minutes   Serves: 4 to 6

1 tablespoon olive oil
2 medium leeks (white and tender green), well rinsed and chopped, or 2 medium onions, chopped
1 medium zucchini, scrubbed and grated
1 medium carrot, grated
2 garlic cloves, minced
1 (14-ounce) can Italian peeled tomatoes, drained
¾ cup fresh bread crumbs

2 eggs
2 tablespoons chopped parsley
1½ teaspoons dried basil
1¼ teaspoons salt
¼ teaspoon pepper
1 pound ground round (85% lean)
½ pound ground pork
½ pound ground veal

1. In a large skillet, heat oil. Add leeks and cook over medium heat, stirring often, until softened, about 3 minutes. Off heat, stir in zucchini, carrot, and garlic; set vegetables aside.

2. In a large bowl, combine tomatoes, bread crumbs, eggs, parsley, basil, salt, and pepper, breaking up tomatoes with a spoon. Add ground round, ground pork, ground veal, and reserved vegetables. Knead with your hands until well blended. Transfer mixture to a 9 x 5 x 3-inch loaf pan.

3. Bake until a meat thermometer inserted in center of loaf reads 160°, about 1¼ hours. Let stand 5 minutes. Drain off excess fat and slice.

---

69   BALL PARK MEATLOAF
Prep: 10 minutes   Cook: 45 minutes   Serves: 4

⅓ cup plus 1 tablespoon spicy brown mustard
½ cup sweet pickle relish with juices
¾ cup fresh bread crumbs
1 egg
1 small onion, chopped

1 teaspoon garlic salt
⅛ teaspoon pepper
¾ pound ground chuck (80% lean) or ground round (85% lean)
¾ pound ground pork
1½ teaspoons brown sugar

1. Preheat oven to 350°. In a medium bowl, combine ⅓ cup mustard, relish, bread crumbs, egg, onion, garlic salt, and pepper. Mix to blend well. Add ground chuck and ground pork and mix until combined.

2. Pack mixture into an 8 x 4 x 2½-inch loaf pan. Place on a baking sheet and bake until a meat thermometer inserted in center of loaf reads 155° to 160°, 35 to 40 minutes.

3. In a small bowl, combine remaining 1 tablespoon mustard with brown sugar. Brush mixture over top of meatloaf and bake until topping is glazed, about 5 minutes. Let stand 5 minutes before slicing.

70 RAVIOLI MEATLOAF
Prep: 10 minutes   Cook: 1 hour   Serves: 4 to 6

1 small onion, chopped
1 garlic clove, minced
½ cup Italian-seasoned bread
  crumbs
¼ cup milk
1 egg

1¼ teaspoons salt
¼ teaspoon pepper
1½ pounds ground round
  (85% lean)
1 (15½-ounce) can ravioli in
  sauce

1. Preheat oven to 350°. In medium bowl, combine onion, garlic, bread crumbs, milk, egg, salt, and pepper. Add ground round and mix well. Transfer half of meat mixture to a lightly oiled 9 x 5 x 3-inch loaf pan. Spread ravioli on top. Cover with remaining meat mixture and press firmly.

2. Bake until a meat thermometer inserted in center of loaf reads 160°, about 1 hour. Let stand 10 minutes. Drain off excess fat and invert onto a serving platter.

---

71 POT ROAST MEATLOAF
Prep: 20 minutes   Cook: 1 hour   Serves: 4 to 6

1 small onion, chopped
1 celery rib, chopped
2 cups tomato sauce
1 cup fresh bread crumbs
⅓ cup chopped parsley
1 egg
1½ teaspoons salt
½ teaspoon celery seed
½ teaspoon pepper
2 pounds ground round
  (85% lean)

3 medium carrots, cut into
  1-inch chunks
4 medium red potatoes (about
  1 pound), quartered
10 small white boiling onions,
  peeled
½ teaspoon marjoram
½ cup beef broth

1. Preheat oven to 450°. In a medium bowl, combine onion, celery, 1 cup tomato sauce, bread crumbs, parsley, egg, 1 teaspoon salt, celery seed, and ¼ teaspoon pepper. Mix well. Add ground round and mix until blended.

2. Rinse a 9 x 5 x 3-inch loaf pan with cold water; shake out excess water but do not dry. Pack meat mixture into rinsed loaf pan. Invert and unmold loaf into a lightly greased 9 x 13-inch baking pan.

3. Surround meatloaf with carrots, potatoes, and onions. Season vegetables with marjoram and remaining ½ teaspoon salt and ¼ teaspoon pepper. Cover pan with aluminum foil.

4. Bake 15 minutes. Reduce oven temperature to 350° and bake 30 minutes. Uncover and drain off excess fat from pan. Pour remaining 1 cup tomato sauce over meatloaf, letting excess run down sides. Pour beef broth over all and bake until a meat thermometer inserted in center of loaf reads 160° to 165°, about 15 minutes longer. Let stand 5 minutes before serving.

72 MEATLOAF ITALIANO
Prep: 10 minutes   Cook: 1 hour   Serves: 4 to 6

1 (15-ounce) can Italian-
flavored stewed tomatoes,
drained and coarsely
chopped
¾ cup Italian-seasoned bread
crumbs
2 eggs
1 teaspoon salt

¼ teaspoon crushed hot red
pepper
1½ pounds ground chuck
(80% lean)
½ pound ground pork
1 cup large-curd cottage
cheese

1. Preheat oven to 350°. In a large bowl, combine stewed tomatoes, bread crumbs, eggs, salt, and hot pepper. Add ground chuck, ground pork, and cottage cheese and knead with your hands until mixed. Transfer to a 9 x 5 x 3-inch loaf pan.

2. Bake until a meat thermometer inserted in center of loaf reads 160°, about 1 hour. Let stand 5 minutes. Pour off excess fat and slice.

73 ITALIAN MEATLOAF ROLLATINI
Prep: 20 minutes   Cook: 1 hour   Serves: 6 to 8

1 cup fresh bread crumbs
2 eggs
1 (28-ounce) jar marinara
sauce
1 teaspoon Italian seasoning
1 teaspoon garlic salt
¼ teaspoon pepper
1 pound ground round
(85% lean)

1 pound ground veal
1 medium onion, finely
chopped
4 ounces sliced mozzarella
cheese
4 ounces sliced hard salami

1. Preheat oven to 350°. Lightly oil a 9 x 13-inch baking dish. In a large bowl, mix bread crumbs, eggs, ⅔ cup marinara sauce, Italian seasoning, garlic salt, and pepper with a fork until well blended. Add ground round, ground veal, and onion and knead with your hands until mixed.

2. Sprinkle a large sheet of wax paper or foil with water. With wet hands, pat out meat mixture into a 9 x 12-inch rectangle. Arrange overlapping mozzarella slices over surface of meat rectangle, leaving a 1-inch border around all sides. Cover cheese with overlapping salami slices.

3. Using wax paper to help lift, roll up into a cylinder and press seams closed. Pick up rolled loaf in wax paper or foil and roll off into prepared baking dish, seam side down.

4. Bake 45 minutes and drain off fat. Pour remaining marinara sauce over top of meat and continue baking until a meat thermometer inserted in center of loaf reads 160°, 15 to 20 minutes longer. Skim off excess fat from surface of sauce. Slice and serve with sauce.

74 SHERRIED SPANISH MEATLOAF

Prep: 10 minutes   Cook: 1 hour   Serves: 4 to 6

1 cup fresh bread crumbs
⅓ cup dry sherry
1 egg
1 pound ground chuck
    (80% lean) or ground
    round (85% lean)
1 pound ground pork
⅓ cup chopped pimiento-
    stuffed green olives
⅓ cup pine nuts (pignoli) or
    chopped slivered
    blanched almonds

¼ cup raisins
1 teaspoon salt
½ teaspoon ground cinnamon
¼ teaspoon black pepper
¼ teaspoon crushed hot red
    pepper
2 medium tomatoes, sliced
    ¼ inch thick

1. Preheat oven to 375°. In a medium bowl, soak bread crumbs in sherry until soft, about 3 minutes. Add egg and beat until mixed. Add ground chuck, ground pork, olives, pine nuts, raisins, salt, cinnamon, black pepper, and hot pepper; mix until well blended.

2. Pack mixture into an 8 x 4 x 2½-inch loaf pan. Place on a baking sheet and bake 30 minutes. Arrange tomato slices, overlapping, in 2 rows on top of loaf and continue baking until a meat thermometer inserted in center of loaf reads 160° to 165°, 25 to 30 minutes longer. Let stand about 10 minutes before serving.

75 CHEESY OLIVE LOAF

Prep: 15 minutes   Cook: 1¼ hours   Serves: 4 to 6

6 ounces sharp Cheddar
    cheese
1 cup Cheddar-flavored mini-
    crackers, crushed (about
    2½ ounces)
3 scallions, chopped
3 tablespoons tomato paste

1 egg
¾ teaspoon salt
¼ teaspoon pepper
1½ pounds ground round
    (85% lean)
½ cup chopped pitted black
    olives

1. Preheat oven to 350°. Cut 4 ounces of Cheddar into ½-inch cubes to make about 1 cup. Coarsely grate remaining Cheddar and set aside.

2. In a large bowl, mix crushed crackers, scallions, tomato paste, egg, salt, and pepper with a fork until blended. Add ground round, diced Cheddar, and chopped olives. Knead with your hands until mixed. Transfer to an 8 x 4 x 2½-inch loaf pan.

3. Bake 1 hour. Sprinkle grated cheese over top of loaf and continue baking until a meat thermometer reads about 160°, 10 to 15 minutes longer. Let stand 5 minutes. Drain off excess fat and slice.

76 MONSTER MEATBALL MEATLOAF
Prep: 15 minutes   Cook: 1¼ hours   Serves: 4 to 6

A fun way to serve three, count 'em, *three* family favorites at once—spaghetti, meatballs, and meatloaf!

1   cup Italian-seasoned bread
    crumbs
1   (8-ounce) can tomato sauce
    with onions and peppers
1   small onion, chopped
2   garlic cloves, minced
2   eggs
¼   cup chopped parsley
1½ teaspoons Italian seasoning
½   teaspoon salt
⅛   teaspoon crushed hot red
    pepper

1   pound sweet or hot Italian
    sausage, casings removed
1   pound ground round
    (85% lean) or ground
    chuck (80% lean)
2   (14-ounce) jars marinara
    sauce
1   pound spaghetti
2   tablespoons olive oil
    Grated Parmesan cheese

1. Preheat oven to 350°. Line an 8-cup bowl with plastic wrap, letting excess wrap hang over sides.

2. In a medium bowl, combine seasoned bread crumbs, tomato sauce, onion, garlic, eggs, parsley, Italian seasoning, salt, and hot pepper. Add Italian sausage and ground round and mix until well blended. Pack meat mixture into lined bowl. Invert bowl into a lightly oiled 9 x 13-inch baking pan. Remove bowl and plastic wrap; smooth over any holes in surface of meat.

3. Bake until a meat thermometer inserted in center of loaf reads 145° to 150°, 45 to 50 minutes. Drain off excess fat in pan. Pour marinara sauce over top of meatloaf, letting excess run down sides. Bake until a meat thermometer inserted in center of loaf reads 160° to 165°, 10 to 15 minutes longer. Let meatloaf stand 5 minutes.

4. After pouring sauce over meatloaf, bring a large pot of salted water to a boil over high heat. Add spaghetti and cook until tender but still firm, 8 to 10 minutes; drain well. Toss spaghetti with olive oil. Cut meatloaf into wedges. Serve with spaghetti and spoon sauce from pan over both. Pass a bowl of grated Parmesan cheese on the side.

77 LITTLE ITALY MEATLOAF
Prep: 15 minutes   Cook: 1¼ hours   Serves: 4 to 6

1 medium onion, chopped	2 tablespoons tomato paste
1 garlic clove, minced	1½ teaspoons basil
1 cup Italian-seasoned bread crumbs	1 teaspoon salt
½ cup chopped black olives	¼ teaspoon crushed hot red pepper
½ cup chopped oil-packed sun-dried tomatoes, drained	2 pounds ground round (85% lean)
½ cup dry red wine	3 tablespoons grated Parmesan cheese
2 eggs	

1. Preheat oven to 350°. In a large bowl, combine onion, garlic, bread crumbs, olives, sun-dried tomatoes, wine, eggs, tomato paste, basil, salt, and hot pepper. Add ground round and knead with your hands until well blended. Transfer mixture to a 9 x 5 x 3-inch loaf pan.

2. Bake 1 hour. Sprinkle Parmesan cheese over top and bake 15 minutes longer, or until cheese melts and a meat thermometer inserted in center of loaf reads 160°. Let stand 5 minutes. Pour off excess fat and slice.

78 SKILLET MEATLOAF
Prep: 10 minutes   Cook: 30 minutes   Serves: 4

1 small onion, chopped	1 teaspoon garlic salt
1 small green bell pepper, chopped	¼ teaspoon pepper
¾ cup dried bread crumbs	1 pound ground round (85% lean)
¼ cup milk	1 tablespoon vegetable oil
1 egg	1½ cups tomato sauce

1. In a medium bowl, combine onion, bell pepper, bread crumbs, milk, egg, garlic salt, and pepper. Add ground round and knead with your hands until well mixed.

2. Put meat mixture in a 9-inch nonstick skillet and form into an 8-inch patty. Add oil to skillet and cook over medium heat, occasionally lifting up patty with a wide spatula and tilting pan to let oil run underneath, until bottom is browned, about 5 minutes.

3. Drain off excess fat. Place a plate over top of skillet and carefully invert skillet and plate together so patty is on plate. Slide patty, uncooked side down, back into skillet and cook until underside is just beginning to brown, about 3 minutes. Drain off excess fat.

4. Pour tomato sauce and ½ cup water over meat and bring to a simmer. Reduce heat to low, cover, and simmer until patty is cooked through, about 20 minutes. Let stand 5 minutes before cutting into wedges and serving with tomato sauce from skillet.

79 MEATLOAF SALUMERIA
Prep: 15 minutes   Cook: 1¾ hours   Serves: 6 to 8

1 cup fresh bread crumbs
1 medium onion, chopped
3 garlic cloves, minced
½ cup dried Italian-seasoned bread crumbs
¼ cup grated Parmesan cheese
2 eggs
2 tablespoons chopped parsley
1½ teaspoons salt
½ teaspoon pepper

2 pounds ground round (85% lean)
1 (10-ounce) package mixed vegetables, thawed
2 ounces boiled ham, cut into ¼-inch dice
2 ounces Genoa salami, cut into ¼-inch dice
½ cup finely diced Cheddar cheese
2 cups tomato sauce

1. Preheat oven to 350°. In a large bowl, mix fresh bread crumbs and ¼ cup water. Let stand 1 minute. Squeeze out excess water; put bread crumbs in a large bowl.

2. Add onion, garlic, dried seasoned bread crumbs, Parmesan cheese, eggs, parsley, salt, and pepper to bowl; mix well. Add ground round, mixed vegetables, ham, salami, and Cheddar cheese. Knead with your hands to mix well. Place meatloaf mixture on a lightly oiled 9 x 13-inch baking pan and form into a 9 x 5-inch loaf.

3. In a medium bowl, combine tomato sauce and 2 cups water. Pour over meatloaf. Bake, basting occasionally with tomato sauce, and adding additional water to pan to avoid scorching, if necessary, until a meat thermometer inserted in center of loaf reads 165°, about 1¾ hours.

4. Let stand 5 minutes. Skim off excess fat from surface of sauce. Slice and serve with tomato sauce from pan.

80 MEATLOAF ALASKA
Prep: 15 minutes   Cook: 1¼ hours   Serves: 4 to 6

1 small onion, chopped
1 egg
⅔ cup rolled oats
½ cup ketchup
1 tablespoon Worcestershire sauce
2 teaspoons salt
½ teaspoon pepper
2 pounds ground round (85% lean)

4 large russet potatoes, (about 2 pounds), peeled and cut into 1-inch chunks
3 tablespoons butter
About ½ cup milk
1 egg yolk, well beaten
⅓ cup finely shredded Cheddar cheese

1. Preheat oven to 375°. In a medium bowl, combine onion, egg, oats, ketchup, Worcestershire sauce, 1 teaspoon salt, and ¼ teaspoon pepper. Stir with a fork until mixed. Add ground round and blend well.

2. Rinse an 8 x 4 x 2½-inch loaf pan with cold water; shake out excess water but do not dry. Pack meat mixture into rinsed pan. Invert and unmold meatloaf onto a lightly oiled baking sheet.

3. Bake until a meat thermometer inserted into center of loaf reads 150° to 155°, about 45 minutes. Let meatloaf stand 5 minutes and drain off excess fat. Leave oven on.

4. Meanwhile, in a large saucepan of boiling salted water, cook potato chunks until just tender when pierced with tip of a sharp knife, 15 to 20 minutes. Drain well.

5. In a medium bowl, mash potatoes with butter and remaining 1 teaspoon salt and ¼ teaspoon pepper, adding enough milk to reach desired consistency. Let cool slightly, then beat in egg yolk. Using a long, narrow metal cake spatula, spread mashed potatoes over top and sides of loaf. (If desired, pipe mashed potatoes through a large pastry bag fitted with a large open star tip.) Sprinkle Cheddar cheese over top of mashed potatoes.

6. Return meatloaf to oven and bake until potatoes are lightly browned and cheese is melted, about 15 minutes. Let stand 5 minutes, then cut into 1-inch-thick slices to serve.

---

81 JIM'S MEATLOAF WITH SKILLET-GLAZED VEGETABLES

Prep: 15 minutes   Cook: 1 hour 25 minutes   Serves: 4 to 6

This is based on Jim Fobel's recipe, from his *Diet Feasts*, where he "beefs up" meatloaf by using lots of browned vegetables.

1 tablespoon olive oil	1 cup tomato sauce
2 cups chopped cabbage (about 8 ounces)	¼ cup chopped parsley
	½ teaspoon basil
2 celery ribs, chopped	½ teaspoon celery seed
1 medium onion, chopped	1 teaspoon salt
1 garlic clove, minced	¼ teaspoon pepper
1 cup dried bread crumbs	1½ pounds ground sirloin (90% lean)
2 eggs	

1. Preheat oven to 350°. In a large nonstick skillet, heat oil over medium-high heat. Add cabbage, celery, onion, and garlic and cook, stirring often, until vegetables are beginning to brown, about 5 minutes. Add 2 tablespoons water and cook until liquid evaporates, about 2 minutes. Add 2 more tablespoons water and cook until liquid evaporates and vegetables are well browned, about 2 minutes longer. Transfer vegetables to a medium bowl.

2. Add bread crumbs, eggs, ½ cup tomato sauce, parsley, basil, celery seed, salt, and pepper to bowl. Blend well. Add ground sirloin and knead in bowl with your hands until mixed. Transfer to a 9 x 5 x 3-inch loaf pan.

3. Bake 1 hour. Spread remaining ½ cup tomato sauce over top of meatloaf. Continue to bake until a meat thermometer inserted in center of loaf reads 160°, about 15 minutes longer. Let stand 5 minutes before serving.

82   GRANT AVENUE MEATLOAF
Prep: 15 minutes   Cook: 1¼ hours   Serves: 4 to 6

2 scallions, minced
1 celery rib, chopped
2 teaspoons minced fresh
    ginger
1 cup crispy rice cereal
½ cup chopped water
    chestnuts

2 eggs
2 tablespoons soy sauce
1 teaspoon salt
¼ teaspoon pepper
1 pound ground round
    (85% lean)
1 pound ground pork

1. Preheat oven to 350°. In a medium bowl, combine scallions, celery, ginger, cereal, water chestnuts, eggs, soy sauce, salt, and pepper. Add ground round and ground pork and knead with your hands until blended. Transfer mixture to a 9 x 5 x 3-inch loaf pan.

2. Bake until a meat thermometer inserted in center of loaf reads 160°, about 1¼ hours. Let stand 5 minutes. Pour off excess fat and slice.

83   MEATLOAF 'N' OVEN FRIES SUPPER
Prep: 15 minutes   Cook: 1¼ hours   Serves: 4 to 6

1¼ cups fresh bread crumbs
1¼ cups tomato-vegetable juice,
    such as V-8
1 small onion, chopped
2 eggs
1½ teaspoons salt
1 teaspoon savory
⅜ teaspoon pepper
2 pounds ground round
    (85% lean)

4 strips of bacon
3 large russet potatoes (about
    1¼ pounds), peeled
2 tablespoons flour
1½ cups beef broth
¼ teaspoon liquid gravy
    seasoning

1. Preheat oven to 350°. In a medium bowl, combine bread crumbs, tomato-vegetable juice, onion, eggs, 1 teaspoon salt, savory, and ¼ teaspoon pepper. Mix well. Add ground round and mix until blended. In a lightly oiled flameproof 10 x 15-inch baking dish, pat meat mixture into a free-form loaf, about 9 x 5 inches. Arrange bacon strips diagonally across top of loaf, tucking ends down sides.

2. Cut each potato lengthwise into eighths. Cut each piece lengthwise in half again, so each potato yields 16 wedges. Arrange potato wedges around meatloaf and season with remaining ½ teaspoon salt and ⅛ teaspoon pepper.

3. Bake until a meat thermometer inserted in center of loaf reads 160° to 165°, 60 to 70 minutes. With a bulb baster, occasionally remove and reserve excess fat from pan and turn potatoes with a metal spatula. Transfer meatloaf and potatoes to a serving platter and cover with foil to keep warm.

4. Place baking dish over 2 burners on top of the stove. Add 2 tablespoons reserved fat. Sprinkle in flour and cook over medium heat, whisking constantly, until mixture is light brown, about 2 minutes. Whisk in beef broth and gravy seasoning and bring to a boil, whisking until smooth and thickened. Reduce heat to low and simmer 3 minutes. Season gravy with additional salt and pepper and serve with meatloaf and potatoes.

---

84 HAM LOAF WITH TANGY PINEAPPLE SAUCE

Prep: 15 minutes   Cook: 1 to 1¼ hours   Serves: 6 to 8

½ pound boiled ham, coarsely chopped	2 teaspoons dry mustard
1½ cups fresh bread crumbs	¼ teaspoon hot pepper sauce
½ cup milk	¼ teaspoon pepper
2 eggs	1 pound ground pork
¼ cup pineapple syrup (reserved from Tangy Pineapple Sauce, below)	Tangy Pineapple Sauce (recipe follows)

1. Preheat oven to 350°. In a food processor, pulse boiled ham until very finely chopped. (Ham can also be ground in a meat grinder.)

2. In a large bowl, mix bread crumbs, milk, eggs, pineapple syrup, mustard, hot sauce, and pepper until blended. Add ground pork and chopped ham; knead with your hands until well mixed. Transfer to an 8 x 4 x 2½-inch loaf pan.

3. Bake until a meat thermometer inserted in center of loaf reads 160°, 1 to 1¼ hours. Let stand 5 minutes. Drain off excess fat and slice. Serve with Tangy Pineapple Sauce.

TANGY PINEAPPLE SAUCE
Makes about 1½ cups

1 (8-ounce) can pineapple chunks in syrup	¼ cup chicken broth
1½ teaspoons cornstarch	2 tablespoons brown sugar
1 tablespoon cider vinegar	1 teaspoon ketchup

1. Drain pineapple chunks, reserving syrup.

2. In a small bowl, dissolve cornstarch in vinegar. In a small saucepan, combine cornstarch mixture, chicken broth, ¼ cup pineapple syrup, brown sugar, and ketchup. Cook over low heat, stirring often, until mixture comes to a simmer and thickens, about 2 minutes. Add drained pineapple chunks and stir until pineapple is heated through, about 1 minute.

85   FRUITED AFRICAN MEATLOAF
Prep: 10 minutes   Cook: 1½ hours   Serves: 4 to 6

This is equally excellent with ground lamb or with a half-and-half combination of lamb and beef.

½ cup chopped dried apricots	1½ teaspoons salt
½ cup orange juice	½ teaspoon ground coriander
1 cup fresh bread crumbs	½ teaspoon ground ginger
1 medium onion, chopped	¼ teaspoon ground allspice
¾ cup chopped roasted	¼ teaspoon pepper
unsalted peanuts	2 pounds ground round
½ cup tomato juice	(85% lean)
2 eggs	2 tablespoons brown sugar

1. Preheat oven to 350°. In a small saucepan, bring apricots and orange juice to a simmer over low heat and cook until apricots are soft, about 10 minutes; drain. Cut apricots into ½-inch pieces.

2. In a medium bowl, combine bread crumbs, chopped onion, chopped apricots, ½ cup peanuts, tomato juice, eggs, salt, coriander, ginger, allspice, and pepper. Add ground round and knead with your hands until well mixed. Transfer to a 9 x 5 x 3-inch loaf pan.

3. Bake 1 hour. Sprinkle brown sugar over top of loaf. Top with remaining ¼ cup peanuts, pressing peanuts lightly into loaf to adhere. Continue to bake until a meat thermometer inserted in center of loaf reads 160°, about 15 minutes longer. Let stand 10 minutes. Pour off excess fat and cut into slices to serve.

86   MUSHROOM AND WHEAT GERM MEATLOAF
Prep: 10 minutes   Cook: 1 hour 20 minutes   Serves: 4 to 6

2 teaspoons butter	2 tablespoons steak sauce
1 medium onion, chopped	1 teaspoon salt
½ pound fresh mushrooms,	¼ teaspoon pepper
sliced	1 pound ground round
1 cup wheat germ	(85% lean)
½ cup milk	½ pound ground pork
2 eggs	½ pound ground veal

1. Preheat oven to 350°F. In a large skillet, melt butter over medium heat. Add onion and mushrooms. Cook, stirring often, until mushrooms begin to brown, about 5 minutes. Transfer mixture to a medium bowl.

2. Add wheat germ, milk, eggs, steak sauce, salt, and pepper to bowl: mix well. Add ground round, ground pork, and ground veal and knead with your hands until well blended. Transfer to a 9 x 5 x 3-inch loaf pan.

3. Bake until a meat thermometer inserted in center of loaf reads 160°, about 1¼ hours. Let stand 5 minutes. Pour off excess fat and slice.

87 DAVID'S GRANOLA LOAF
Prep: 10 minutes   Cook: 1¼ hours   Serves: 4 to 6

Be sure to seek out unsweetened granola at your favorite natural foods store. While the grocery store variety may be okay at the breakfast table, it's too sweet to use here.

1 medium onion, chopped	2 teaspoons salt
2 medium carrots, grated	½ teaspoon pepper
1½ cups unsweetened granola	2 pounds ground sirloin
½ cup milk	(90% lean)
2 eggs	
3 tablespoons Worcestershire sauce	

1. Preheat oven to 350°. In a medium bowl, combine onion, carrots, granola, milk, eggs, Worcestershire sauce, salt, and pepper. Add ground sirloin and knead with your hands until well blended. Transfer mixture to a 9 x 5 x 3-inch loaf pan.

2. Bake until a meat thermometer inserted in center of loaf reads 160°, about 1¼ hours. Let stand about 5 minutes before slicing.

---

88 FAT TUESDAY'S MEATLOAF
Prep: 15 minutes   Cook: 1 hour 20 minutes   Serves: 4 to 6

2 tablespoons vegetable oil	1½ teaspoons garlic salt
1 medium onion, chopped	1 teaspoon thyme
1 medium red bell pepper, chopped	½ teaspoon oregano
	½ teaspoon basil
1 medium celery rib, chopped	¼ teaspoon cayenne
1 cup fresh bread crumbs	1 pound ground round
1 cup tomato sauce	(85% lean)
2 eggs	1 pound ground pork
2 tablespoons Worcestershire sauce	

1. Preheat oven to 350°. Heat oil in a large skillet over medium-high heat. Add onion, bell pepper, and celery and cook, stirring often, until onion is lightly browned, about 6 minutes.

2. In a medium bowl, combine bread crumbs, ½ cup tomato sauce, eggs, Worcestershire sauce, garlic salt, thyme, oregano, basil, and cayenne; blend until mixed. Add ground beef and ground pork and knead with your hands until well blended. Transfer mixture to a 9 x 5 x 3-inch loaf pan. Spread remaining tomato sauce over top of loaf.

3. Bake until a meat thermometer inserted in center of loaf reads 160°, about 1¼ hours. Let stand 5 minutes. Drain off excess fat and slice.

89   ED DEBEVIC'S BURNT MEATLOAF

Prep: 20 minutes   Cook: 55 minutes   Serves: 8 to 12

This is a double-loaf batch, but it can easily be halved. "Ed" recommends cooling the meatloaf, chilling it overnight, and reheating it to allow the flavors to blend. We couldn't wait that long to sample it, and it was just as delicious served the same day it was made.

¼ cup vegetable oil	2 tablespoons soy sauce
1 large onion, finely chopped	2 eggs
2 medium bell peppers, preferably 1 red and 1 green, finely chopped	1 tablespoon salt
	1½ teaspoons pepper
	3½ pounds ground round (85% lean)
3 garlic cloves, minced	1½ pounds ground pork
1 cup dried bread crumbs	2 (3-ounce) cans tomato paste
3 tablespoons heavy cream	

1. Preheat oven to 475°. In a large skillet, heat oil. Add onion, bell peppers, and garlic and cook over medium heat, stirring often, until vegetables are just softened, but not browned, about 5 minutes.

2. In a large bowl, combine bread crumbs, cream, soy sauce, eggs, salt, and pepper with cooked vegetables. Mix well. Add ground round and ground pork and knead with your hands until well blended. Pack half of meat mixture into a rinsed 9 x 5 x 3-inch loaf pan.

3. Invert to unmold loaf onto a foil-lined baking sheet. Rinse loaf pan and repeat with remaining meat mixture. Using a rubber spatula, spread a thick layer of tomato paste over the top and sides of each loaf.

4. Bake until tomato paste layer is browned and a meat thermometer inserted in center of loaf reads 160°, about 50 minutes. (Tomato paste should be slightly charred.) Let stand 10 minutes before slicing.

90   DILLY MINI-MEATLOAVES

Prep: 10 minutes   Cook: 35 minutes   Serves: 6

1 cup saltine cracker crumbs	2 eggs
½ cup chopped dill pickles	1½ teaspoons celery salt
¼ cup dill pickle juice	½ teaspoon pepper
2 tablespoons chopped parsley	2 pounds ground round (85% lean)

1. Preheat oven to 375°. In a large bowl, mix cracker crumbs, pickles, pickle juice, parsley, eggs, celery salt, and pepper. Add ground round and knead with your hands until blended.

2. On a baking sheet, form meat mixture into 3 mini-loaves, each about 5 x 3 inches. Bake until a meat thermometer inserted in center of a loaf reads 160°, about 35 minutes.

91 ALMOST LIL'S MEATLOAF
Prep: 10 minutes   Cook: 1¼ hours   Serves: 4

My friend Lil makes this with ground beef, but I found it was fantastic with the "new ground meat"—chicken. Lil warns, "Don't add salt to the recipe—canned soup has enough."

- 1 **medium onion, chopped**
- 1 **celery rib, chopped**
- 3 **garlic cloves, minced**
- 1 **(10¾-ounce) can chicken and rice soup**
- ½ **cup fresh bread crumbs**
- ¼ **cup grated Parmesan cheese**
- ¼ **teaspoon pepper**
- 1½ **pounds ground chicken.**

1. Preheat oven to 350°. In a medium bowl, combine onion, celery, garlic, soup, bread crumbs, Parmesan cheese, and pepper. Add ground chicken and mix well. Transfer to an 8 x 4 x 2½-inch loaf pan.

2. Bake until a meat thermometer inserted in center of loaf reads 160°, about 1¼ hours. Let stand 5 minutes before slicing.

---

92 CHICKEN COUSCOUS LOAF WITH ALMOND CRUST
Prep: 20 minutes   Cook: 1 hour 10 minutes   Serves: 4 to 6

- ¾ **cup reduced-sodium chicken broth or water**
- 1 **teaspoon butter**
- 1⅛ **teaspoons salt**
- ½ **cup instant couscous**
- 1 **medium carrot, grated**
- 1 **medium zucchini, grated**
- 1 **small onion, chopped**
- ⅓ **cup raisins**
- ½ **teaspoon turmeric**
- ½ **teaspoon ground ginger**
- ¼ **teaspoon cinnamon**
- ⅛ **teaspoon crushed hot red pepper**
- 2 **eggs—1 whole, 1 separated**
- 1¼ **pounds ground chicken**
- ¾ **cup blanched almonds, finely chopped**

1. Preheat oven to 350°. In a small saucepan, bring chicken broth, butter, and ⅛ teaspoon salt to a boil; stir in couscous. Cover immediately, remove from heat, and let stand 5 minutes. Fluff couscous with a fork and let cool slightly.

2. In a medium bowl, combine couscous, grated carrot and zucchini, chopped onion, raisins, remaining 1 teaspoon salt, turmeric, ginger, cinnamon, and hot pepper. With a fork, stir in 1 whole egg plus 1 egg yolk until lightly beaten. Add ground chicken and mix until well blended. Pack mixture into a lightly oiled 8 x 4 x 2½-inch loaf pan.

3. Place loaf pan on a baking sheet and bake 45 minutes. In a small bowl, beat egg white until foamy. Stir in chopped almonds. Remove loaf from oven and spread almond mixture evenly over top. Bake 15 minutes longer, or until almond crust is lightly browned. Let loaf stand 5 minutes. Run a knife around inside of pan to loosen, invert loaf onto a serving platter, and serve immediately.

93   RICE AND CHEDDAR–STUFFED TURKEY LOAF

Prep: 20 minutes   Cook: 1¼ hours   Serves: 4 to 6

1 cup cooked rice	¼ cup evaporated milk
½ cup shredded sharp Cheddar cheese	1 small onion, minced
	1 egg
¼ cup finely chopped sweet red or green bell pepper	1 teaspoon chili powder
	½ teaspoon salt
½ cup fresh whole wheat bread crumbs	¼ teaspoon pepper
	1½ pounds ground turkey

1. Preheat oven to 350°. In a small bowl, combine rice, Cheddar cheese, and chopped bell pepper.

2. In a medium bowl, combine bread crumbs, evaporated milk, onion, egg, chili powder, salt, and pepper. Add ground turkey and mix well. Transfer half of turkey mixture to a lightly oiled 8 x 4 x 2½-inch loaf pan. Cover with rice mixture, then top with remaining turkey mixture.

3. Bake until a meat thermometer inserted in center of loaf reads 160°, about 1¼ hours.

94   MINI-LOAVES ABERDEEN

Prep: 20 minutes   Cook: 50 minutes   Serves: 6

1 medium onion, finely chopped	1 pound ground pork
	6 hard-boiled eggs, shelled
½ cup saltine cracker crumbs	1 (15-ounce) can stewed tomatoes, with their juice
3 tablespoons milk	
1 egg	1 cup tomato sauce
¾ teaspoon sage	6 thin slices of Cheddar cheese (about 4 ounces)
½ teaspoon salt	
¼ teaspoon pepper	

1. In a medium bowl, combine onion, cracker crumbs, milk, egg, sage, salt, and pepper. Add ground pork and mix well to combine.

2. Divide meat mixture into 6 equal parts. Using wet hands, pat one part of meat mixture evenly around a hard-boiled egg to cover it completely, and form into a small oval. Transfer to a lightly oiled 12 x 8-inch baking dish. Repeat with remaining meat mixture and eggs.

3. In a medium bowl, combine stewed tomatoes and tomato sauce. Pour tomato mixture over meatloaves. Bake until meatloaves show no trace of pink when prodded with tip of a knife, about 45 minutes.

4. Top each mini-loaf with a slice of Cheddar, trimming cheese, if necessary, to fit. Bake until cheese melts, about 5 minutes. Let stand 5 minutes. Skim off fat from surface of sauce and serve.

95 MINNESOTA TURKEY LOAF WITH WILD RICE

Prep: 15 minutes   Cook: 2 hours   Serves: 4 to 6

1½ cups reduced-sodium
    chicken broth
½ cup wild rice
1 small onion, minced
1 small carrot, grated
2 eggs
⅓ cup milk

¼ cup chopped parsley
¾ teaspoon thyme
½ teaspoon marjoram
1 teaspoon salt
¼ teaspoon pepper
2 pounds ground turkey

1. In a medium saucepan, bring chicken broth to a boil. Stir in wild rice, reduce heat to low, and cover. Simmer until rice is barely tender, 45 to 50 minutes. Drain off any excess liquid.

2. Preheat oven to 350°. In a large bowl, combine onion, carrot, eggs, milk, parsley, thyme, marjoram, salt, and pepper. Add ground turkey and wild rice and knead with your hands until well blended. Transfer mixture to a 9 x 5 x 3-inch loaf pan.

3. Bake until a meat thermometer inserted in center of loaf reads 160°, about 1¼ hours. Let stand 5 minutes. Drain off excess liquid and slice.

---

96 KIELBASA LOAF

Prep: 15 minutes   Cook: 1 hour 20 minutes   Serves: 4 to 6

1 tablespoon vegetable oil
¼ pound kielbasa, cut into
    ½-inch dice
1 medium onion, chopped
1 small red bell pepper,
    chopped
2 garlic cloves, minced
1 cup rye bread crumbs
½ cup milk

2 eggs
1 teaspoon paprika,
    preferably hot
1 teaspoon salt
¼ teaspoon pepper
1½ pounds ground round
    (85% lean)
2 tablespoons spicy brown
    mustard

1. Preheat oven to 350°. Heat oil in a large skillet. Add kielbasa, onion, bell pepper, and garlic and cook over medium-high heat, stirring often, until onion is lightly browned, about 6 minutes.

2. In a medium bowl, combine bread crumbs, milk, eggs, paprika, salt, and pepper. Add ground round and kielbasa mixture and knead with your hands until well mixed. Transfer to a 9 x 5 x 3-inch loaf pan.

3. Bake 1 hour. Spread mustard over top of loaf and bake until a meat thermometer inserted in center of loaf reads 160°, about 15 minutes longer.

97   PORK LOAF WITH APPLESAUCE GLAZE
Prep: 15 minutes   Cook: 1 hour   Serves: 4 to 6

1 tablespoon vegetable oil	1 teaspoon sage
1 medium onion, finely chopped	¾ teaspoon salt
1 cup fresh bread crumbs	¼ teaspoon pepper
1½ cups prepared chunky applesauce	⅛ teaspoon ground allspice
1 egg	1 pound ground pork
	1 teaspoon Dijon mustard

1. Preheat oven to 375°. In a small skillet, heat oil until hot. Add onion and cook over medium heat, stirring often, until lightly browned, about 4 minutes.

2. In a medium bowl, combine bread crumbs, 1 cup applesauce, egg, sage, salt, pepper, and allspice; stir with a fork until mixed. Add ground pork and onions and mix until blended. Pack mixture into an 8 x 4 x 2½-inch loaf pan.

3. In a small bowl, stir together remaining ½ cup applesauce and Dijon mustard. Spread applesauce mixture over top of loaf and cover pan with aluminum foil. Place on a baking sheet and bake for 30 minutes. Remove foil and continue baking until a meat thermometer inserted in center of loaf reads 160° to 165°, about 30 minutes. Let stand 5 minutes before slicing.

---

98   WASHINGTON STATE TURKEY LOAF
Prep: 15 minutes   Cook: 1 hour 10 minutes   Serves: 4 to 6

2 medium Granny Smith apples, peeled, cored, and chopped	¼ cup evaporated milk
	1 egg
1 medium onion, chopped	1 teaspoon poultry seasoning
⅓ cup reduced-sodium chicken broth	¾ teaspoon salt
	¼ teaspoon pepper
½ cup fresh bread crumbs	1¼ pounds ground turkey

1. Preheat oven to 350°. In a large nonstick skillet, combine apples, onion, and broth. Bring to a simmer over medium heat. Cover and cook for 5 minutes. Remove cover and cook until liquid evaporates, about 2 minutes. Transfer to a medium bowl.

2. Add bread crumbs, evaporated milk, egg, poultry seasoning, salt, and pepper to apple mixture in bowl; stir until blended. Add ground turkey and mix well. Using wet hands, form into a 7 x 4-inch free-form loaf on a lightly greased baking sheet.

3. Bake until a meat thermometer inserted in center of loaf reads 160°, about 1 hour. Let stand 5 minutes before slicing.

99 BARBECUED CHICKEN LOAF
Prep: 15 minutes   Cook: 1¼ hours   Serves: 4 to 6

1 medium onion, chopped
1 medium bell pepper, green or red, chopped
1 jalapeño pepper, seeded and minced
¾ cup barbecue sauce
¾ cup rolled oats
⅔ cup corn kernels, fresh or thawed frozen

2 eggs
1 tablespoon chili powder
1 tablespoon Worcestershire sauce
1 teaspoon garlic salt
2 pounds ground chicken

1. Preheat oven to 350°. In a medium bowl, combine onion, bell pepper, jalapeño pepper, ½ cup barbecue sauce, rolled oats, corn, eggs, chili powder, Worcestershire sauce, and garlic salt. Add ground chicken and mix well. Transfer to a 9 x 5 x 3-inch loaf pan.

2. Bake 1 hour. Spread remaining ¼ cup barbecue sauce over top of loaf and bake until a meat thermometer inserted in center of loaf reads 160°, about 15 minutes longer. Let stand 5 minutes. Drain off excess liquid and slice.

100 MEATLOAF A LA CROISSANT
Prep: 15 minutes   Cook: 1 hour   Serves: 4 to 6

1 small onion, finely chopped
¾ cup fresh bread crumbs
⅓ cup heavy cream
¼ cup dry white wine or dry vermouth
1 egg
2 tablespoons chopped parsley

1 teaspoon salt
¾ teaspoon thyme
¼ teaspoon pepper
⅛ teaspoon ground allspice
1 pound ground veal
1 pound ground pork
1 (8-ounce) package refrigerated crescent rolls

1. Preheat oven to 375°. In a medium bowl, combine onion, bread crumbs, heavy cream, wine, egg, parsley, salt, thyme, pepper, and allspice. Stir with a fork until mixed. Add ground veal and ground pork and blend well.

2. Rinse an 8 x 4 x 2½-inch loaf pan with cold water; shake out excess water but do not dry. Pack meat mixture into rinsed pan. Invert and unmold meatloaf onto a lightly oiled baking sheet.

3. Bake until a meat thermometer inserted in the center of loaf reads 150° to 155°, about 45 minutes. Let stand 5 minutes, then drain off excess fat.

4. Unroll and separate crescent roll dough sections. Drape dough over top and down sides of meatloaf, overlapping slightly. Don't worry about completely covering loaf.

5. Return to oven and bake until dough is golden brown, about 15 minutes. Let stand 5 minutes before cutting into 1-inch-thick slices to serve.

101   MINESTRONE MEATLOAF PRESTO
Prep: 10 minutes   Cook: 55 minutes   Serves: 4 to 6

1½ pounds ground chuck
      (80% lean) or ground
      round (85% lean)
1   cup Italian-seasoned bread
      crumbs
1   (10½-ounce can) condensed
      minestrone soup

1   cup tomato sauce
1   small onion, minced
¼   teaspoon crushed hot red
      pepper

1. Preheat oven to 375°. In a medium bowl, combine ground chuck, bread crumbs, minestrone, ½ cup tomato sauce, onion, and hot pepper. Mix with a fork until well blended.

2. Pack mixture into an 8 x 4 x 2½-inch loaf pan. Place on a baking sheet and bake 40 minutes. Spread remaining ½ cup tomato sauce over top of loaf and bake until a meat thermometer inserted into center of loaf reads 160° to 165°, about 15 minutes longer. Let meatloaf stand 5 minutes before slicing.

102   CHILLED VITELLO TONNATO LOAF WITH HERB MAYONNAISE
Prep: 15 minutes   Cook: 1 hour   Chill: 8 hours   Serves: 4 to 6

1   cup fresh bread crumbs
½   cup evaporated milk
1   egg
1   pound ground veal
2   (6½-ounce) cans tuna packed
      in water, drained and
      well flaked
1   small onion, finely chopped
1   garlic clove, minced
2   tablespoons olive oil
¼   cup chopped parsley

2   tablespoons drained capers,
      coarsely chopped if large
    Grated zest of 1 medium
      lemon
¾   teaspoon salt
¼   teaspoon pepper
1   cup mayonnaise
2   tablespoons chopped fresh
      basil or 1 teaspoon dried
1   tablespoon Dijon mustard
2   teaspoons lemon juice

1. Preheat oven to 350°. In a medium bowl, soak bread crumbs in evaporated milk until soft, about 5 minutes. Add egg and beat lightly. Add ground veal and tuna and mix until well blended. Stir in onion, garlic, olive oil, 2 tablespoons parsley, capers, lemon zest, salt, and pepper; mix well.

2. Pack mixture into a lightly oiled 8 x 4 x 2½-inch loaf pan. Place on a baking sheet and bake until a meat thermometer inserted in center of loaf reads 160° to 165°, about 1 hour. Let cool completely on a wire rack. Cover and refrigerate for at least 8 hours, or overnight, to allow flavors to blend.

3. In a small bowl, combine mayonnaise, remaining 2 tablespoons parsley, basil, mustard, and lemon juice. Mix to blend well. Unmold meatloaf and cut into ¾-inch slices. Serve meatloaf chilled or at room temperature. Pass herbed mayonnaise on the side.

103 MOO SHU MEATLOAF

Prep: 20 minutes   Cook: 1 hour 20 minutes   Serves: 4 to 6

This dish is inspired by my favorite Chinese takeout food—moo shu pork. The loaf is so delicious, you'll never miss the Peking pancakes. If you cannot locate five-spice powder, which is available in Chinese markets and in many supermarkets, substitute ¼ teaspoon ground allspice mixed with a pinch of ground cloves.

2 tablespoons vegetable oil
2 cups shredded Chinese cabbage (napa) cabbage (about ¾ pound)
½ pound fresh mushrooms, sliced
3 scallions, chopped
1 teaspoon minced fresh ginger
1 garlic clove, minced
2 tablespoons soy sauce
2 tablespoons dry sherry

¼ cup plus 2 tablespoons hoisin sauce
1 cup fresh bread crumbs
2 eggs
¾ teaspoon salt
½ teaspoon Chinese five-spice powder
¼ teaspoon crushed hot red pepper
2 pounds ground pork

1. Preheat oven to 350°. In a large skillet, heat oil over high heat. Add cabbage, mushrooms, scallions, ginger, and garlic and stir-fry until cabbage is wilted, about 5 minutes. Off heat, stir in soy sauce, sherry, and 2 tablespoons hoisin sauce.

2. In a medium bowl, combine bread crumbs, eggs, salt, five-spice powder, and hot pepper. Add ground pork and vegetable mixture and knead with your hands until well mixed. Transfer mixture to a 9 x 5 x 3-inch loaf pan.

3. Bake until a meat thermometer inserted in center of loaf reads 140°, about 1 hour. Spread remaining ¼ cup hoisin sauce over top of loaf and continue baking until a meat thermometer reads 160°, about 15 minutes longer. Let stand 5 minutes. Pour off excess fat and slice.

104 CALIFORNIA DIP MEATLOAF

Prep: 10 minutes   Cook: 1¼ hours   Serves: 4 to 6

2 pounds ground round (85% lean)
1 (1-ounce) envelope dry onion soup mix

1½ cups crushed salt-free potato chips (about 6½ ounces)
¾ cup sour cream
2 eggs

1. Preheat oven to 375°. In a medium bowl, knead ground round, onion soup, potato chips, sour cream, eggs, and ¼ cup water with your hands until well mixed. Transfer to an 8 x 4 x 2½-inch loaf pan.

2. Bake until a meat thermometer inserted in center of loaf reads 160°, about 1¼ hours. Let stand 5 minutes. Drain off excess fat and slice.

105   SPA-STYLE TURKEY LOAF
Prep: 10 minutes   Cook: 1¼ hours   Serves: 4 to 6

1 medium onion, finely chopped	2 egg whites
1 medium celery rib, finely chopped	2 tablespoons chopped parsley
1 medium carrot, grated	2 teaspoons poultry seasoning
1 cup fresh whole-wheat bread crumbs	1½ teaspoons salt
½ cup canned reduced-sodium chicken broth	¼ teaspoon pepper
	1½ pounds ground turkey
	2 tablespoons tomato paste

1. Preheat oven to 350°. In a large bowl, combine onion, celery, carrot, bread crumbs, chicken broth, egg whites, parsley, poultry seasoning, salt, and pepper. Add ground turkey and mix well. Transfer mixture to a 9 x 5 x 3-inch loaf pan.

2. Bake 1 hour. Spread tomato paste over top of loaf. Continue to bake until a meat thermometer inserted in center of loaf reads 160°, about 15 minutes longer. Let stand 10 minutes. Pour off excess liquid and cut into slices to serve.

106   CORNBREAD-STUFFED PORK ROULADE WITH ORANGE-BOURBON GLAZE
Prep: 15 minutes   Cook: 50 minutes   Serves: 4 to 6

1½ teaspoons cornstarch	1 egg
¼ cup bourbon or apple juice	1½ teaspoons sage
½ cup orange marmalade	¾ teaspoon salt
7 tablespoons butter	¼ teaspoon pepper
1 (7-ounce) package cornbread stuffing mix	1½ pounds ground pork
1 small onion, chopped	1 celery rib, chopped
⅓ cup milk	¾ cup chicken broth or water

1. In a small saucepan, dissolve cornstarch in 2 tablespoons bourbon. Add marmalade and 1 tablespoon butter and cook over low heat, stirring, until butter is melted and glaze is thickened, about 2 minutes. Set glaze aside.

2. Preheat oven to 350°. In a blender or food processor, grind ¾ cup cornbread stuffing into fine crumbs. In a medium bowl, combine stuffing crumbs with onion, milk, egg, remaining 2 tablespoons bourbon, ½ teaspoon sage, salt, and pepper. Mix well. Add ground pork and mix until blended. Sprinkle a large sheet of wax paper or aluminum foil with water. With wet hands, pat out pork mixture into a 9 x 13-inch rectangle.

3. In a large skillet, melt remaining 6 tablespoons butter over medium heat. Add celery and cook, stirring occasionally, until softened, about 3 minutes. Add chicken broth and bring to a boil. In a medium bowl, combine remaining cornbread stuffing and sage with celery mixture. Pat cornbread mixture evenly over surface of pork rectangle, leaving a 1-inch border around edges. Using wax paper or foil to help lift, roll up into a cylinder and press seams closed. Pick up roulade in wax paper or foil and roll off onto a foil-lined, lightly oiled 10 x 15-inch baking sheet, seam side down.

4. Bake 35 minutes. Meanwhile, reheat glaze over low heat. Brush glaze over loaf. Continue to bake until a meat thermometer reads 160° to 165°, 10 to 15 minutes longer. (If glaze threatens to scorch, tent roulade with aluminum foil.)

---

107 SAUSAGE LOAF WITH SWEET POTATO AND PEAR WHIP
Prep: 20 minutes   Cook: 40 minutes   Serves: 6

1   medium onion, chopped
1   cup herb-seasoned stuffing mix, crushed
2   eggs
2   teaspoons sage
2   teaspoons salt
½   teaspoon pepper
¼   teaspoon ground coriander
¼   teaspoon ground ginger
¼   teaspoon ground allspice
2   pounds ground pork
    Sweet Potato and Pear Whip (recipe follows)

1. Preheat oven to 350°. In a medium bowl, combine onion, stuffing crumbs, eggs, sage, salt, pepper, coriander, ginger, and allspice. Blend well. Add ground pork and knead with your hands until well mixed. Transfer mixture to a 2-quart ring mold.

2. Bake until a meat thermometer inserted in center of meat reads 160°, about 40 minutes. Let stand 5 minutes. Drain off excess fat.

3. Invert sausage ring to unmold onto a large round platter. Fill center of ring with hot Sweet Potato and Pear Whip and serve immediately.

SWEET POTATO AND PEAR WHIP
Makes about 2½ cups

4   large sweet potatoes (about 2 pounds total), peeled and cut into 1-inch chunks
3   medium pears, peeled, quartered, and cored
2   tablespoons butter

In a large saucepan of lightly salted boiling water, cook sweet potatoes until almost tender, 20 to 25 minutes. Add pears and cook until both are tender, about 5 minutes. Drain well; transfer to a medium bowl. Using an electric hand mixer, mash together sweet potatoes and pears with butter until whipped and smooth.

108   BUTTERMILK PORK LOAF
Prep: 15 minutes   Cook: 1 hour 19 minutes   Serves: 6 to 8

1 cup fresh bread crumbs	2 eggs
1 cup buttermilk	1½ teaspoons salt
1 tablespoon butter	½ teaspoon pepper
1 medium onion, minced	1½ pounds ground pork
1 small red or green bell pepper, chopped	½ pound boiled ham, ground

1. In a medium bowl, combine bread crumbs and buttermilk. Let stand 10 minutes.

2. In a medium skillet, melt butter over medium heat. Add onion and bell pepper and cook, stirring often, until vegetables are softened, about 4 minutes. Let cool slightly, then add to buttermilk mixture. Stir in eggs, salt, and pepper. Add ground pork and ham and mix well. Transfer to a 9 x 5 x 3-inch loaf pan.

3. Bake until a meat thermometer inserted in center of loaf reads 160°, about 1¼ hours. Let stand 5 minutes. Pour off excess fat and slice.

---

109   SOUTH AMERICAN MEATLOAF ROULADE
Prep: 15 minutes   Cook: 1 hour   Serves: 6 to 8

In South America, this dish would traditionally be prepared as a rolled, stuffed flank steak. This budget version is equally appetizing.

2 pounds ground round (85% lean)	1 (10-ounce) package frozen chopped spinach, thawed and squeezed dry
2 garlic cloves, minced	
1 teaspoon thyme	¼ cup milk
2¼ teaspoons salt	1 egg, beaten
½ teaspoon pepper	¼ teaspoon crushed hot red pepper
1 cup fresh bread crumbs	
3 medium carrots, grated	1 hard-boiled egg, sliced
1 medium onion, finely chopped	Quick Brown Gravy (page 182)

1. Preheat oven to 350°. In a large bowl, combine ground round, garlic, thyme, 2 teaspoons salt, and pepper. Moisten a large sheet of wax paper or foil lightly with water. With wet hands, pat out meat mixture on sheet into a 9 x 12-inch rectangle.

2. In a medium bowl, combine bread crumbs, carrots, onion, spinach, milk, egg, remaining ¼ teaspoon salt, and hot pepper. Mix to blend stuffing well. Pat stuffing evenly over meat mixture, leaving a 1-inch border around all sides. Arrange hard-boiled egg slices down center of stuffing.

3. Starting at a long end and using wax paper or foil to help lift, roll up into a cylinder and press seams closed. Pick up roulade in wax paper or foil and roll off onto a lightly oiled baking sheet, seam side down.

4. Bake until a meat thermometer inserted in center of roulade reads 160°, about 1 hour. Let stand 5 minutes. Transfer to a serving platter and serve with Quick Brown Gravy.

---

110 KASHA AND MEATLOAF WITH MUSHROOM GRAVY

Prep: 20 minutes   Cook: 1½ hours   Serves: 4 to 6

½ cup kasha (roasted buckwheat kernels)
1 egg, beaten
1 cup beef broth
1 tablespoon butter
1¼ teaspoons salt
⅜ teaspoon pepper
1 medium onion, minced
2 eggs

¼ cup chopped parsley
¾ teaspoon mace
¾ teaspoon ground coriander
1 pound ground round (85% lean)
1 pound lean ground lamb
Mushroom Sauce (recipe follows)

1. In a medium bowl, combine kasha and beaten egg. Mix to coat kasha well with egg. In a large skillet, cook kasha mixture over medium heat, stirring, pressing, and breaking up lumps constantly with a spoon, until kasha kernels are mostly separated. Add broth, butter, ½ teaspoon salt, and ⅛ teaspoon pepper. Bring to a boil, reduce heat to low, cover tightly, and simmer until liquid is absorbed and kasha is tender, about 3 minutes. Fluff kasha with a fork and let cool until tepid, about 10 minutes.

2. In a large bowl, combine onion, eggs, parsley, mace, coriander, and remaining ¾ teaspoon salt and ¼ teaspoon pepper. Add ground round, ground lamb, and kasha and knead with your hands until well blended. Transfer mixture to a 9 x 5 x 3-inch loaf pan.

3. Bake until a meat thermometer inserted in center of loaf reads 160°, about 1¼ hours. Let stand 5 minutes. Drain off excess fat and slice. Serve with hot Mushroom Sauce.

MUSHROOM SAUCE
Makes about 2 cups

3 tablespoons butter
¼ pound fresh mushrooms, sliced
3 tablespoons flour
2 cups beef broth

2 tablespoons port or sherry
1 bay leaf
Pinch of thyme
¼ teaspoon salt
¼ teaspoon pepper

1. In a medium saucepan, melt 1 tablespoon butter over medium heat. Add mushrooms and cook, stirring often, until mushrooms have given off their liquid and are lightly browned, about 5 minutes.

2. Add remaining 2 tablespoons butter and melt. Sprinkle on flour and cook, stirring constantly, 1 minute. Whisk in broth and port and add bay leaf, thyme, salt, and pepper. Bring to a boil, whisking until liquid is thickened and smooth. Reduce heat to low and simmer 15 minutes.

111   MEATLOAF SQUARES
Prep: 10 minutes   *Cook: 45 minutes*   *Serves: 4 to 6*

1 small onion, chopped
1 egg
1 cup crushed corn flakes
¾ cup chili sauce
1 teaspoon celery salt

¼ teaspoon pepper
2 pounds ground round
   (85% lean)
4 strips of bacon

1. Preheat oven to 375°. In a medium bowl, combine onion, egg, corn flakes, ½ cup chili sauce, celery salt, and pepper. Stir with a fork until mixed. Add the ground round and blend well. Transfer to a 9-inch square baking pan and spread evenly.

2. Spread remaining chili sauce over top. Crisscross bacon strips over chili sauce, tucking ends of bacon down into sides of pan to fit, if necessary. Cover with aluminum foil.

3. Bake 15 minutes. Uncover and bake until a meat thermometer inserted in center reads 155°, about 30 minutes longer. Let stand 5 minutes. Pour off excess fat, and cut into squares to serve.

112   MEATLOAF SPUD-WICHES
Prep: 10 minutes   *Cook: 1 hour 35 minutes*   *Serves: 4*

1 small onion, chopped
1 egg
¾ cup dried bread crumbs
½ cup ketchup
1 tablespoon Worcestershire
   sauce
1¾ teaspoons salt
½ teaspoon pepper
2 pounds ground round
   (85% lean)

4 medium russet potatoes
   (about 1½ pounds),
   peeled and cut into 1-inch
   chunks
2 tablespoons butter
   About ¼ cup milk
   Quick Brown Gravy
   (page 182)

1. Preheat oven to 375°. In a medium bowl, combine onion, egg, bread crumbs, ketchup, Worcestershire sauce, 1 teaspoon salt, and ¼ teaspoon pepper. Stir with a fork until mixed. Add the ground round and blend well. Transfer to a 9 x 5 x 3-inch loaf pan.

2. Bake until a meat thermometer inserted in center of loaf reads 155°, about 1¼ hours. Let stand 5 minutes. Drain off excess fat, then cut into 8 slices, about ¾ inch thick.

3. Meanwhile, in a large saucepan of boiling salted water, cook the potato chunks until just tender when pierced with tip of a sharp knife, 15 to 20 minutes. Drain well.

4. In a medium bowl, mash potatoes with butter and remaining ¾ teaspoon salt and ¼ teaspoon pepper. Blend in ¼ cup milk. Add enough additional milk if necessary to reach desired consistency.

5. Spread hot mashed potatoes over 4 hot meatloaf slices. Top with remaining meatloaf slices to make "sandwiches." Using a spatula, transfer to dinner plates. Pass a gravyboat of Quick Brown Gravy on the side.

---

113 GREEK LAMB LOAF WITH HONEYED TOMATO SAUCE

Prep: 25 minutes   Cook: 1 hour 20 minutes   Serves: 4 to 6

½ cup orzo (rice-shaped pasta)
1 (10-ounce) package frozen chopped spinach, thawed and squeezed dry
1 medium onion, chopped
2 garlic cloves, minced
1 cup tomato sauce
2 teaspoons salt

1 teaspoon oregano
½ teaspoon pepper
¼ teaspoon cinnamon
2 pounds lean ground lamb or ground round (85% lean), or a combination of both
Honeyed Tomato Sauce (recipe follows)

1. In a medium saucepan of boiling salted water, cook orzo 5 minutes. Drain, rinse under cold water, and drain again.

2. In a large bowl, mix spinach, onion, garlic, tomato sauce, salt, oregano, pepper, and cinnamon with a fork until well blended. Add ground lamb and orzo; knead with your hands until mixed. Transfer to a 9 x 5 x 3-inch loaf pan.

3. Bake until a meat thermometer inserted in center of loaf reads 160°, about 1 hour 15 minutes. Let stand 5 minutes. Drain off excess fat and slice. Top each serving with a dollop of Honeyed Tomato Sauce.

HONEYED TOMATO SAUCE
Makes about 1 ½ cups

1 tablespoon olive oil
1 small onion, chopped
1 cup tomato sauce
¾ cup beef broth

2 teaspoons honey
½ teaspoon oregano
¼ teaspoon cinnamon

1. In a small nonreactive saucepan, heat oil. Add onion and cook, stirring often, until softened, about 3 minutes.

2. Stir in tomato sauce, beef broth, honey, oregano, and cinnamon and bring to a simmer. Reduce heat to low and cook, stirring often, until thickened, about 20 minutes.

114   LAMB MEATLOAF WITH PINE NUT STUFFING AND MINTED CUCUMBER SAUCE

Prep: 10 minutes   Stand: 10 minutes   Cook: 55 minutes   Serves: 6

1½ cups bulgur	½ teaspoon cinnamon
2 pounds lean ground lamb	¼ teaspoon cayenne
3 medium onions, finely chopped	¼ cup olive oil
¼ cup ice water	½ cup pine nuts (pignoli)
1¼ teaspoons ground allspice	¼ cup chopped parsley
1¼ teaspoons salt	Minted Cucumber Sauce (recipe follows)

1. Preheat oven to 350°. Lightly oil a 9-inch square baking dish. In a medium bowl, soak bulgur 10 minutes in enough cold water to cover by 1 inch. Drain well. One handful at a time, squeeze out excess water.

2. In a large bowl, place bulgur, 1½ pounds ground lamb, 2 chopped onions, ice water, 1 teaspoon each allspice and salt, cinnamon, and cayenne. Using a hand-held electric mixer set at high speed, beat meat mixture until light in color and sticky, about 2 minutes.

3. In a large skillet, heat 2 tablespoons olive oil. Add remaining onion and cook over medium heat, stirring often, until softened, about 3 minutes. Transfer onion to a medium bowl. Do not clean skillet.

4. In same skillet, cook pine nuts over medium heat, stirring often, until lightly browned, 2 to 3 minutes. Combine pine nuts and onion. Add remaining ½ pound lamb, ¼ teaspoon each allspice and salt, and parsley. Knead mixture with your hands until well mixed.

5. Pat half of lamb-bulgur mixture in an even layer in prepared baking dish. Form lamb-pine nut mixture into patties and arrange over lamb-bulgur layer. Join patties together to form a second, thinner layer. Form remaining lamb-bulgur mixture into patties and arrange over lamb-pine nut layer. Join patties together to form last layer. Score top of loaf in a diamond pattern, and drizzle with remaining 2 tablespoons oil.

6. Bake until a meat thermometer inserted in center reads 155°, about 45 minutes. Let stand 5 minutes. Drain excess fat from loaf, cut into squares, and serve with Minted Cucumber Sauce.

MINTED CUCUMBER SAUCE
Makes about 1¼ cups

1 medium cucumber, peeled, seeded, and chopped	¾ cup plain low-fat yogurt
½ teaspoon salt	1 teaspoon dried mint

1. In a fine-meshed sieve, toss cucumber with salt; let stand 15 minutes. Rinse cucumber well and squeeze with your hands to remove excess liquid.

2. In a small bowl, combine cucumber, yogurt, and mint. Cover and refrigerate at least 15 minutes before serving.

115 TURKEY AND OYSTER STUFFING LOAF

Prep: 10 minutes   Cook: 1¼ hours   Serves: 4 to 6

If you can't wait until Thanksgiving for your annual serving of turkey with oyster stuffing, here's the meatloaf for you!

1 pint shucked oysters	2 eggs
1 medium onion, chopped	1¼ teaspoons salt
1¼ cups crushed herb-seasoned stuffing mix	½ teaspoon poultry seasoning
¼ cup milk	¼ teaspoon pepper
	1½ pounds ground turkey

1. Preheat oven to 350°. Drain oysters in a sieve set over a bowl; reserve ¼ cup oyster liquor. Coarsely chop oysters.

2. In a medium bowl, combine onion, stuffing mix, chopped oysters with reserved liquor, milk, eggs, salt, poultry seasoning, and pepper. Add ground turkey and mix well. Transfer to a 9 x 5 x 3-inch loaf pan.

3. Bake until a meat thermometer inserted in center of loaf reads 160°, about 1¼ hours. Let stand 5 minutes. Drain off excess liquid and slice.

116 PILGRIM TURKEY LOAF

Prep: 10 minutes   Cook: 1 hour   Serves: 4 to 6

1 cup herb-seasoned stuffing mix	1 teaspoon poultry seasoning
½ cup milk	¾ teaspoon salt
1 egg	¼ teaspoon pepper
1 small onion, chopped	1½ pounds ground turkey
1 celery rib, chopped	Cranberry sauce (optional)
2 tablespoons chopped parsley	

1. Preheat oven to 375°. In a medium bowl, blend together stuffing mix, milk, and egg; let stand 5 minutes. Stir in onion, celery, parsley, poultry seasoning, salt, and pepper. Add ground turkey and mix until well blended.

2. Pack mixture into an 8 x 4 x 2½-inch loaf pan. Place on a baking sheet and bake until a meat thermometer inserted in center of loaf reads 160° to 165°, about 1 hour. Let stand 10 minutes before slicing. Serve turkey loaf with cranberry sauce, if desired.

117   CHICKEN LOAF PESTO
Prep: 10 minutes   Cook: 1 hour 20 minutes   Serves: 4 to 6

1¼ cups fresh bread crumbs	¼ teaspoon pepper
¾ cup pesto (about 6 ounces)	2 pounds ground chicken
2 eggs	2 tablespoons grated Romano
1 teaspoon salt	cheese

1. Preheat oven to 350°. In a large bowl, combine bread crumbs, pesto, eggs, salt, and pepper. Add ground chicken and knead with your hands until well blended. Transfer mixture to a lightly oiled 8 x 4 x 2½-inch loaf pan.

2. Bake 1 hour. Sprinkle cheese over top and bake 20 minutes longer, or until cheese melts and a meat thermometer inserted in loaf reads 165°. Let stand 5 minutes. Pour off excess liquid and slice.

118   VEAL LOAF CORDON BLEU
Prep: 15 minutes   Cook: 1¼ hours   Serves: 4 to 6

1 cup fresh bread crumbs	1 teaspoon tarragon
2 eggs	¼ teaspoon pepper
2 scallions, minced	1½ pounds ground veal
¼ cup milk	½ pound boiled ham, ground
1 tablespoon Dijon mustard	1 cup finely diced Swiss
1¼ teaspoons salt	cheese (4 ounces)

1. In a medium bowl, combine bread crumbs, eggs, scallions, milk, mustard, salt, tarragon, and pepper. Add ground veal and ham and knead with your hands until well mixed. Transfer half of meat mixture to a lightly oiled 9 x 5 x 3-inch loaf pan. Layer with diced Swiss cheese, then top with remaining meat mixture.

2. Bake until a meat thermometer inserted in center of loaf reads 160°, about 1¼ hours. Let stand 5 minutes. Pour off excess fat and serve.

119 FRENCH MUSHROOM AND TARRAGON MEATLOAF

Prep: 15 minutes   Cook: 1 hour 10 minutes   Serves: 4 to 6

Reminiscent of a pâté, this meatloaf is fancy enough for company when served with glazed baby carrots and mashed potatoes. It is also delicious cold with French bread and pickles.

¾ cup fresh bread crumbs
⅓ cup heavy cream
1 egg
2 tablespoons butter
2 shallots or 1 scallion, chopped
10 ounces fresh mushrooms, finely chopped
¼ cup port or dry vermouth

2 tablespoons chopped parsley
1 tablespoon chopped fresh tarragon or 1 teaspoon dried
1 teaspoon salt
¼ teaspoon pepper
1½ pounds ground veal
⅓ cup sour cream

1. Preheat oven to 350°. In a medium bowl, blend together bread crumbs, cream, and egg. Set aside while preparing mushrooms.

2. In a large skillet, melt butter over low heat. Add shallots and cook, stirring often, until softened, about 1 minute. Increase heat to medium-high and add mushrooms. Cook, stirring often, until mushrooms give off some of their liquid, about 2 minutes. Add port, parsley, tarragon, ½ teaspoon salt, and ⅛ teaspoon pepper. Cook, stirring often, until liquid evaporates and mushrooms are beginning to brown lightly, about 4 minutes. Transfer mushrooms to bowl with softened bread crumbs and mix well. Add ground veal, remaining ½ teaspoon salt, and ¼ teaspoon pepper; mix until blended.

3. Pack mixture into an 8 x 4 x 2½-inch loaf pan. Place on a baking sheet and bake 45 minutes. Spread sour cream over top of loaf and bake until a meat thermometer inserted in the center of meatloaf reads 160° to 165°, about 15 minutes longer. Let stand about 5 minutes before slicing.

Chapter 5

Around the World in 21 Meatballs

Although spaghetti and meatballs is one of the glories of Italian-American cooking, Italy certainly does not have a corner on the world meatball market. Indians and the Middle East share the same word for meatball, *kofta*, although the seasonings are totally different. The Moroccan word is also similar, *kefta*. The Germans serve *kloppsingers* in a zesty lemon and caper sauce. And what would a smorgasbord be without Scandinavian meatballs? Among other variations, Northern European meatballs can be nestled in cream or accented by lingonberries.

Many recipes call for browning meatballs in a skillet before making the sauce. Do this in batches, if necessary, so the meatballs will brown nicely. If they are crowded, they will steam and will not develop a crust. Some cooks prefer to drop their meatballs into simmering sauce, which results in a tender-textured meatball while the meat flavor is infused in the sauce. In fact, many of the Italian cooks I spoke to considered this trick to be the secret of their world-class spaghetti and meatball recipe.

Herbed tomato sauces are always a popular medium for cooking meatballs, but you'll also find sweet-and-sour sauces, like Mrs. Haines's Hawaiian Meatballs, Spinach and Beef Meatballs in Cilantro Sauce, and Viennese Meatballs with Gingersnap Sauce. Many meatball dishes are enhanced if they are served spooned with their sauce over hot cooked noodles or rice, so keep this in mind when planning a side dish.

Tiny cocktail meatballs, perfect for entertaining, can be found in Chapter 1, Appetizers and Hors d'Oeuvres, on page 21. And many soup recipes feature meatballs, too (pages 23 to 36). So pick up some ground meat and have a ball!

120 TANGY BEEF MEATBALLS IN HORSERADISH SAUCE

Prep: 10 minutes   Cook: 14 minutes   Serves: 4

1 cup rye bread crumbs	1½ pounds ground round
¼ cup milk	(85% lean)
¼ cup prepared white	2 tablespoons vegetable oil
horseradish	2 tablespoons flour
1 egg	1 (13¾-ounce) can beef broth
1 teaspoon salt	¾ cup sour cream
¼ teaspoon pepper	

1. In a medium bowl, combine rye bread crumbs, milk, 2 tablespoons horseradish, egg, salt, and pepper. Add ground round and mix well. Using about 1 tablespoon for each, form into meatballs.

2. In a large skillet, heat oil. Add meatballs and cook over medium-high heat, turning often, until browned all over, about 8 minutes.

3. Sprinkle flour over meatballs in skillet and turn them to coat. Add beef broth and bring to a boil. Reduce heat to low and simmer until sauce is thickened and meatballs are cooked through, about 5 minutes.

4. Stir in sour cream and remaining 2 tablespoons horseradish. Cook without boiling just until heated through, about 1 minute.

121 GERMAN MEATBALLS IN CAPER SAUCE

Prep: 15 minutes   Cook: 30 to 35 minutes   Serves: 4 to 6

Giant meatballs are poached in a spicy broth, then the broth is transformed into lots of tangy sauce. Be sure to serve plenty of boiled potatoes or noodles to soak up all the flavor.

¾ cup fresh bread crumbs	1 pound ground round
1 small onion, finely chopped	(85% lean)
¼ cup heavy cream	½ pound ground pork
2 whole eggs plus 2 egg yolks	2 cups beef broth
Grated zest of 1 small lemon	2 bay leaves
3 anchovy fillets, rinsed and	3 tablespoons flour
mashed	3 tablespoons lemon juice
1½ teaspoons salt	¼ cup sour cream
½ teaspoon pepper	2 tablespoons capers, drained
¼ teaspoon ground cloves	

1. Preheat oven to 200°. In a large bowl, mix bread crumbs, onion, heavy cream, whole eggs, lemon zest, anchovies, salt, pepper, and ⅛ teaspoon cloves until well blended. Add ground round and ground pork and knead with your hands until mixed.

2. In a large saucepan, bring 1 quart water, beef broth, bay leaves, and remaining ⅛ teaspoon cloves to a boil over high heat. Reduce heat to medium, keeping broth at a simmer. Using about 2 tablespoons for each, form meat mixture into large meatballs, dropping as formed into simmering broth. Simmer, uncovered, until meatballs are cooked through, about 20 minutes. Using a slotted spoon, transfer meatballs to a deep serving dish, cover with aluminum foil, and keep warm in oven while making sauce.

3. Strain cooking liquid, return to large saucepan, and boil over high heat until evaporated to 3 cups, 5 to 10 minutes. In a small bowl, whisk flour and lemon juice until smooth. Whisk flour mixture into reduced cooking liquid and boil until slightly thickened, about 5 minutes.

4. In a small bowl, whisk together sour cream and egg yolks. Gradually whisk in about 1 cup of hot cooking liquid. Whisk sour cream mixture into cooking liquid and cook, stirring, until thickened, about 1 minute. Do not let sauce come to a boil after adding sour cream mixture. Stir in capers and pour sauce over meatballs.

---

122 MRS. HAINES'S HAWAIIAN MEATBALLS

Prep: 10 minutes   Cook: 21 minutes   Serves: 4

1 (8-ounce) can crushed pineapple in syrup
1¼ cups pineapple juice
2 tablespoons dried bread crumbs
1 egg
1 teaspoon salt
¼ teaspoon pepper
1 pound ground round (85% lean)

2 tablespoons vegetable oil
1 medium onion, sliced
1 medium green bell pepper, cut into ½-inch-thick strips
¼ cup steak sauce, such as Heinz 57
2 teaspoons cornstarch

1. In a sieve set over a bowl, drain crushed pineapple, reserving syrup. Stir pineapple juice into syrup and set aside.

2. In a medium bowl, combine drained pineapple, bread crumbs, egg, salt, and pepper. Add ground round and mix well. Using about 1 tablespoon meat mixture for each, form into 18 meatballs.

3. In a large skillet, heat oil. Add meatballs and cook over medium-high heat, stirring often, until browned all over, about 8 minutes. Using a slotted spoon, transfer browned meatballs to a plate.

4. Add onion and bell pepper to skillet. Cook, stirring often, until vegetables are crisp-tender, about 2 minutes. Stir in pineapple juice mixture and steak sauce. Return meatballs to skillet and bring to a boil. Reduce heat to low, cover, and simmer until meatballs are cooked through, about 10 minutes.

5. In a small bowl, dissolve cornstarch in 2 tablespoons water. Add cornstarch mixture to skillet, bring to a boil, and cook, stirring, until sauce is thickened, about 1 minute.

123   VIENNESE MEATBALLS WITH GINGERSNAP SAUCE

Prep: 15 minutes   Cook: 20 minutes   Serves: 4

1 egg	2 medium carrots, thinly
1 teaspoon salt	sliced
¼ teaspoon pepper	1 (13¾-ounce) can beef broth
1 pound ground round	3 tablespoons brown sugar
(85% lean)	2 tablespoons lemon juice
½ pound ground veal	⅓ cup crushed gingersnap
2 tablespoons vegetable oil	cookies

1. In a large bowl, lightly beat egg with salt and pepper. Add ground round and ground veal and knead with your hands until well blended. Using about 1 tablespoon for each, form into meatballs.

2. Heat oil in a large skillet. Add meatballs and cook over medium heat, turning often, until browned all over, about 8 minutes. Add carrots, beef broth, brown sugar, and lemon juice. Bring to a simmer, reduce heat to low, cover tightly, and cook until carrots are crisp-tender, about 10 minutes.

3. Using a slotted spoon, transfer meatballs to a deep serving dish; cover with foil to keep warm. Stir gingersnaps into simmering sauce and cook until thickened, about 1 minute.

124   SPINACH AND BEEF MEATBALLS IN CILANTRO SAUCE

Prep: 10 minutes   Cook: 20 minutes   Serves: 4 to 6

1 cup fresh bread crumbs	⅛ teaspoon cayenne
1 (10-ounce) package frozen	1¼ pounds ground round
chopped spinach, thawed	(85% lean)
and squeezed dry	2 tablespoons vegetable oil
¼ cup milk	½ cup reduced-sodium
1 egg	chicken broth
1 teaspoon salt	3 tablespoons lemon juice
½ teaspoon ground cumin	3 tablespoons chopped fresh
½ teaspoon ground coriander	cilantro or parsley

1. In a medium bowl, mix bread crumbs, spinach, milk, egg, salt, cumin, coriander, and cayenne. Add ground round and blend well. Using 1 tablespoon for each, form meat mixture into meatballs.

2. In a large skillet, heat oil over medium heat. Add meatballs and cook, turning often, until browned all over, 8 to 10 minutes. Transfer meatballs to paper towels to drain briefly.

3. Return meatballs to skillet and add chicken broth, lemon juice, and ½ cup water. Bring to a boil over high heat, reduce heat to low, and simmer, covered, until meatballs are cooked through, about 10 minutes. Stir in cilantro.

125 MOROCCAN MEATBALLS WITH SWEET ONION SAUCE ON COUSCOUS

Prep: 20 minutes   Cook: 1 hour 10 minutes   Serves: 4 to 6

1 small onion, minced
½ cup fresh bread crumbs
1 cup tomato sauce
1 egg
2 teaspoons salt
¼ teaspoon cayenne
1½ pounds lean ground lamb or ground sirloin (90% lean)
6 tablespoons butter
4 large onions, sliced
2 large carrots, cut into 1-inch pieces
2 large zucchini, cut into 1-inch pieces

2 cups reduced-sodium beef broth
4 ounces dried apricots (about ¾ cup)
½ cup packed brown sugar
1 teaspoon cinnamon
1 cup canned chick-peas, drained
6 cups chicken stock or reduced-sodium canned broth
10 ounces couscous (1⅓ cups)
2 tablespoons chopped fresh mint or parsley

1. Preheat oven to 375°. In a large bowl, mix onion, bread crumbs, ½ cup tomato sauce, egg, salt, and cayenne until blended. Add ground lamb and knead with your hands until well mixed. Set meat mixture aside.

2. In a 5- to 6-quart ovenproof Dutch oven, heat 3 tablespoons butter over medium-high heat. Add onions and carrots, partially cover, and cook, stirring often, until onions are lightly browned, about 10 minutes.

3. Add zucchini, beef broth, and 2 cups water. Bring to a boil, then reduce heat to low. Using about 1 tablespoon for each, form meat mixture into meatballs and drop as formed into simmering liquid. Simmer 15 minutes. Add remaining ½ cup tomato sauce, apricots, brown sugar, and cinnamon. Bring to a simmer, stirring gently to dissolve sugar.

4. Transfer pot to oven and bake, uncovered, until liquid is reduced by half, 30 to 40 minutes. During last 5 minutes of cooking, gently stir in chick-peas.

5. Meanwhile, in a large saucepan, bring chicken stock, remaining 3 tablespoons butter, and remaining ½ teaspoon salt to a boil. Gradually stir in couscous, cover tightly, and remove from heat. Let stand until liquid is absorbed and couscous is tender, about 6 minutes.

6. Arrange cooked couscous in a large mound in center of a heated platter and make a well in center. With a slotted spoon, transfer meatballs and vegetables to well. Spoon sauce over couscous, sprinkle mint over top, and serve.

126 SYRIAN LEEK MEATBALLS
Prep: 15 minutes   Cook: 40 minutes   Serves: 4

2 medium leeks (white part
   only), well rinsed and
   coarsely chopped
1 pound ground round
   (85% lean)
2 tablespoons dried bread
   crumbs

1¼ teaspoons salt
¼ teaspoon pepper
2 (15-ounce) cans stewed
   tomatoes, drained
¼ teaspoon cayenne
3 tablespoons grated
   Parmesan cheese

1. Preheat oven to 375°. In a medium saucepan of boiling salted water, cook leeks until tender, about 5 minutes. Drain in a sieve, rinse under cold water, and drain well. Press leeks in sieve to remove excess liquid.

2. In a medium bowl, combine leeks, ground round, bread crumbs, salt and pepper. Using about 1 tablespoon for each, form into meatballs and place in a lightly oiled 9 x 13-inch baking dish.

3. Bake, turning once, until meatballs are browned, about 20 minutes. Add stewed tomatoes and cayenne to baking dish. Sprinkle Parmesan cheese over meatballs. Bake for 15 minutes, or until tomatoes are heated through and cheese is melted.

127 MEATBALLS BURGUNDY
Prep: 20 minutes   Cook: 25 minutes   Serves: 4

4 slices of bacon, cut into
   1-inch pieces
⅓ cup flour
1 pound ground round
   (85% lean)
½ cup fresh bread crumbs
2 small onions, chopped
2 tablespoons chopped
   parsley

1 teaspoon salt
½ teaspoon thyme
⅜ teaspoon pepper
½ pound fresh mushrooms,
   sliced
1 medium carrot, sliced
   ½ inch thick
¾ cup beef broth
½ cup dry red wine

1. In a large skillet, cook bacon over medium heat until crisp, about 5 minutes. Remove from heat. Using a slotted spoon, transfer bacon to paper towels to drain, leaving fat in skillet.

2. Place flour on a plate. In a large bowl, combine ground round, bread crumbs, 1 chopped onion, parsley, ¾ teaspoon salt, thyme, and ¼ teaspoon pepper. Mix until well blended. Using about 1 tablespoon for each, form mixture into about 18 meatballs. Roll meatballs in flour; reserve 1 tablespoon of flour.

3. Reheat fat in skillet, if necessary. Add meatballs and cook over medium heat, turning often, until browned all over, about 8 minutes. Using a slotted spoon, transfer meatballs to a plate. Pour off all but 2 tablespoons fat.

4. Add mushrooms, carrot, and remaining onion to fat in skillet. Cook over medium heat, stirring often and scraping up browned bits from bottom of pan, until mushrooms are lightly browned, about 5 minutes. Sprinkle reserved 1 tablespoon flour over vegetables and cook, stirring, 1 minute.

5. Stir in beef broth, wine, and ¾ cup water. Return meatballs to pan and bring to a boil. Reduce heat to low and simmer, uncovered, until sauce is thickened, 8 to 10 minutes. Add bacon and season sauce with remaining ¼ teaspoon salt and ⅛ teaspoon pepper.

---

128 SWEDISH MEATBALLS WITH MUSHROOM SAUCE

Prep: 15 minutes   Cook: 20 minutes   Serves: 4

1 tablespoon butter	¼ teaspoon ground allspice
½ pound fresh mushrooms, sliced	¼ teaspoon grated nutmeg
¾ teaspoon salt	¼ teaspoon pepper
⅓ cup crushed crisp rye crackers	1 pound ground round (85% lean)
½ cup heavy cream	1 tablespoon vegetable oil
1 egg	2 tablespoons flour
2 tablespoons minced onion	¾ cup beef broth
2 tablespoons chopped parsley	

1. In a large skillet, melt butter over medium heat. Add mushrooms and ¼ teaspoon salt. Cook, stirring often, until mushrooms have given off their liquid and have browned slightly, about 6 minutes. Transfer mushrooms to a plate and set aside.

2. In a medium bowl, combine rye cracker crumbs, ¼ cup cream, egg, onion, parsley, remaining ½ teaspoon salt, allspice, nutmeg, and ⅛ teaspoon pepper; stir with a fork until mixed. Add ground round and mix until well blended. Using about 1 tablespoon of mixture for each, form into meatballs.

3. In a large skillet, heat oil over medium-high heat. Add meatballs and cook, turning occasionally, until browned all over, about 8 minutes.

4. Sprinkle flour over meatballs and gently turn meatballs until coated flour is absorbed. Add broth and ¾ cup water. Bring to a simmer, scraping up browned bits from bottom of pan with a wooden spoon. Reduce heat to low, cover, and simmer 5 minutes.

5. Gently stir in mushrooms, remaining ¼ cup cream, and ⅛ teaspoon pepper. Cook just until heated through, about 2 minutes.

129 LION'S HEAD MEATBALLS WITH CHINESE CABBAGE

Prep: 10 minutes   Cook: 30 minutes   Serves: 4 to 6

Large pork meatballs are nestled on a bed of Chinese cabbage and simmered until both are tender. The poetically minded see the curly leaves of the cabbage surrounding the oversized meatballs as resembling the lion's mane curling around his head—hence the name of the dish.

1 scallion, minced	⅛ teaspoon pepper
¼ cup minced water chestnuts	1 pound ground pork
1 egg	⅓ cup cornstarch
3 tablespoons soy sauce	3 tablespoons vegetable oil
1 tablespoon dry sherry	1 pound Chinese (napa)
1 tablespoon dark Asian	cabbage (about ½ large
sesame oil (optional)	head)
2 teaspoons minced fresh	¾ cup reduced-sodium
ginger	chicken broth
½ teaspoon salt	½ teaspoon sugar

1. In a medium bowl, mix together scallion, water chestnuts, egg, 2 tablespoons soy sauce, sherry, sesame oil, ginger, salt, and pepper. Add ground pork and blend well. Using ⅓ cup meat mixture for each, form into 6 large meatballs. Place cornstarch on a plate. Roll each meatball in cornstarch to coat completely; reserve cornstarch remaining on plate.

2. In a 12-inch skillet or flameproof casserole, heat oil over moderately high heat. Add meatballs and cook, turning occasionally, until browned all over, about 8 minutes. Using a slotted spoon, transfer meatballs to a plate. Pour off all but 1 tablespoon oil from skillet.

3. Remove core from cabbage and cut leaves crosswise into ½-inch-wide strips. One handful at a time, add cabbage to skillet and cook over medium-high heat, stirring and letting each addition wilt before adding more. Return meatballs to skillet, setting them on top of cabbage. Cover, reduce heat to low, and simmer until cabbage is tender and meatballs are cooked through, about 20 minutes. Transfer meatballs and cabbage to a bowl and cover with foil to keep warm.

4. Add chicken broth to skillet and bring to a boil over high heat. Add 1 tablespoon reserved cornstarch to 2 tablespoons cold water; stir to dissolve cornstarch. Stir cornstarch mixture, sugar, and remaining 1 tablespoon soy sauce into broth. Cook, sitrring, until sauce boils and thickens, about 30 seconds. Pour sauce over meatballs and serve.

130 PERSIAN LAMB-STUFFED MEATBALLS
Prep: 30 minutes   Cook: 5 minutes   Serves: 6

Every Middle Eastern country has a version of *kufta*—meat-stuffed meatballs. They can be deep-fried, sautéed, simmered in sauce, or as in this recipe, poached in broth and topped with a tangy yogurt dressing.

1 cup plain low-fat yogurt	1½ pounds lean ground lamb, from the leg
1 scallion, minced	
3 garlic cloves—1 crushed through a press, 2 minced	2 tablespoons chopped parsley
2 teaspoons dried mint	2¼ teaspoons salt
3 tablespoons olive oil	1 teaspoon paprika
3 medium onions—2 finely chopped, 1 quartered	¼ teaspoon ground allspice
	½ teaspoon pepper
1 small green bell pepper, finely chopped	½ cup bulgur
	1 quart beef broth

1. In a small bowl, combine yogurt, scallion, crushed garlic, and 1 teaspoon mint. Cover and refrigerate until ready to serve.

2. In a large skillet, heat olive oil. Add chopped onions, bell pepper, and minced garlic. Cook over medium heat, stirring often, until vegetables are softened, about 5 minutes. Add ½ pound ground lamb and cook, stirring often to break up lumps of meat, until lamb loses its pink color, about 5 minutes. Add remaining 1 teaspoon mint, parsley, 1 teaspoon salt, paprika, allspice, and ¼ teaspoon pepper. Cook 1 minute. Transfer spiced meat mixture to a medium bowl and let cool completely.

3. In another medium bowl, combine bulgur and 2 cups cold water. Let stand 20 minutes, then drain well through a fine-mesh sieve. One handful at a time, squeeze drained bulgur in a kitchen towel to remove excess water. Transfer to a food processor.

4. Add remaining 1 pound ground lamb, quartered onion, and remaining 1¼ teaspoons salt and ¼ teaspoon pepper to food processor. Process until mixture becomes a fine paste, about 1 minute. Transfer meat paste to a small bowl.

5. Working with hands rinsed often under cold water, form 2 tablespoons of meat paste into a ball, then flatten into a patty about 4 inches wide. Place about 2 teaspoons of cooled spiced meat mixture in center of patty. Bring edges of patty up to enclose filling and smooth into a large meatball about 2½ inches in diameter. Transfer meatball to a baking sheet. Repeat with remaining paste and spiced meat mixture.

6. In a large pot, bring beef broth and 4 cups water to a boil over high heat. One at a time, rolling between your hands to reform into spheres, drop meatballs into boiling water. Reduce heat to medium-low and simmer until meatballs are completely heated through and outer meat layer shows no sign of pink when prodded with tip of a sharp knife, about 12 minutes.

7. To serve, transfer meatballs with broth to individual soup bowls. Pass minted yogurt on the side.

131   VEAL MEATBALLS IN LEMON-DILL SAUCE
Prep: 10 minutes   Cook: 20 minutes   Serves: 4

½ cup fresh bread crumbs	½ cup flour
1 small onion, chopped	1 tablespoon butter
1 egg	1 tablespoon vegetable oil
1¾ teaspoons dried dill	1 cup beef broth
1 teaspoon salt	1½ teaspoons cornstarch
½ teaspoon pepper	Grated zest of 1 lemon
1½ pounds ground veal	½ cup plain low-fat yogurt

1. In a medium bowl, combine bread crumbs, onion, egg, ¾ teaspoon dill, salt, and ¼ teaspoon pepper. Add ground veal and mix well. Using about 1 tablespoon of meat mixture for each, roll into meatballs. Place flour on a plate. Dredge meatballs in flour, shaking off excess.

2. In a large skillet, melt butter in oil over medium-high heat. Add meatballs and cook, turning often, until browned all over, about 8 minutes.

3. Add broth, remaining 1 teaspoon dill, and ¼ teaspoon pepper to skillet. Bring to a boil, stirring to scrape up browned bits from bottom of pan. Reduce heat to low, cover, and simmer until meatballs are cooked through, about 10 minutes.

4. In a small bowl, dissolve cornstarch in 2 tablespoons cold water. Stir dissolved cornstarch and lemon zest into sauce and bring to a boil, stirring until thickened, about 1 minute. Add yogurt and cook, without boiling, just until heated through, about 30 seconds.

132   ISRAELI TURKEY MEATBALLS WITH SWEET-AND-SOUR RAISIN SAUCE
Prep: 10 minutes   Cook: 25 minutes   Serves: 4

Israel has the largest turkey consumption per capita in the world, over 27 pounds per person.

3 tablespoons rendered chicken fat or vegetable oil	1 egg
	¼ cup chopped parsley
	1 teaspoon salt
1 small onion, minced	¼ teaspoon pepper
1 medium carrot, grated	1¼ pounds ground turkey
1 garlic clove, minced	⅓ cup raisins
½ cup matzoh meal	2 tablespoons lemon juice
2¼ cups chicken stock or reduced-sodium canned broth	2 tablespoons sugar
	1 tablespoon cornstarch

1. In a large skillet, heat 1 tablespoon fat. Add onion, carrot, and garlic. Cook over medium heat, stirring often, until onion is softened, about 4 minutes. Transfer vegetables to a medium bowl.

2. Add matzoh meal, ¼ cup stock, egg, parsley, salt, and pepper to vegetables in bowl; mix well. Add ground turkey and blend well. Using about 1 tablespoon for each, form turkey mixture into meatballs.

3. Heat remaining 2 tablespoons fat in skillet over medium heat. Add meatballs and cook, turning often, until browned all over, 8 to 10 minutes.

4. Stir in remaining 2 cups stock, raisins, lemon juice, and sugar. Bring to a boil, reduce heat to low, cover, and simmer for 10 minutes, or until meatballs are cooked through.

5. In a small bowl, dissolve cornstarch in 1 tablespoon water. Stir cornstarch mixture into cooking liquid, raise heat to medium-high, and cook until thickened, about 1 minute.

---

133 CHICKEN CHOW MEIN MEATBALLS
Prep: 15 minutes   Cook: 15 minutes   Serves: 4

2 tablespoons soy sauce	3 medium carrots, sliced
2 tablespoons dry sherry	diagonally ¼ inch thick
2 tablespoons cornstarch	3 celery ribs, sliced diagonally
1 tablespoon grated fresh	½ inch thick
ginger	1 medium onion, sliced
2 scallions, minced	1½ cups reduced-sodium
2 garlic cloves, minced	chicken broth
1 egg white	Hot cooked thin egg
¼ teaspoon salt	noodles, preferably fresh
¼ teaspoon pepper	Chinese or canned crispy
1 pound ground chicken	chow mein noodles
¼ cup vegetable oil	

1. In a medium bowl, combine 1 tablespoon each soy sauce and sherry, 1 teaspoon each cornstarch and ginger, 1 minced scallion and 1 minced garlic clove, egg white, salt, and pepper. Stir with a fork until mixed. Add ground chicken and mix until blended. Form mixture into 12 to 14 meatballs.

2. In a large skillet, heat 2 tablespoons oil over high heat until very hot but not smoking. Add remaining scallion, garlic, and ginger and stir-fry until fragrant, about 15 seconds. Add carrots, celery, and onion and stir-fry until vegetables are crisp-tender, about 3 minutes. Transfer vegetables to a large plate.

3. Add remaining 2 tablespoons oil to skillet. Reduce heat to medium-high and add meatballs. Cook, turning until browned all over, about 8 minutes.

4. In a small bowl, dissolve remaining 1 tablespoon plus 2 teaspoons cornstarch in chicken broth. Return vegetables to skillet. Add remaining 1 tablespoon each soy sauce and sherry and cook for 15 seconds. Add chicken broth mixture and cook, stirring gently, until sauce boils and thickens, about 1 minute. Place noodles on a serving platter, spoon the meatballs and vegetables onto noodles, and serve immediately.

134 EGYPTIAN GARLIC MEATBALLS

Prep: 20 minutes   Cook: 30 minutes   Serves: 4

3 medium onions	¼ teaspoon pepper
2 tablespoons butter	1 tablespoon olive oil
1 pound ground round	2 cups tomato juice
(85% lean)	2 teaspoons lemon juice
3 garlic cloves, minced	2 teaspoons sugar
1 teaspoon salt	1 tablespoon cornstarch

1. Mince 1 onion and reserve. Slice remaining 2 onions. In a large skillet melt butter. Add sliced onions and cook over medium heat, stirring often, until golden brown, about 8 minutes. Transfer to a plate; set skillet aside.

2. In a medium bowl, combine ground round, minced onion, garlic, salt, and pepper. Using about 2 tablespoons for each, form into 12 large meatballs.

3. In same skillet as onions were cooked, heat oil. Add meatballs and cook over medium-high heat, turning often, until browned all over, about 8 minutes. Return cooked onions to skillet. Stir in tomato juice, lemon juice, and sugar. Bring to a boil, reduce heat to low, cover, and simmer until meatballs are cooked through, about 10 minutes.

4. In a small bowl, dissolve cornstarch in 2 tablespoons cold water. Stir into tomato sauce and cook, stirring, until thickened, about 1 minute.

135 LAMB AND ROSEMARY MEATBALLS WITH ARTICHOKES

Prep: 15 minutes   Cook: 20 to 24 minutes   Serves: 4

½ cup fresh bread crumbs	2 tablespoons olive oil
3 tablespoons grated	1 small onion, chopped
Parmesan cheese	1 medium carrot, chopped
1 egg	1 (16-ounce) package frozen
1 garlic clove, minced	artichoke hearts, thawed
1¼ teaspoons rosemary	1 cup beef broth
¾ teaspoon salt	½ cup dry white wine
⅜ teaspoon pepper	1 teaspoon lemon juice
1 pound ground lamb	1 teaspoon tomato paste
¼ cup flour	

1. In a medium bowl, combine bread crumbs, Parmesan cheese, egg, garlic, 1 teaspoon rosemary, ½ teaspoon salt, and ¼ teaspoon pepper. Stir with a fork until mixed. Add ground lamb and mix until blended. Using about 2 tablespoons of mixture for each, form into meatballs.

2. Place flour on a plate; roll meatballs in flour to coat lightly, reserving any flour remaining on plate. In a large skillet, heat oil over medium heat. Add meatballs and cook, turning often, until browned all over, about 8 minutes. With a slotted spoon, transfer meatballs to a plate. Drain off all but 1 tablespoon fat from pan.

3. Add onion, carrot, and artichoke hearts to skillet and cook over medium heat, stirring often, until onions are softened, 3 to 5 minutes. Sprinkle 1 tablespoon reserved flour over vegetables and cook, stirring often, 1 minute. Stir in beef broth, wine, lemon juice, tomato paste, and remaining ¼ teaspoon each rosemary and salt and ⅛ teaspoon pepper. Bring to a simmer, reduce heat to low, and cook, partially covered, until sauce has thickened slightly and meatballs are cooked through, 8 to 10 minutes.

---

136   MIDEASTERN LAMB MEATBALLS WITH SPINACH

Prep: 15 minutes   Cook: 30 minutes   Serves: 4

½ cup fresh bread crumbs
2 scallions, minced
3 garlic cloves—1 minced, 2 crushed through a press
1 egg
½ teaspoon ground cumin
¾ teaspoon salt
¼ teaspoon pepper
1 pound lean ground lamb
3 tablespoons olive oil

1 medium onion, chopped
1 medium carrot, chopped
2 pounds fresh spinach, well rinsed, stemmed, and shredded
1 cup beef broth
1 teaspoon ground coriander
Hot cooked rice and chopped fresh parsley

1. In a medium bowl, combine bread crumbs, scallions, minced garlic, egg, cumin, salt, and pepper. Add ground lamb and mix well. Using about 1 tablespoon for each, form into meatballs.

2. In a large Dutch oven, heat 1 tablespoon olive oil. Add meatballs and cook over medium-high heat, turning often, until browned all over, about 8 minutes. Transfer meatballs to a plate and set aside.

3. Heat 1 more tablespoon oil in Dutch oven. Add onion and carrot and cook over medium heat, stirring often, until onion is softened, about 4 minutes. Stir in beef broth, scraping up browned bits from bottom of pan. Bring to a boil.

4. Return meatballs to Dutch oven and top with half of spinach. Cover, reduce heat to low, and simmer until spinach is wilted, about 5 minutes. Stir in remaining spinach, cover and simmer, stirring often, until spinach is tender and meatballs are cooked through, about 10 minutes.

5. In a small skillet, heat remaining 1 tablespoon olive oil over low heat. Add crushed garlic and coriander and stir until fragrant but not browned, about 1 minute. Add to meatballs. Serve over bowls of cooked rice, garnished with parsley.

137 SCANDINAVIAN MEATBALLS WITH LINGONBERRY SAUCE

Prep: 15 minutes   Cook: 22 minutes   Serves: 4 to 6

2 medium russet potatoes,
  peeled and cut into
  chunks
1 small onion, minced
⅓ cup evaporated milk
¼ cup dried bread crumbs
1 egg
1 teaspoon salt

¼ teaspoon ground allspice
¼ teaspoon pepper
1 pound ground round
  (85% lean)
1 tablespoon butter
1 tablespoon vegetable oil
  Lingonberry preserves or
  cranberry sauce

1. In a medium saucepan of boiling salted water, cook potatoes just until tender enough to be pierced with tip of a knife, about 12 minutes. Drain well. Using a ricer or masher, mash potatoes.

2. In a medium bowl, mix onion, evaporated milk, bread crumbs, egg, salt, allspice, and pepper with a fork until blended. Add ground round and mashed potatoes and blend well. Using 1 heaping teaspoon for each, form into about 4 dozen meatballs.

3. In a 12-inch skillet, heat butter and oil. Add meatballs and cook over medium heat, turning often, until meatballs are browned all over and cooked through, about 10 minutes. Serve hot with lingonberry preserves, if desired.

138 SOUPER TOMATO MEATBALLS

Prep: 10 minutes   Cook: 23 minutes   Serves: 4

1 (10 ¾-ounce) can tomato
  soup
1 small onion, minced
1 garlic clove, minced
¼ cup Italian-seasoned bread
  crumbs
1 egg

½ teaspoon basil
¼ teaspoon salt
¼ teaspoon pepper
1 pound ground round
  (85% lean)
1 tablespoon vegetable oil
¾ cup milk

1. In a medium bowl, combine ¼ cup tomato soup, onion, garlic, bread crumbs, egg, basil, salt, and pepper. Add ground round and mix well. Using about 2 tablespoons meat mixture for each, form into meatballs.

2. In a large skillet, heat oil. Add meatballs and cook over medium-high heat, turning often, until browned all over, about 8 minutes.

3. Stir in remaining soup and milk. Bring to a boil, reduce heat to low, cover, and simmer until meatballs are cooked through, about 15 minutes.

139 LAMB KOFTAS IN SPICY YOGURT SAUCE
Prep: 25 minutes   Cook: 40 minutes   Serves: 4

1 pound lean ground lamb
¼ cup minced onion plus 2 medium onions, chopped
3 garlic cloves, minced
4 teaspoons curry powder
1 tablespoon ground cumin
2 teaspoons ground coriander
1½ teaspoons salt
½ teaspoon crushed hot red pepper

2 tablespoons vegetable oil
1 tablespoon grated fresh ginger
2 medium tomatoes, seeded and chopped
½ cup plain low-fat yogurt
2 teaspoons cornstarch
¼ cup raisins
¼ cup sliced almonds

1. Preheat oven to 350°. In a medium bowl, combine lamb, minced onion, 1 garlic clove, 2 teaspoons curry powder, 1 teaspoon each cumin, coriander, and salt, and ¼ teaspoon hot pepper. Knead with your hands until well mixed. Set meat mixture aside.

2. In a large ovenproof skillet or flameproof casserole, heat oil. Add 2 chopped onions and cook over medium heat, stirring often, until softened, about 5 minutes. Add ginger and remaining garlic and cook 1 minute. Add remaining 2 teaspoons curry powder, 1 teaspoon each cumin and coriander, ½ teaspoon salt, and ¼ teaspoon hot pepper. Cook, stirring, 30 seconds. Stir in chopped tomatoes and cook 1 minute. Stir in 1½ cups water and bring to a boil. Reduce heat and simmer, partially covered, 15 minutes.

3. In a small bowl, whisk together yogurt and cornstarch. Whisk yogurt mixture into sauce, increase heat to medium, and return to a simmer.

4. Using about 1 tablespoon for each, form meat mixture into meatballs, dropping as formed into simmering sauce. Bake 15 minutes, until sauce is thickened and meatballs are cooked through. Garnish with raisins and almonds before serving.

140 ROZ'S LAMB KEFTEDES WITH CHEESE SAUCE

Prep: 20 minutes   Cook: 35 minutes   Serves: 4

2 medium onions, finely chopped	1¼ teaspoons salt
2 garlic cloves, minced	½ teaspoon pepper
1 egg	1 pound lean ground lamb
¼ cup pine nuts (pignoli)	2 tablespoons butter
1 tablespoon lemon juice	2 tablespoons flour
2 teaspoons dried mint	2 cups milk
	½ cup grated Parmesan cheese

1. Preheat oven to 375°. In a medium bowl, combine onions, garlic, egg, pine nuts, lemon juice, mint, 1 teaspoon salt, and ¼ teaspoon pepper. Add ground lamb and mix well.

2. Using about 1 tablespoon for each, form into 32 meatballs; place as formed on a large lightly oiled baking sheet.

3. Bake meatballs, turning once, until browned, about 20 minutes. With a slotted spoon, transfer meatballs to a flameproof 11 x 7-inch baking dish or oval gratin. Position a broiler rack about 4 inches from source of heat and preheat broiler.

4. Meanwhile, in a heavy medium saucepan, melt butter over medium heat. Whisk in flour and cook, stirring, about 1 minute without letting mixture brown. Whisk in milk, increase heat to medium-high, and bring to a boil, whisking until smooth and thick. Reduce heat to low and simmer, whisking often, until sauce has no trace of raw flour taste, about 5 minutes. Remove from heat and stir in ¼ cup Parmesan cheese and remaining ¼ teaspoon each salt and pepper. Pour sauce over meatballs and sprinkle ¼ cup Parmesan cheese over top.

5. Broil until top is lightly browned, about 3 minutes.

Chapter 6

Pasta Perfect

Pasta, of course, is merely the Italian name for "noodles," a culinary staple the world over. While Italian-style pasta dishes like Penne with Herbed Veal Meatballs and Artichokes, Fresh Fettuccine with Bolognese Sauce, and My Favorite Lasagne, are well represented here, other countries' noodle classics also make a showing, such as Egg Noodles in Peking Meat Sauce with Crunchy Toppings, Mrs. Foreman's Iowa Spaghetti, and Greek Orzo Pie.

Versatility is one of pasta's most admirable traits. Whether you're looking for a quick nourishing supper, like Linguine with Turkey Marsala Sauce, or an ornate oven-baked crowd pleaser, like Johnny Mazetti Spaghetti Casserole, it always fills the bill. Pasta can be the canvas for a whole palette of flavors, textures, and seasonings, from Southwestern Chicken Pasta Roll-Ups to Penne with Creamy Moussaka Sauce.

Pasta and ground meat are each inexpensive, absolutely delicious ways to stretch a dollar; combined, they are even more of a terrific value. Think of how much pasta sauce you can make from one pound of ground meat! Ground beef is often used in traditional pasta sauce recipes, but ground turkey and ground veal, in particular, make superlative sauces, as well.

While many of the dishes in this chapter feature the familiar dried pastas, I haven't neglected the fresh pastas that you may have noticed in your supermarket's refrigerator case. Remember that these delicate pastas cook quickly, so watch them with care. For the adventurous cook, I've even given instructions on how to make your own tortellini from won ton wrappers (which are nothing more than pasta squares, if you think about it) in the recipes for Veal and Ricotta Tortellini in Parmesan Cream Sauce (page 117).

141 SUNDAY NIGHT SPAGHETTI AND MEATBALLS

Prep: 20 minutes   Cook: 1 hour   Serves: 6 to 8

2 slices firm-textured white bread, crumbled
⅓ cup milk
1 egg
¼ cup grated Parmesan cheese
1 tablespoon Italian seasoning
¼ teaspoon salt
¼ teaspoon black pepper
¾ pound ground round (85% lean) or ground sirloin (90% lean)
¾ pound sweet Italian sausage, casings removed

¼ cup olive oil
1 medium onion, chopped
1 garlic clove, minced
1 (35-ounce) can crushed tomatoes
1 (6-ounce) can tomato paste
½ cup dry red wine
¼ teaspoon crushed hot red pepper
1½ pounds spaghetti
Grated Parmesan cheese

1. In a medium bowl, soak bread in milk until softened; squeeze out and discard excess milk. Add egg, ¼ cup Parmesan cheese, 1 teaspoon Italian seasoning, salt, and black pepper to bread. Stir with a fork until well mixed. Add ground round and sausage and mix until blended. Using about 1 tablespoon for each, form meat mixture into 14 to 16 meatballs.

2. In a large skillet, or flameproof casserole, heat oil over medium heat. In batches, if necessary, add meatballs and cook, turning, until browned and crusty all over, about 8 minutes per batch. With a slotted spoon, transfer meatballs to a plate and set aside. Discard all but 2 tablespoons fat from skillet.

3. Add onion and cook, stirring often, until softened, about 3 minutes. Add garlic and cook, stirring, 1 minute. Add tomatoes, tomato paste, wine, remaining 2 teaspoons Italian seasoning, hot pepper, and ½ cup water. Reduce heat to low, partially cover, and simmer 30 minutes. Return meatballs to skillet and cook, uncovered, 15 minutes.

4. Meanwhile, in a large pot of boiling water, cook spaghetti until just tender, 8 to 10 minutes; drain well. Place pasta in a warm serving dish. Pour sauce and meatballs over spaghetti. Pass a bowl of grated Parmesan cheese on the side.

Variation: **HIDDEN TREASURE MEATBALLS**

1. Cut ½ pound mozzarella cheese into ½-inch cubes. Place a cheese cube in center of each uncooked meatball, covering cube completely with meatball mixture.

142 JOHNNY MAZETTI SPAGHETTI CASSEROLE

Prep: 15 minutes   Cook: 1 hour 10 minutes   Serves: 6 to 8

Just about everyone in Columbus, Ohio, has a recipe for an enormous, rib-sticking spaghetti casserole based on the original from Mazetti's, a well-known Italian restaurant there. When you first assemble the dish, it will seem as if there is too much sauce, but remember, the sauce will be absorbed during baking.

1½ cups ground chuck (80% lean)	1 teaspoon basil
1 large onion, chopped	1 teaspoon oregano
1 large green bell pepper, chopped	1 bay leaf
½ pound fresh mushrooms, sliced	¾ teaspoon salt
2 garlic cloves, minced	¼ teaspoon pepper
1 (35-ounce) can Italian peeled tomatoes, coarsely chopped, juice reserved	1 (3.8-ounce) can sliced black olives
1 (12-ounce) can tomato sauce	1 pound spaghetti
	2 cups shredded sharp Cheddar cheese (8 ounces)
	1 cup fresh bread crumbs

1. In a 5- to 6-quart Dutch oven, cook ground chuck, onion, bell pepper, mushrooms, and garlic over medium-high heat, stirring often to break up lumps of meat, until beef loses its pink color, about 8 minutes.

2. Add tomatoes with their juice, tomato sauce, basil, oregano, bay leaf, salt, and pepper. Bring to a boil, reduce heat to medium-low, and simmer, stirring often, until slightly thickened, about 20 minutes.

3. Meanwhile, in a large pot of lightly salted water, cook spaghetti until just tender, about 9 minutes. Drain well.

4. Preheat oven to 350°. Add olives, spaghetti, and 1 cup Cheddar cheese to sauce; stir gently to mix. Transfer to a lightly oiled 10 x 15-inch baking dish. Sprinkle bread crumbs and remaining cheese over top.

5. Bake until top is lightly browned and casserole is bubbling throughout, about 30 minutes. Let stand 5 minutes before serving.

143 EASY BAKED ZITI

Prep: 10 minutes   Cook: 45 minutes   Serves: 6 to 8

1 pound ziti or other tubular
   pasta
1 pound ground chuck
   (80% lean) or ground
   round (85% lean)
1 medium onion, chopped
2 garlic cloves, minced
1 (35-ounce) can Italian peeled
   tomatoes, with their juice
1 cup tomato sauce
1 (6-ounce) can tomato paste

2 teaspoons oregano
2 teaspoons basil
1 teaspoon salt
¼ teaspoon crushed hot red
   pepper
2 cups part-skim ricotta cheese
1½ cups shredded part-skim
   mozzarella cheese
   (6 ounces)
½ cup grated Parmesan cheese

1. Preheat oven to 350°. In a large pot of boiling salted water, cook ziti until barely tender, about 8 minutes. Drain well. Return ziti to empty pot.

2. In a large skillet, cook ground chuck, onion, and garlic over medium heat, stirring often to break up lumps, until meat loses its pink color, about 5 minutes. Stir in tomatoes with their juice, tomato sauce, tomato paste, oregano, basil, salt, and hot pepper; break up tomatoes in skillet with a spoon. Bring tomato sauce to a simmer.

3. Pour tomato sauce over ziti in pot. Add ricotta and stir to mix. Pour half of ziti mixture into a lightly oiled 3-quart casserole. Sprinkle on 1 cup mozzarella. Pour in remaining ziti and sprinkle remaining mozzarella and Parmesan cheese over top. Bake, uncovered, 30 to 40 minutes, or until casserole is bubbling and cheese has melted.

144 MRS. FOREMAN'S IOWA SPAGHETTI

Prep: 15 minutes   Soak: 20 minutes   Cook: 45 minutes
Serves: 4 to 6

1 (1-ounce) package dried
   imported mushrooms
½ cup boiling water
1 pound spaghetti
1 pound ground round
   (85% lean)
1 large onion, chopped
2 medium green bell peppers,
   chopped

3 garlic cloves, minced
4 cups (1 quart) tomato sauce
1 (16-ounce) can creamed corn
½ teaspoon salt
½ teaspoon pepper
1 cup grated Parmesan cheese
   (4 ounces)

1. In a small bowl, soak mushrooms in boiling water until softened, about 20 minutes. Lift out mushrooms and strain liquid through a sieve lined with moistened paper towels; reserve liquid. Rinse soaked mushrooms well under cold water to remove any hidden grit.

2. Meanwhile, in a large saucepan of boiling salted water, cook spaghetti until just tender, 9 to 10 minutes. Drain well, rinse under cold water, and drain again.

3. Preheat oven to 350°. In a large skillet, cook ground round, onion, bell peppers, and garlic over medium-high heat, stirring often to break up lumps of meat, until beef loses its pink color, about 5 minutes.

4. Stir in tomato sauce, creamed corn, salt, and pepper. Bring to a simmer, stirring often. In a lightly oiled 9 x 13-inch baking dish, combine cooked spaghetti, meat mixture, and ½ cup Parmesan cheese. Toss to mix. Sprinkle remaining cheese over top. Bake until sauce is bubbling, about 30 minutes.

---

145 LINGUINE WITH TURKEY MARENGO
Prep: 15 minutes   Cook: 1 hour 25 minutes   Serves: 4 to 6

½ cup fresh bread crumbs
1 egg
1 teaspoon salt
¼ teaspoon pepper
1¼ pounds ground turkey
3 tablespoons olive oil
1 large onion, chopped
½ pound fresh mushrooms, quartered
2 garlic cloves, minced
1 (28-ounce) can tomato puree
1 (15-ounce) can Italian peeled tomatoes, with their juice

½ cup dry white wine
½ cup chicken broth
1 teaspoon basil
½ teaspoon thyme
½ teaspoon grated orange zest
1 (16-ounce) package frozen small white onions, thawed
½ cup pimiento-stuffed olives
1½ pounds linguine
Grated Parmesan cheese

1. In a medium bowl, mix bread crumbs, egg, salt, and pepper. Add ground turkey and mix until well blended. Using about 1 tablespoon for each, form turkey mixture into meatballs. (Rinse hands occasionally in cold water to help avoid sticking.)

2. In a 5- to 6-quart Dutch oven, heat olive oil. Add meatballs and cook over medium-high heat, turning often, until browned all over, 8 to 10 minutes. With a slotted spoon, transfer meatballs to a plate, leaving oil behind in Dutch oven.

3. Add additional oil, if necessary, to measure 2 tablespoons, and reduce heat to medium. Add onion and mushrooms. Cook, stirring often, until onion is softened, about 5 minutes. Add garlic and cook 1 minute. Stir in tomato puree, tomatoes with their juice, wine, broth, basil, thyme, and orange zest; break up tomatoes with a large spoon. Bring to a boil, reduce heat to low, and simmer, uncovered, until sauce is slightly thickened, about 45 minutes.

4. Add meatballs to sauce. Gently stir in small white onions and olives. Simmer 15 minutes, or until meatballs are cooked through.

5. Meanwhile, cook linguine in a large pot of boiling salted water until tender, about 8 minutes. Drain well and transfer to a large heated bowl. Add sauce and toss until coated. Arrange meatballs on top. Pass a bowl of grated Parmesan cheese on the side.

146   JIFFY BEEF, MACARONI, AND CHEESE
Prep: 10 minutes   Cook: 45 minutes   Serves: 4

1½ cups elbow macaroni
1 pound ground round
   (85% lean)
1 medium onion, chopped
1 medium green bell pepper,
   chopped
1 (10¾-ounce) can Cheddar
   cheese soup

1 cup milk
½ teaspoon salt
¼ teaspoon hot pepper sauce
1 cup fresh bread crumbs
½ cup grated Parmesan cheese
¼ teaspoon paprika
1 tablespoon butter

1. Preheat oven to 350°. In a large pot of boiling salted water, cook macaroni just until tender, about 8 minutes. Drain well.

2. Meanwhile, in a large skillet, cook ground round, onion, and bell pepper over medium heat, stirring often to break up meat, until it loses its pink color, about 5 minutes. Drain off excess fat.

3. In a lightly buttered deep 2-quart baking dish, combine macaroni and beef. Stir in soup, milk, salt, and hot sauce. Sprinkle bread crumbs, Parmesan cheese, and paprika over top and dot with butter.

4. Bake until top is browned and casserole is bubbling, about 30 minutes.

---

147   GOLDEN POLENTA WEDGES WITH QUICK BOLOGNESE SAUCE
Prep: 10 minutes   Cook: 35 to 40 minutes   Chill: 2 hours   Serves: 8

Quick Bolognese Sauce
   (page 112)
1½ teaspoons salt
1¼ cups yellow cornmeal,
   preferably stone-ground

2 tablespoons olive oil
2 tablespoons butter
1 cup grated Parmesan cheese

1. Prepare Quick Bolognese Sauce. In a heavy medium saucepan, bring 4 cups water and salt to a boil over high heat. Pouring in a slow, steady stream, stir in cornmeal. Reduce heat to low and cook, stirring very often to avoid sticking, until cornmeal is thick enough to support a freestanding spoon, 25 to 30 minutes. Transfer polenta to a well-buttered 9-inch pie plate, spreading evenly. Let cool completely, then chill until firm, about 2 hours.

2. Preheat oven to 400°. Cut chilled polenta into 8 wedges. In a large skillet, heat olive oil and butter. In batches, add polenta wedges and cook over medium heat, turning once, until golden brown, about 6 minutes. Transfer browned wedges to a baking sheet. Sprinkle ½ cup Parmesan cheese over polenta.

3. Bake until cheese melts, about 5 minutes. Serve polenta wedges with hot bolognese sauce spooned on top. Pass remaining Parmesan cheese on the side.

148 NEW ENGLAND CHOP SUEY
Prep: 10 minutes   Cook: 20 minutes   Serves: 4

In New England, "chop suey" is not an Asian vegetable stir-fry with noodles, but elbow macaroni with a gently seasoned tomato sauce. It is a dish most often found in diners, not in Chinese restaurants.

1 pound ground round
(85% lean)
1 medium onion, chopped
2 celery ribs, thinly sliced
1 (35-ounce) can Italian peeled
tomatoes, drained and
coarsely chopped

1 teaspoon Worcestershire
sauce
¼ teaspoon salt
¼ teaspoon pepper
12 ounces elbow macaroni
1 cup shredded Cheddar
cheese (4 ounces)

1. In a large skillet, cook ground round, onion, and celery over medium-high heat, stirring often to break up lumps of meat, until beef loses its pink color, about 5 minutes.

2. Stir in tomatoes, Worcestershire sauce, salt, and pepper. Bring to a boil, reduce heat to medium, and cook, stirring often, until liquid is slightly reduced, about 5 minutes.

3. Meanwhile, cook macaroni in a large pot of boiling salted water until tender, about 9 minutes. Drain well and transfer to a warmed serving bowl. Add sauce and cheese and toss.

149 CABBAGE AND PASTA SURPRISE
Prep: 15 minutes   Cook: 35 minutes   Serves: 3 or 4

1 pound ground round
(85% lean)
1 medium onion, chopped
2 cups chopped cabbage
1 (28-ounce) can Italian peeled
tomatoes, with their juice
2 teaspoons Worcestershire
sauce

1 teaspoon celery salt
¼ teaspoon sugar
¼ teaspoon pepper
8 ounces elbow macaroni
1 cup shredded Cheddar
cheese (4 ounces)

1. In a large skillet, cook ground round, onion, and cabbage over medium heat, stirring often to break up lumps of meat, until beef loses its pink color and cabbage is wilted, about 6 minutes.

2. Stir in tomatoes with their juice, Worcestershire sauce, celery salt, sugar, and pepper. Bring to a boil, reduce heat to low, and simmer, uncovered, until thickened, about 20 minutes.

3. Meanwhile, cook macaroni in a large pot of boiling salted water until tender, about 8 minutes. Drain well.

4. In a warm serving bowl, toss macaroni, cabbage sauce, and Cheddar cheese until cheese is melted.

150 MIXED-UP RAVIOLI
Prep: 10 minutes Cook: 1 hour Serves: 4 to 6

A casserole that has all of the ingredients of ravioli, but isn't ravioli, is obviously all mixed-up!

1 pound ground chicken or
    ground veal
1 medium onion, chopped
1 garlic clove, minced
1 (32-ounce) jar marinara
    sauce
1 cup tomato sauce
¼ teaspoon pepper

1 (10-ounce) package frozen
    chopped spinach, thawed
    and squeezed dry
1 cup low-fat cottage cheese or
    ricotta cheese
2 eggs
8 ounces bow-tie pasta
½ cup grated Parmesan cheese

1. In a 5-quart Dutch oven, cook ground chicken, onion, and garlic over medium heat, stirring often to break up lumps of meat, until chicken has lost its pink color, about 5 minutes. Drain off excess liquid.

2. Stir in marinara sauce, tomato sauce, and pepper. Bring to a boil, reduce heat to low, and simmer 10 minutes. Stir in spinach, cottage cheese, and eggs.

3. Meanwhile, in a large pot of boiling salted water, cook pasta just until barely tender, about 8 minutes. Drain well. Add cooked pasta to sauce and mix well. Transfer mixture to a lightly oiled 2-quart casserole placed on a baking sheet. Sprinkle Parmesan cheese over top.

4. Bake, uncovered, until bubbling, about 30 minutes. Let stand about 10 minutes before serving.

151 QUICK BOLOGNESE SAUCE
Prep: 5 minutes Cook: 35 minutes
Makes: 2 cups, enough for 1 pound cooked pasta

1 pound ground round
    (85% lean)
1 medium onion, finely
    chopped
1 garlic clove, minced
1 (6-ounce) can tomato paste

½ cup beef broth
½ cup dry red wine
1 teaspoon basil
⅛ teaspoon pepper
2 tablespoons heavy cream

1. In a medium saucepan, cook ground round, onion, and garlic over medium-high heat, stirring often to break up lumps of meat, until beef loses its pink color, about 5 minutes.

2. Stir in tomato paste, beef broth, wine, ½ cup water, basil, and pepper. Bring to a boil, reduce heat to medium-low, and simmer, uncovered, stirring often, until thickened, about 30 minutes. Stir in heavy cream.

152   MY FAVORITE LASAGNE

Prep: 20 minutes   Cook: 1¾ hours   Stand: 10 minutes
Serves: 6 to 8

¾ pound ground round
    (85% lean)
¾ pound ground pork
1 large onion, chopped
2 garlic cloves, minced
1 (28-ounce) can tomatoes
    with added puree
1 (6-ounce) can tomato paste
½ cup dry red wine
1 teaspoon basil
1 teaspoon oregano
¼ teaspoon crushed hot red
    pepper

2 tablespoons olive oil
12 lasagne noodles (9 ounces)
1 (15-ounce) container part-
    skim ricotta cheese
½ cup grated Parmesan cheese
2 eggs
¼ cup chopped parsley
1 teaspoon salt
¼ teaspoon black pepper
1 pound part-skim
    mozzarella, sliced

1. In a 5- to 6-quart Dutch oven, cook ground round, ground pork, onion, and garlic over medium-high heat, stirring often to break up lumps of meat, until beef and pork lose their pink color, about 7 minutes. Drain off excess fat.

2. Stir in tomatoes with puree, tomato paste, wine, basil, oregano, and hot pepper. Bring to a boil, breaking up tomatoes with a large spoon. Reduce heat to low and simmer, uncovered, until meat sauce is slightly thickened, about 45 minutes.

3. Meanwhile, bring a large pot of salted water to a boil; add 1 tablespoon olive oil. Add lasagne noodles and boil until just tender, about 10 minutes. Drain, rinse under cold water, and drain again. Toss noodles in colander with remaining 1 tablespoon olive oil. Let noodles stand at room temperature until ready to layer lasagne.

4. Preheat oven to 375°. In a large bowl combine, ricotta cheese, Parmesan cheese, eggs, parsley, salt, and black pepper.

5. Cover bottom of a lightly oiled 9 x 13-inch baking dish with a thin layer of meat sauce. Arrange 4 lasagne noodles, slightly overlapping, in dish. Spoon half of ricotta filling over noodles. Cover with half of mozzarella slices. Spread one-third of meat sauce over cheese. Arrange another layer of 4 overlapping lasagne noodles in dish. Cover with remaining ricotta filling, remaining mozzarella, then half of remaining sauce, and a final layer of noodles. Top with remaining meat sauce. Cover with aluminum foil.

6. Bake lasagne 30 minutes. Remove foil and bake 15 minutes, until bubbling throughout. Let stand about 10 minutes before serving.

153 RISOTTO BOLOGNESE

Prep: 10 minutes   Soak: 20 minutes   Cook: 30 minutes
Serves: 4 to 6

1 ounce dried mushrooms, such as porcini or Polish	1½ cups Italian Arborio rice
5 cups veal or beef stock or 3 cups canned beef broth mixed with 2 cups water	¼ cup grated Parmesan cheese
	2 tablespoons butter
	¼ teaspoon pepper
1¼ cups Quick Bolognese Sauce (page 112)	

1. Rinse dried mushrooms well under cold water. In a medium saucepan, combine rinsed mushrooms with stock and bring to a simmer over low heat. Remove from heat, cover, and let stand until mushrooms are softened, about 20 minutes. Lift out mushrooms and strain broth through a moist paper towel–lined sieve set over a bowl; reserve soaking broth. Rinse soaked mushrooms to remove any hidden grit; chop coarsely.

2. Return soaking broth to saucepan and bring to a simmer. Keep liquid at a low simmer while making risotto.

3. In a large, heavy saucepan or Dutch oven, bring Quick Bolognese Sauce and chopped mushrooms to a simmer over medium-low heat. Add rice and cook, stirring, for 2 minutes. Using a ladle, stir in about ½ cup of simmering broth. Cook, stirring very often, until broth is absorbed. Repeat procedure, adding about ½ cup broth at a time, until all broth is used and risotto is barely tender, 15 to 20 minutes. (If broth is used up before rice is tender, continue with hot water.)

4. Stir in Parmesan cheese, butter, and pepper. Taste and season with salt only if necessary. Serve immediately.

154 FRESH FETTUCCINE WITH CLASSIC BOLOGNESE SAUCE

Prep: 15 minutes   Cook: 1¾ to 3 hours   Serves: 4 to 6

½ pound ground round (85% lean)	1 (35-ounce) can Italian peeled tomatoes, coarsely chopped, juice reserved
½ pound ground veal	
1 small onion, chopped	1 teaspoon basil
1 small carrot, chopped	¼ teaspoon salt
1 small celery rib, chopped	¼ teaspoon pepper
1 garlic clove, minced	1 pound fresh fettuccine
½ cup dry white wine	Grated Parmesan cheese
½ cup heavy cream	

1. In a medium saucepan, cook ground round, ground veal, onion, carrot, celery, and garlic over medium-high heat, stirring often to break up lumps, until meats lose their pink color, about 5 minutes.

2. Add wine, bring to a boil, and cook until liquid is almost completely evaporated, about 6 minutes. Add cream, bring to a boil, and cook until reduced to ¼ cup, about 4 minutes.

3. Stir in tomatoes with their juice, basil, salt, and pepper. Bring to a boil, reduce heat to very low, and simmer gently (a flame tamer is useful here), stirring occasionally, at least 1½ hours and up to 3 hours, the longer the better for flavor.

4. When ready to serve, cook fettuccine in a large pot of boiling salted water, until just tender, about 4 minutes. Drain well and transfer to a warmed serving bowl. Add sauce and toss. Pass a bowl of grated Parmesan cheese on the side.

---

155 SOUTHWESTERN CHICKEN PASTA ROLL-UPS

Prep: 30 minutes   Cook: 45 minutes   Serves: 8 to 12

2 tablespoons olive oil	1 cup cottage cheese
12 lasagne noodles (9 ounces)	1 cup shredded Monterey Jack
1 pound ground chicken	cheese
1 medium onion, chopped	1 (3.8-ounce) can sliced black
1 medium zucchini, cut into	olives
¼-inch dice	2 cups tomato salsa
1 garlic clove, minced	½ cup shredded Cheddar
1 teaspoon chili powder	cheese
1 teaspoon salt	

1. Preheat oven to 350°. Bring a large pot of salted water to a boil; add 1 tablespoon olive oil. One at a time, add lasagne noodles. Cook until tender, about 10 minutes. Drain, rinse under cold water, and drain again. Toss noodles with remaining olive oil.

2. In a large skillet, cook ground chicken, onion, zucchini, and garlic over medium heat, stirring often to break up lumps of meat, until chicken loses its pink color, about 5 minutes. Drain off excess liquid. Add chili powder and salt and cook, stirring, 1 minute.

3. In a medium bowl, combine chicken mixture, cottage cheese, Monterey Jack, and olives. Mix well.

4. Spread about ½ cup salsa over bottom of a lightly oiled 9 x 13-inch baking dish. Place 1 lasagne noodle flat on a work surface. Spread about ⅓ cup filling over noodle, leaving 1 inch uncovered at one end. Starting from covered end, roll up noodle and place seam side down in prepared baking dish. Repeat with remaining noodles and filling. Pour remaining 1½ cups salsa over roll-ups and cover with aluminum foil.

5. Bake 25 minutes. Uncover and sprinkle Cheddar cheese over top. Bake until cheese is melted, about 5 minutes.

156 LINGUINE WITH TURKEY MARSALA SAUCE

Prep: 10 minutes   Cook: 30 minutes   Serves: 4

2 tablespoons butter	½ teaspoon salt
1 small onion, chopped	⅛ teaspoon pepper
10 ounces fresh mushrooms, sliced	1 cup heavy cream
	½ cup chicken broth
1 garlic clove, minced	1 pound linguine
1 pound ground turkey or ground veal	¼ cup chopped parsley
	Grated Parmesan cheese
½ cup dry Marsala wine	

1. In a large skillet, heat 1 tablespoon butter. Add onion and cook over medium heat until softened, about 3 minutes. Add remaining 1 tablespoon butter, mushrooms, and garlic. Cook, stirring often, until mushrooms have given off their liquid, the liquid evaporates, and the mushrooms are beginning to brown, about 6 minutes.

2. Add ground turkey and cook, stirring often to break up lumps, just until meat loses its pink color, about 4 minutes. Increase heat to high and add Marsala, salt, and pepper. Cook until wine is almost evaporated, about 2 minutes. Add heavy cream and chicken broth and cook until liquid is evaporated by half, about 4 minutes.

3. Meanwhile, in a large pot of boiling salted water, cook linguine until tender but still firm, 8 to 9 minutes. Drain well.

4. In a heated serving dish, toss hot cooked linguine, sauce, and parsley. Pass a bowl of grated Parmesan cheese on the side.

157 TURKEY TETRAZZINI SUPPER

Prep: 10 minutes   Cook: 40 minutes   Serves: 4

8 ounces ziti or other tubular pasta	2 cups half-and-half
	2 tablespoons dry sherry
1 pound ground turkey	¾ teaspoon salt
½ pound fresh mushrooms, sliced	¼ teaspoon pepper
	¾ cup grated Parmesan cheese
3 scallions, chopped	¼ cup fresh bread crumbs
3 tablespoons flour	1 tablespoon butter, cut up

1. Preheat oven to 400°. In a large saucepan of boiling salted water, cook ziti until tender but still firm, 10 to 12 minutes. Drain well, rinse under cold water, and set aside.

2. In a large skillet, cook ground turkey, mushrooms, and scallions over medium heat, stirring often to break up lumps of meat, until turkey loses its pink color, about 5 minutes.

3. Sprinkle flour over meat and mushroom mixture and cook, stirring, 1 minute. Stir in half-and-half, sherry, salt, and pepper. Bring to a boil, reduce heat to low, and simmer until thickened, about 3 minutes. Remove from heat and stir in ½ cup Parmesan cheese.

4. In a lightly oiled 2-quart casserole, combine cooked ziti and turkey mixture; toss to mix. Sprinkle remaining ¼ cup Parmesan and bread crumbs over top; dot with butter. Bake until casserole is bubbling and top is browned, about 20 minutes.

---

158 VEAL AND RICOTTA TORTELLINI IN PARMESAN CREAM SAUCE

Prep: 45 minutes   Cook: 10 minutes   Serves: 4 to 6

6 tablespoons unsalted butter	1 teaspoon basil
1 small onion, minced	⅛ teaspoon grated nutmeg
½ pound ground veal	½ teaspoon salt
¼ cup fresh bread crumbs	½ teaspoon pepper
¼ cup ricotta cheese	50 won ton wrappers
¾ cup grated Parmesan cheese	1 cup heavy cream
1 egg yolk	Grated Parmesan cheese and
2 tablespoons chopped parsley	freshly ground pepper

1. In a small skillet, melt 2 tablespoons butter over low heat. Add onion and cook, stirring often, until onion is golden but not browned, about 5 minutes.

2. In a medium bowl combine ground veal, cooked onion with butter, bread crumbs, ricotta cheese, ¼ cup grated Parmesan cheese, egg yolk, parsley, basil, nutmeg, salt, and pepper. Blend filling well.

3. Place 1 won ton wrapper on a work surface, with points at 12, 3, 6, and 9 o'clock. Moisten edges of wrapper with water. Place about 1 teaspoon filling in center of wrapper. Fold 12 o'clock point down to meet 6 o'clock point, enclosing filling. Press edges to seal. Bring 3 and 9 o'clock points together to meet, dab with water, and press to seal. (The tortellini will resemble a nurse's cap.) Transfer filled tortellini to a wax paper–lined baking sheet. Repeat procedure with remaining wrappers and filling.

4. Bring a large pot of salted water to a boil over high heat. Gradually add tortellini, trying to keep water at a boil. Cook until filling is cooked through, about 2 minutes. Carefully drain tortellini, preferably removing them in batches with a large skimmer to a large bowl.

5. In a 12-inch skillet or large flameproof casserole, bring heavy cream and remaining 4 tablespoons butter to a boil over high heat. Boil until evaporated by one-fourth, 1 to 2 minutes. Add tortellini and bring to a boil. Gently stir in remaining ½ cup Parmesan cheese, and cook until sauce is thickened, about 1 minute. Serve immediately, with a bowl of Parmesan cheese and a pepper mill passed on the side.

159   VEAL PATTIES PIZZAIOLA WITH FRESH LINGUINE

Prep: 5 minutes   Cook: 18 minutes   Serves: 4

1½ pounds ground veal
1 teaspoon Italian seasoning
1 teaspoon salt
¼ teaspoon pepper
1 tablespoon olive oil
1 (15-ounce) jar marinara sauce

½ cup shredded mozzarella cheese
9 ounces fresh linguine
Grated Parmesan cheese

1. In a medium bowl, mix veal, Italian seasoning, salt, and pepper. Form into 4 patties about 1 inch thick.

2. In a large skillet, heat olive oil over medium-high heat. Add veal patties and cook, turning once, until medium-well done, about 4 minutes per side. Transfer patties to paper towels to drain briefly.

3. Pour off all fat from skillet. Wipe out skillet with paper towels. Return patties to skillet and add marinara sauce. Bring to a simmer, reduce heat to low, and cook 5 minutes. Sprinkle mozzarella over tops of patties. Cover skillet and cook until cheese melts, about 2 minutes.

4. Meanwhile, in a large saucepan of boiling salted water, cook linguine just until tender, 2 to 3 minutes. Divide linguine evenly among 4 dinner plates. Spoon sauce over pasta, then top each serving with a veal patty. Pass a bowl of grated Parmesan cheese on the side.

160   VEAL AND RICOTTA MANICOTTI

Prep: 15 minutes   Cook: 1 hour 50 minutes   Serves: 6

4 tablespoons olive oil
1 medium onion, chopped
1 garlic clove, minced
2 (28-ounce) cans Italian peeled tomatoes, with their juice
1 teaspoon rosemary
¼ teaspoon pepper
8 ounces manicotti shells

1½ pounds ground veal
1 cup part-skim ricotta cheese
1 cup shredded mozzarella cheese (4 ounces)
¼ cup grated Parmesan cheese
1 whole egg plus 1 egg yolk, beaten
¼ cup chopped parsley
2 teaspoons basil

1. In a large nonreactive saucepan or flameproof casserole, heat 2 tablespoons oil. Add onion and cook over medium heat, stirring often, until softened, about 4 minutes. Add garlic and cook 1 minute. Add tomatoes with their juice, rosemary, and pepper; break up tomatoes in saucepan with a large spoon. Bring to a boil, reduce heat to low, and simmer, stirring often, until slightly thickened, about 1 hour.

2. Meanwhile, in a large saucepan of boiling salted water, cook manicotti shells until barely tender, 10 to 12 minutes. Drain well, rinse under cold water.

3. Preheat oven to 350°. In a large skillet, heat remaining 2 tablespoons oil. Add veal and cook over medium heat, stirring often to break up lumps of meat, until veal loses its pink color, about 5 minutes.

4. In a large bowl, combine cooked veal with ricotta, mozzarella, Parmesan, beaten eggs, parsley, and basil. Stuff manicotti shells with veal mixture.

5. Spread a thin layer of tomato sauce over bottom of a lightly oiled 9 x 13-inch baking dish. Place stuffed shells in dish, pour remaining tomato sauce on top, and cover with foil. Bake until sauce is bubbling, 25 to 35 minutes.

---

161 PENNE WITH CREAMY MOUSSAKA SAUCE

Prep: 10 minutes   Stand: 30 minutes   Cook: 1 hour 20 minutes
Serves: 6 to 8

This recipe makes enough sauce for 2 pounds of pasta. If you are serving less people, divide the amount of pasta and cheeses in half. Use only 2 cups of the lamb-eggplant sauce and freeze the remainder for another meal.

1 large eggplant (1¼ to 1½ pounds)	1 (6-ounce) can tomato paste
1 tablespoon plus ¼ teaspoon salt	1½ teaspoons basil
	1½ teaspoons oregano
2 tablespoons olive oil	⅛ teaspoon allspice
1 large onion, chopped	¼ teaspoon pepper
1½ pounds ground lamb or ground sirloin (90% lean)	2 pounds penne or other tubular pasta
2 garlic cloves, minced	1 cup part-skim ricotta cheese
1 cup dry red wine	6 ounces feta cheese, crumbled
1 (28-ounce) can crushed tomatoes	Grated Parmesan cheese

1. Cut unpeeled eggplant into ¾-inch cubes. In a colander, toss eggplant cubes with 1 tablespoon salt. Place colander in sink and let drain for 30 minutes. Rinse eggplant well with cold water and drain again. Pat dry with paper towels.

2. In a 6-quart Dutch oven, heat oil until hot. Add onion and eggplant and cook over medium-high heat, stirring often, until onion is softened, about 5 minutes. Add ground lamb and garlic and cook, stirring often, until meat is no longer pink, about 3 minutes. Drain off excess fat. Stir in wine, crushed tomatoes, tomato paste, basil, oregano, remaining ¼ teaspoon salt, allspice, and pepper. Bring lamb-eggplant sauce to a simmer, reduce heat to low, and cook, partially covered, 1 hour, stirring often to prevent scorching.

3. Meanwhile, in a very large pot of boiling salted water, cook penne just until tender, 9 to 12 minutes. Scoop out and reserve ½ cup of pasta cooking water; drain pasta well.

4. In a large heated bowl, toss pasta, reserved cooking water, and ricotta and feta cheeses until cheeses are slightly melted and mixture is creamy. Add hot lamb-eggplant sauce and toss well. Pass a bowl of grated Parmesan cheese on the side.

162 GREEK ORZO PIE
Prep: 20 minutes   Cook: 40 minutes   Serves: 6

2 cups orzo (rice-shaped pasta)	1 (10-ounce) package frozen
⅔ cup grated Parmesan cheese	chopped spinach, thawed
1 egg, lightly beaten	and squeezed dry
2 tablespoons butter, softened	1 cup tomato sauce
1½ cups cream-style cottage	1 teaspoon oregano
cheese	½ teaspoon salt
1 pound lean ground lamb or	¼ teaspoon cinnamon
ground sirloin (90% lean)	¼ teaspoon pepper
1 medium onion, chopped	½ cup crumbled feta cheese
1 garlic clove, minced	

1. Preheat oven to 350°. In a medium saucepan of boiling salted water, cook orzo until tender, 5 to 6 minutes. Drain well.

2. In a medium bowl, mix cooked orzo, Parmesan cheese, egg, and softened butter until butter melts. Spread into a well-buttered 10-inch pie plate, pushing mixture up sides to form a shell. Spoon cottage cheese onto bottom of orzo shell, spread evenly, and refrigerate while making filling.

3. In a large nonreactive skillet, cook ground lamb, onion, and garlic over medium-high heat, stirring to break up lumps, until meat loses its pink color, about 5 minutes. Drain off excess fat. Stir in spinach, tomato sauce, oregano, salt, cinnamon, and pepper. Bring to a simmer, stirring constantly. Heap meat mixture into orzo shell, leaving a 1-inch border of cottage cheese visible.

4. Bake until orzo shell is set and beginning to brown lightly, about 25 minutes. Sprinkle feta cheese over top of meat mixture and bake until cheese melts, about 5 minutes. Let stand 5 minutes, then cut into wedges to serve.

163 LAMB AND ZITI PASTITSIO
Prep: 15 minutes   Cook: 1½ hours   Stand: 10 minutes
Serves: 6 to 8

1 stick (4 ounces) butter	1 (6-ounce) can tomato paste
½ cup flour	½ cup dry red wine
4 cups milk, scalded	½ cup beef broth
¼ teaspoon grated nutmeg	1 teaspoon basil
6 eggs, at room temperature	1 teaspoon oregano
2 cups grated Parmesan	½ teaspoon cinnamon
cheese (8 ounces)	½ teaspoon salt
1½ pounds lean ground lamb	¼ teaspoon pepper
1 large onion, chopped	1 pound ziti or other tubular
2 garlic cloves, minced	pasta

1. Preheat oven to 350°. In a medium saucepan, melt butter over medium-low heat. Add flour and cook, whisking frequently, for 2 minutes without letting mixture brown. Whisk in hot milk, bring to a boil, and cook, whisking often, until thickened, about 2 minutes. Season with nutmeg.

2. In a large bowl, beat eggs well. Gradually beat sauce into eggs. Stir in 1 cup Parmesan cheese.

3. In a large skillet, cook ground lamb, onion, and garlic over medium-high heat, stirring often to break up lumps of meat, until lamb loses its pink color, about 5 minutes. Drain off excess fat. Stir in tomato paste, wine, beef broth, basil, oregano, cinnamon, salt, and pepper. Bring to a boil, reduce heat to low, and simmer until thickened, about 15 minutes.

4. Meanwhile, in a large saucepan of boiling salted water, cook pasta until just tender, 10 to 12 minutes. Drain, rinse under cold water, and drain again.

5. In a lightly oiled 9 x 13-inch baking dish, place half of cooked macaroni. Spread half of Parmesan sauce over macaroni. Cover with all of lamb mixture. Top with remaining macaroni, then spoon remaining sauce over macaroni, and sprinkle with remaining 1 cup Parmesan cheese.

6. Bake until sauce is bubbling and top is golden brown, about 50 minutes. Let stand 10 minutes before cutting into squares to serve.

---

164 ANTS CLIMBING A TREE
Prep: 15 minutes   Cook: 20 minutes   Serves: 3 or 4

Chinese cooks colorfully remark that the ground pork clinging to the noodles resembles "ants climbing a tree." Be sure to use bean threads (*sai fun*), also known as glass, or cellophane, noodles.

4 ounces bean threads
2 cups boiling water
½ pound ground pork
2 tablespoons soy sauce
1 tablespoon dry sherry
1 teaspoon cornstarch
½ teaspoon sugar
2 tablespoons vegetable oil
1 tablespoon minced fresh ginger

1 scallion, chopped
1 small carrot, finely chopped
1 tablespoon spicy brown bean sauce (Szechuan sauce)
1 cup reduced-sodium chicken broth

1. In a medium heatproof bowl, cover bean threads with boiling water and let stand until noodles are supple (like rubber bands), about 10 minutes. Drain well.

2. In a small bowl, combine ground pork, 1 tablespoon soy sauce, sherry, cornstarch, and sugar. Stir to blend well.

3. In a wok or 12-inch skillet, heat oil over high heat until very hot but not smoking. Add ginger and scallion and stir-fry until fragrant, about 30 seconds. Add pork mixture and carrot. Stir-fry until meat loses its pink color, about 3 minutes. Stir in bean sauce.

4. Add chicken broth and remaining 1 tablespoon soy sauce and bring to a boil. Add noodles, reduce heat to low, and simmer, stirring occasionally, until noodles are tender and liquid is mostly absorbed, about 5 minutes.

165 PENNE WITH HERBED VEAL MEATBALLS AND ARTICHOKES

Prep: 20 minutes   Cook: 2 hours   Serves: 6 to 8

2 tablespoons olive oil
1 medium onion, chopped
2 garlic cloves, minced
2 (28-ounce) cans Italian peeled tomatoes, with their juice
½ cup dry white wine
2 teaspoons basil
2 teaspoons rosemary
2 teaspoons tarragon
½ teaspoon pepper

2 (16-ounce) packages frozen artichoke hearts, thawed
1 pound ground veal
1 cup fresh bread crumbs
½ cup grated Parmesan cheese
3 eggs
1½ teaspoons salt
1½ pounds penne or other tubular pasta
Grated Parmesan cheese

1. In a 5-quart Dutch oven, heat oil over medium heat. Add onion and cook, stirring often, until softened, 3 to 5 minutes. Add garlic and cook, stirring, 1 minute .

2. Add tomatoes with their juice, wine, basil, 1 teaspoon each rosemary and tarragon, and ¼ teaspoon pepper. Bring to a boil, breaking up tomatoes with a large spoon. Reduce heat to low and simmer 1½ hours. Add artichoke hearts.

3. In a medium bowl, mix ground veal, bread crumbs, Parmesan cheese, eggs, salt, and remaining 1 teaspoon each rosemary and tarragon and ¼ teaspoon pepper. Drop mixture by heaping tablespoons into simmering sauce. Cook, covered, until meatballs are cooked through, about 15 minutes.

4. In a large pot of boiling salted water, cook penne just until tender, about 10 minutes. Drain well. Transfer pasta to a large heated serving bowl. Add meatballs and sauce and toss. Pass a bowl of grated Parmesan cheese on the side.

166 HERBED TURKEY LASAGNE

Prep: 15 minutes   Cook: 1 hour 10 minutes   Stand: 10 minutes
Serves: 8 to 12

2 pounds ground turkey
1 medium onion, finely chopped
1 teaspoon rosemary
1 teaspoon tarragon
2¼ teaspoons salt
½ teaspoon pepper
1 stick (4 ounces) butter
½ cup flour

2 cups chicken stock or reduced-sodium canned broth
1¼ cups milk
¾ cup dry white wine
1¼ cups grated Parmesan cheese (about 5 ounces)
12 lasagne noodles (9 ounces)
2 cups (1 pint) low-fat cottage cheese

1. Preheat oven to 350°. In a large skillet or flameproof casserole, cook ground turkey and onion over medium-high heat, stirring often to break up lumps of meat, until turkey loses its pink color, about 5 minutes. Drain off excess liquid. Stir in rosemary, tarragon, 1½ teaspoons salt, and ¼ teaspoon pepper.

2. In a heavy medium saucepan, melt butter over medium-low heat. Whisk in flour and cook, stirring, for 2 minutes without letting mixture brown. Whisk in stock, milk, and wine. Bring to a boil, whisking until smooth and thick. Reduce heat to low and simmer, whisking often, for 3 minutes. Stir in 1 cup Parmesan cheese. Set sauce aside.

3. Cook lasagne noodles in a large pot of salted boiling water until just tender, about 9 minutes. Drain, rinse under cold water, and drain again.

4. Cover bottom of a lightly buttered 9 x 13-inch baking dish with a thin layer of sauce. Arrange a single layer of 4 slightly overlapping lasagne noodles over it. Cover with half of turkey mixture. Spoon on 1 cup cottage cheese, then spoon on a third of sauce. Arrange another layer of noodles in dish. Cover with remaining turkey mixture and cottage cheese. Spoon on half of remaining sauce. Top with a final layer of noodles, then cover with remaining sauce. Sprinkle remaining ¼ cup Parmesan cheese over top.

5. Bake until lasagne is bubbling and top is lightly browned, about 50 minutes. Let stand about 10 minutes before serving.

167 EGG NOODLES IN PEKING MEAT SAUCE WITH CRUNCHY TOPPINGS

Prep: 15 minutes   Cook: 15 minutes   Serves: 4

⅓ cup brown bean sauce
(found in Chinese
markets and most
supermarkets)
2 tablespoons dry sherry
2 teaspoons sugar
¼ teaspoon crushed hot red
pepper
1 pound ground pork
2 scallions, chopped
1 tablespoon grated fresh
ginger

2 garlic cloves, minced
½ cup reduced-sodium
chicken broth
1 pound egg noodles,
preferably fresh Chinese
2 teaspoons Asian sesame oil
or peanut oil
Fresh bean sprouts, sliced
celery, chopped
cucumber, hot chili oil

1. In a small bowl, whisk together bean sauce, sherry, sugar, and hot pepper. Set sauce aside.

2. In a large skillet, cook ground pork over medium-high heat, breaking up lumps with a spoon, until meat just loses its pink color, about 3 minutes. Add scallions, ginger, and garlic; stir-fry 30 seconds. Stir in chicken broth and reserved sauce. Reduce heat to medium-low, and simmer until liquid is reduced by half, about 5 minutes. (Meat sauce can be made up to 2 days ahead, covered, and refrigerated. Reheat gently over low heat.)

3. Meanwhile, cook noodles in boiling salted water just until tender, about 3 minutes for fresh or 8 minutes for dried. Drain noodles well.

4. Place noodles in a large serving bowl and toss with sesame oil. Top with hot meat sauce and toss well. Place garnishes in small bowls. Serve noodles in individual bowls and let guests choose their own toppings.

Chapter 7

Heavy on the Veggies

It's amazing what you can do with a pound of ground meat. One of the best—and most nutritious—ways I know to stretch ground meat is to combine it with vegetables or grains. Stuffed eggplants, peppers, cabbage leaves, and even whole cabbages are featured in many countries, imaginatively sauced and seasoned. These dishes, which use meat in a co-starring role, are perfect for today's menus, as they allow us to increase our vegetable and grain intake in flavorful ways. For those who are watching their diets, many of these vegetable-meat dishes are excellent ways to trim calories and cholesterol without skimping on meaty flavor.

Stuffed cabbage is one of the glories of ethnic cooking, and almost every country has a variation on this theme. This chapter offers a stuffed cabbage recipe for every taste. Lamb and Bulgur–Stuffed Cabbage, with a hint of mint, has a sweet-and-sour character. Vodka-Spiked Beef and Cabbage Rolls are made with both ground beef and pork, and there is a tantalizing sour cream fillip in the sauce. Sauerkraut lovers (count me in) will favor the Cabbage Rolls with Sauerkraut and Bacon, which comes from an old Romanian recipe. Stuffed Whole Cabbage Campagne offers a show-stopping presentation.

Stuffed peppers come in many guises, too, and there are several of my favorites here. If you like your sweet peppers fork-tender, but don't want to overcook the filling, partially cook the trimmed peppers in boiling salted water for 5 minutes before stuffing. Without the extra boiling, the peppers will cook to crisp-tender consistency. The choice is yours.

168 TURKEY SALAD ARIZONA
Prep: 10 minutes   Cook: 5 minutes   Serves: 4

1¼ pounds ground turkey
1 cup corn kernels, fresh or
   thawed frozen
1 cup tomato salsa
½ teaspoon salt
2 cups shredded lettuce

2 medium ripe tomatoes,
   sliced
1 small red onion, sliced
Lime wedges
¼ cup sour cream

1. In a large nonstick skillet, cook ground turkey and corn, stirring often to break up lumps of meat, until turkey loses its pink color, about 5 minutes. Drain off excess liquid. Stir in ½ cup salsa and salt.

2. Divide lettuce evenly among 4 dinner plates. Mound hot turkey mixture in center of lettuce. Garnish with tomato slices, red onion slices, and lime wedges. Top each serving with 1 tablespoon sour cream. Pass remaining salsa on the side.

---

169 SZECHUAN GREEN BEANS AND PORK
Prep: 10 minutes   Cook: 10 minutes   Serves: 2 to 4

2 tablespoons soy sauce
2 tablespoons chicken broth
   or water
2 tablespoons dry sherry
1 teaspoon Asian sesame oil
1 teaspoon rice vinegar or
   distilled white vinegar
1 teaspoon sugar
½ teaspoon salt
½ teaspoon crushed hot red
   pepper

⅓ cup vegetable oil
1¼ pounds green beans,
   trimmed
½ pound ground pork
3 garlic cloves, minced
1 teaspoon minced fresh
   ginger
1 scallion, chopped

1. In a small bowl, combine soy sauce, chicken broth, sherry, sesame oil, vinegar, sugar, salt, and hot pepper; set sauce aside.

2. In a wok or a 12-inch skillet, heat oil until very hot but not smoking. In 2 batches, fry green beans over high heat, turning often with kitchen tongs, until bright green and just beginning to brown, about 2 minutes. Transfer beans to paper towels to drain. Discard oil remaining in wok.

3. Reduce heat to medium. Add ground pork, garlic, and ginger and cook, stirring to break up lumps of meat, until pork loses its pink color, about 3 minutes. Add green beans and stir-fry 1 minute longer. Stir in reserved sauce and cook until liquid is almost evaporated, about 1 minute. Transfer to a serving dish, sprinkle scallion over top, and serve.

170   GREEK GREEN BEANS WITH SIRLOIN TOMATO SAUCE

Prep: 15 minutes   Cook: 15 minutes   Serves: 4

¾ pound ground sirloin
    (90% lean)
1 small onion, chopped
1 garlic clove, minced
1 (15-ounce) can Italian-style
    stewed tomatoes, with
    their juice
1 tablespoon tomato paste

½ teaspoon oregano
½ teaspoon salt
¼ teaspoon ground allspice
¼ teaspoon pepper
1 pound green beans,
    trimmed
¼ cup grated Parmesan cheese

1. In a large nonstick skillet, cook ground sirloin, onion, and garlic over medium-high heat, stirring often to break up lumps of meat, until beef loses its pink color, about 5 minutes.

2. Stir in stewed tomatoes with their juice, tomato paste, oregano, salt, allspice, and pepper. Bring to a boil, reduce heat to medium, and cook until liquid is evaporated by half, about 8 minutes.

3. Meanwhile, in a large saucepan of boiling salted water, cook green beans until just tender, 3 to 5 minutes. Drain well.

4. In a large serving bowl, toss green beans with meat sauce. Sprinkle cheese over top and serve.

171   HILL COUNTRY FOUR-BEAN BAKE

Prep: 10 minutes   Cook: 25 to 35 minutes   Serves: 4 to 6

Lone Star State barbecues would be incomplete without chuckwagon beans as a side dish. I think it's hefty enough to be a suppertime main course, too.

1 pound ground chuck
    (80% lean)
1 medium onion, chopped
1 (16-ounce) can pork and
    beans
1 (16-ounce) can pinto beans,
    rinsed and drained
1 (16-ounce) can cannellini
    beans, rinsed and drained

1 (16-ounce) can red kidney
    beans, rinsed and drained
¾ cup barbecue sauce
¾ cup maple syrup
2 tablespoons prepared
    mustard
½ teaspoon salt
½ teaspoon pepper

1. Preheat oven to 400°. In a 5-quart Dutch oven, cook ground chuck and onion over medium-high heat, stirring often to break up lumps of meat, until beef loses its pink color, about 5 minutes. Add all remaining ingredients and bring to a boil, stirring constantly.

2. Bake, uncovered, stirring occasionally, until casserole is bubbling, 20 to 30 minutes.

172 WARM CHICKEN AND BASIL SALAD BANGKOK

Prep: 15 minutes   Cook: 10 minutes   Serves: 3

1 tablespoon vegetable oil
4 shallots or 1 small red onion, thinly sliced
1 tablespoon grated fresh ginger
3 garlic cloves, minced
1 jalapeño pepper, thinly sliced into rounds, or ¼ teaspoon crushed hot red pepper
1 pound ground chicken

¼ cup chopped fresh basil
1 tablespoon Asian fish sauce (see Note)
1 teaspoon sugar
½ teaspoon salt
6 romaine lettuce leaves
2 medium ripe tomatoes, chopped
2 Kirby cucumbers, sliced

1. In a large nonstick skillet, heat oil over medium heat. Add sliced shallots and cook, stirring often, until lightly browned, about 3 minutes. Add ginger, garlic, and jalapeño. Cook, stirring, 1 minute.

2. Add ground chicken and cook, stirring often to break up lumps of meat, until chicken loses its pink color, about 5 minutes. Drain off excess liquid.

3. Add basil, fish sauce, sugar, and salt to ground chicken mixture. Cook, stirring, 1 minute.

4. Arrange 2 lettuce leaves on each of 3 dinner plates. Place a mound of hot chicken mixture on lettuce. Garnish with chopped tomatoes and cucumber slices.

NOTE: *Fish sauce is available in Asian markets and in many supermarkets. It is called nuoc mam in Vietnam, nam pla in Thailand, and pastis in Indonesia. If unavailable, substitute a mixture of equal parts soy sauce, Worcestershire sauce, and water.*

173 HOPPIN' JOHN CASSEROLE

Prep: 10 minutes   Cook: 40 minutes   Serves: 4 to 6

4 slices of bacon
1 pound ground pork
1 medium onion, chopped
3 (16-ounce) cans black-eyed peas, rinsed and drained
2 cups cooked rice
1 (10-ounce) package frozen chopped collard greens, thawed

1 (13¾-ounce) can beef broth
2 teaspoons red wine vinegar
½ teaspoon salt
¼ teaspoon crushed hot red pepper
½ cup fresh bread crumbs

1. Preheat oven to 350°. In a medium skillet, cook bacon over medium-high heat until crisp and browned, about 4 minutes. Transfer bacon to paper towels to drain briefly. Crumble and set aside.

2. Drain off all but 1 tablespoon bacon fat from skillet. Add ground pork and onion and cook, stirring often to break up lumps of meat, until pork loses its pink color, about 5 minutes. Drain off excess fat.

3. In a 2-quart casserole, combine black-eyed peas, pork mixture, crumbled bacon, rice, collard greens, beef broth, vinegar, salt, and hot pepper. Stir to mix. Sprinkle bread crumbs over top. Bake until top is browned and casserole is bubbling, about 30 minutes.

---

174 STUFFED WHOLE CABBAGE CAMPAGNE
Prep: 20 minutes   Cook: 1½ hours   Stand: 10 minutes   Serves: 6

As you may have noticed in this book, practically every cuisine salutes the combination of ground meat and cabbage. But leave it to the French to create such a spectacular presentation.

1 medium green cabbage (1½ to 2 pounds)	1 teaspoon tarragon
1 tablespoon butter	1 teaspoon salt
1 medium onion, chopped	¼ teaspoon pepper
1 cup fresh bread crumbs	1 pound ground pork
½ cup milk	1 (13¾-ounce) can beef broth
1 egg	Quick Brown Gravy (page 182)

1. In a large pot of boiling salted water, cook cabbage, covered, until outside leaves are tender, about 10 minutes. Drain, rinse under cold water, and drain again.

2. Leaving leaves attached to cabbage base, peel back as many tender leaves as possible. Using a sharp knife, cut a "lid" from cabbage, about 2 inches from top, reserve lid. Using a large metal spoon, hollow out cabbage leaving a 1-inch-thick shell; save inside of cabbage for another use.

3. In a medium skillet, melt butter. Add onion and cook over medium heat, stirring often, until lightly browned, about 5 minutes. Transfer to a medium bowl. Add bread crumbs, milk, egg, tarragon, salt, and pepper. Stir to mix. Add ground pork and blend well.

4. Lightly spoon meat mixture into cabbage shell and replace cabbage lid. Beginning with inside leaves, fold leaves over meat mixture, continuing until cabbage is reassembled. Tie up well with kitchen string to keep lid in place.

5. Place stuffed cabbage in a large Dutch oven. Add beef broth and bring to a boil over high heat. Reduce heat to low, cover tightly, and simmer until a meat thermometer inserted into center of stuffing (through cabbage top) reads 160°, about 1 hour 10 minutes. Remove cabbage from pot and let stand 10 minutes. Cut into wedges and serve with Quick Brown Gravy.

175 CABBAGE ROLLS WITH SAUERKRAUT AND BACON

Prep: 35 minutes   Cook: 1¾ hours   Chill: 6 hours   Serves: 4 to 6

Pork and rice–stuffed rolls are a national specialty in Romania, where they are called *sarmale*. There, they are made with pickled cabbage leaves, but I use fresh cabbage and chill the casserole overnight to allow the sauerkraut flavor to permeate.

¼ cup converted rice	1 pound fresh sauerkraut,
2 tablespoons butter	(bottled or refrigerated,
2 medium onions, chopped	not canned)
1 pound ground pork	1 cup tomato puree
1 pound ground chuck	1 cup tomato juice
(80% lean) or ground	¼ teaspoon crushed hot red
round (85% lean)	pepper
1 teaspoon thyme	1 medium head of cabbage
1½ teaspoons salt	(about 1½ pounds)
¼ teaspoon pepper	6 slices of bacon

1. In a small saucepan of lightly salted boiling water, cook rice 5 minutes. Drain, rinse under cold water, and drain again.

2. In a large skillet, melt butter over moderate heat. Add onions and cook, stirring often, until onions are lightly browned, about 8 minutes. Transfer half of cooked onions to a large bowl, leaving remaining onions in skillet.

3. Add ground pork, ground chuck, boiled rice, thyme, 1 teaspoon salt, and pepper to onions in bowl. Mix well until blended. Set filling aside.

4. Drain sauerkraut into a colander set over a bowl; reserve sauerkraut juice. Rinse sauerkraut under cold water and drain. One handful at a time, squeeze out excess water. Add sauerkraut, tomato puree, tomato juice, remaining ½ teaspoon salt, and crushed hot pepper to remaining onions in skillet. Bring to a simmer over medium heat, stirring often. Set sauce aside.

5. In a large pot of boiling salted water, cook cabbage until outer leaves peel off easily, about 5 minutes. Peel off tender cabbage leaves and choose largest 12. With a small sharp knife, trim thick rib in center of each leaf by cutting parallel to work surface to shave off about half of rib's thickness.

6. Place about ¼ cup of filling in center of a cabbage leaf, fold in sides, and roll up into a cylinder. Place roll, seam side down, on a plate or baking sheet. Repeat procedure with remaining cabbage leaves and filling.

7. Lightly oil a deep 2½-quart casserole. Line bottom of casserole with 3 strips of bacon. Pour one-third of sauce into bottom of casserole. Tightly arrange 6 cabbage rolls in casserole and pour on half of remaining sauce. Top with remaining rolls and sauce. Place remaining 3 bacon strips over top layer. Add enough of reserved sauerkraut juice (and water, if necessary) to reach 1 inch from top of casserole. Cover tightly with aluminum foil and a lid. Refrigerate at least 6 hours, or overnight. Remove from refrigerator 1 hour before baking; leave cover on.

8. Preheat oven to 375°. Place casserole on a baking sheet and bake, covered, 30 minutes. Reduce heat to 325° and uncover. Continue baking until tops of rolls are beginning to brown, about 1 hour.

---

176 VODKA-SPIKED BEEF AND CABBAGE ROLLS

Prep: 30 minutes   Cook: 1 hour 20 minutes   Serves: 5 to 6

1 small head of cabbage (about 1¼ pounds)	1 teaspoon salt
½ cup rice	½ teaspoon pepper
4 tablespoons butter	½ pound fresh mushrooms, sliced
2 large onions, chopped	1 (13¾-ounce) can beef broth
1 garlic clove, minced	1 (3-ounce) can tomato paste
1½ pounds ground round (85% lean)	⅓ cup vodka
1½ pounds ground pork	1 teaspoon dried dill
1 egg	2 bay leaves
1 teaspoon caraway seeds, crushed	⅓ cup sour cream, at room temperature

1. Preheat oven to 350°. Cook cabbage in a large pot of lightly salted boiling water until outer leaves peel off easily, about 5 minutes; drain. Peel off tender cabbage leaves and choose largest 14. With a small sharp knife, trim thick rib in center of each leaf by cutting parallel to work surface, shaving off about half of rib's thickness.

2. In a medium saucepan, cook rice in 1 quart lightly salted boiling water 5 minutes. Drain, rinse under cold water, and drain well.

3. In a large skillet, melt 2 tablespoons butter over medium-high heat. Add 1 chopped onion and cook, stirring often, until softened, about 4 minutes. Add garlic and cook 1 minute longer. In a large bowl, combine ground round, ground pork, rice, cooked onion and garlic, egg, caraway seeds, salt, and ¼ teaspoon pepper.

4. Lightly oil a 10 x 15-inch baking dish. Place about ⅓ cup of filling in center of a cabbage leaf, fold in sides, and roll up into a cylinder. Place roll, seam side down, in baking dish; repeat with remaining cabbage leaves and filling.

5. In skillet, melt remaining 2 tablespoons butter over medium-high heat. Add mushrooms and remaining chopped onion and cook, stirring often, until onion is softened, about 5 minutes. Stir in beef broth, tomato paste, vodka, dill, bay leaves, and remaining ¼ teaspoon pepper. Bring sauce to a simmer and pour over cabbage rolls.

6. Cover baking dish with aluminum foil and bake 30 minutes. Remove foil and bake until rolls are beginning to brown, about 30 minutes. With a slotted spoon, transfer cabbage rolls to a serving platter. Discard bay leaves. Skim any fat off surface of sauce, whisk in sour cream, and pour sauce over cabbage rolls.

177 POLISH CABBAGE BAKE
Prep: 15 minutes   Cook: 1½ hours   Serves: 6 to 8

Just right for when you want to enjoy the flavors of stuffed cabbage, but aren't up to fussing with rolling leaves.

1 large cabbage about (2 pounds), cored and coarsely chopped	2 teaspoons salt
	1½ teaspoons thyme
	½ teaspoon pepper
½ cup rice	1½ pounds ground round
1 medium onion, chopped	(85% lean)
2 cups tomato sauce	½ pound ground pork
2 large eggs	½ cup beef broth

1. Preheat oven to 350°. In a large pot of boiling salted water, cook cabbage until just crisp-tender, about 10 minutes. Drain well, rinse under cold water, and drain again.

2. In a small saucepan of boiling salted water, cook rice 5 minutes. Drain, rinse under cold water, and drain again.

3. In a large bowl, combine onion, ¾ cup tomato sauce, eggs, salt, thyme, and pepper; mix with a fork. Add rice, ground round, and ground pork and blend well.

4. In a lightly greased 9 x 13-inch baking dish, spread half of cabbage in an even layer. Cover with all of meat mixture. Spread remaining cabbage on top. Combine remaining 1¼ cups tomato sauce and beef broth and pour over casserole. Cover tightly with aluminum foil.

5. Bake 1 hour. Remove foil and bake 15 minutes longer.

178 LAMB AND BULGUR–STUFFED CABBAGE
Prep: 25 minutes   Cook: 1 hour 10 minutes   Serves: 4 to 6

1 medium head cabbage (1½ to 2 pounds)	2½ teaspoons dried mint
	1 teaspoon salt
1 cup bulgur	½ teaspoon pepper
2 tablespoons vegetable oil	1 pound ground lamb
1 large onion, chopped	1 (28-ounce) can peeled
1 large carrot, chopped	tomatoes, with added
2 scallions, chopped	puree
2 garlic cloves, minced	⅓ cup honey

1. Preheat oven to 350°. Cook cabbage in a large pot of boiling salted water until outer layers peel off easily, about 5 minutes; drain. Peel off tender cabbage leaves and choose largest 12. Cut out and discard core; coarsely chop remaining cabbage. Cut away and discard thick rib in each leaf.

2. In a medium bowl, combine bulgur with enough cold water to cover by 1 inch. Let stand 10 minutes. Drain well in a sieve and squeeze out excess water.

3. In a large skillet, heat oil over medium-high heat. Add onion, carrot, scallions, garlic, 1½ teaspoons mint, salt, and ¼ teaspoon pepper. Cook, stirring often, until onion is softened, 3 to 5 minutes. In a large bowl, combine ground lamb, bulgur, and cooked vegetables.

4. Lightly oil a 9 x 13-inch baking dish. Scatter chopped cabbage over bottom of dish. Place about ⅓ cup of stuffing in center of a cabbage leaf, fold in sides, and roll up into a cylinder. Place roll, seam side down, in baking dish and repeat with remaining leaves and filling.

5. In a blender, combine tomatoes with puree, honey, and remaining 1 teaspoon mint and ¼ teaspoon pepper; puree until smooth. Pour tomato sauce over cabbage rolls. Cover dish with aluminum foil and bake 40 minutes. Remove foil and bake until rolls are beginning to brown, 20 minutes longer.

---

179 TURKISH MEAT AND RICE–STUFFED PEPPERS

Prep: 15 minutes   Cook: 1 hour 10 minutes   Serves: 6

Serve these crisp-tender peppers in bowls with spoons to sip the tart, tomatoey cooking liquid.

6 medium green bell peppers	2 tablespoons tomato paste
½ cup rice	1 teaspoon dried mint
1 (14-ounce) can Italian peeled tomatoes, with their juice	¾ teaspoon salt
	¼ teaspoon paprika
1 pound lean ground lamb or ground round (85% lean)	¼ teaspoon pepper
	2 teaspoons lemon juice
1 large onion, minced	1 beef bouillon cube
2 garlic cloves, minced	
2 tablespoons chopped parsley	

1. Preheat oven to 375°. Slice tops off peppers and scoop out seeds. Stand peppers up in a 9-inch square baking dish.

2. In a medium saucepan of boiling salted water, cook rice 7 minutes. Drain, rinse under cold water, and drain again. Drain tomatoes in a sieve placed over a bowl, squeezing tomatoes in sieve to remove all juice. Reserve juice and tomato pulp separately.

3. In a large bowl, combine rice, tomato pulp, ground lamb, onion, garlic, parsley, tomato paste, mint, salt, paprika, and pepper. Knead with your hands until well mixed. Stuff peppers with meat mixture, dividing evenly. Pour reserved tomato juice and lemon juice around peppers. Add bouillon cube and cover dish tightly with aluminum foil.

4. Bake 45 minutes. Remove foil from dish, reduce oven temperature to 350°, and continue baking, basting a few times with sauce, 15 minutes, or until rice and peppers are tender.

180 CHINESE STUFFED PEPPERS
Prep: 15 minutes   Cook: 1 hour 10 minutes   Serves: 6

6 medium red or green bell peppers	1 cup frozen peas, thawed
¼ cup long-grain white rice	3 tablespoons soy sauce
1 tablespoon vegetable oil	3 tablespoons dry sherry
1 medium scallion, chopped	¾ teaspoon sugar
1 tablespoon minced fresh ginger	½ teaspoon pepper
1 garlic clove, minced	¼ teaspoon salt
1½ pounds ground pork	1½ cups beef broth
	¼ cup dry sherry
	1 tablespoon cornstarch

1. Preheat oven to 375°. Slice tops off peppers and scoop out seeds. Stand peppers up in a 9-inch square baking dish.

2. In a medium saucepan of boiling salted water, cook rice 7 minutes. Drain, rinse under cold water, and drain again.

3. In a medium skillet, heat oil. Add scallion, ginger, and garlic and cook over medium-high heat until vegetables are softened and fragrant but not browned, about 1 minute. Transfer to a medium bowl. Add ground pork, peas, rice, 2 tablespoons soy sauce, 1 tablespoon sherry, ¼ teaspoon sugar, ¼ teaspoon pepper, and salt to bowl. Mix gently but thoroughly to avoid crushing peas. Stuff peppers with meat mixture, dividing evenly.

4. In a 2-cup glass measure, combine beef broth, remaining 2 tablespoons sherry, 1 tablespoon soy sauce, ½ teaspoon sugar, and ¼ teaspoon pepper. Pour sauce over stuffed peppers and cover dish tightly with aluminum foil.

5. Bake 45 minutes. Remove foil from dish, reduce oven temperature to 350°, and continue baking, basting a few times with sauce, 15 minutes, or until rice and peppers are tender and pork shows no trace of pink. Using a slotted spoon, transfer peppers to a serving platter, cover with foil, and keep warm.

6. Place baking dish on top of stove. In a small bowl, dissolve cornstarch in 2 tablespoons water. Whisk into liquid in baking dish, and cook over medium heat until sauce boils and thickens, about 2 minutes. Serve sauce with stuffed peppers.

181   HUNGARIAN STUFFED PEPPERS WITH PAPRIKA SAUCE

Prep: 20 minutes   Cook: 1½ hours   Serves: 6

These peppers will turn out crisp-tender. If you like them soft, parboil first for 5 minutes in boiling salted water. The spicy paprika sauce can be used to gild meatloaves, hamburger patties, and other main dishes, too.

3 **medium sweet red peppers, (about 1¼ pounds)**	½ **cup fresh bread crumbs**
1½ **pounds ground chuck (80% lean)**	¾ **teaspoon marjoram**
1 **medium onion, finely chopped**	1¼ **teaspoons salt**
2 **garlic cloves, minced**	½ **teaspoon pepper**
	Paprika Sauce (recipe follows)

1. Preheat oven to 375°. Using a sharp knife, halve peppers lengthwise through stems. Cut out seeds, seed pods, and ribs, keeping stems attached to peppers.

2. In a medium bowl, combine ground chuck, onion, garlic, bread crumbs, marjoram, salt, and pepper. Mix until well blended. Stuff peppers with meat mixture. Place in a 9 x 13-inch baking dish and pour in 1 cup water.

3. Bake until a meat thermometer inserted in center of meat stuffing reads 160°, about 40 minutes. Using a slotted spoon, transfer peppers to a serving platter. Serve hot with a bowl of Paprika Sauce passed on the side.

PAPRIKA SAUCE
Makes about 2 cups

2 **tablespoons butter**	1 **garlic clove, minced**
1 **small onion, chopped**	2 **tablespoons flour**
1 **medium Italian frying pepper or green bell pepper, seeded and chopped**	2 **tablespoons paprika**
	1 **cup beef broth**
	¼ **teaspoon salt**
	¼ **teaspoon pepper**

1. In a medium saucepan, melt butter over medium heat. Add onion, pepper, and garlic and cook, stirring often, until vegetables are softened, about 5 minutes.

2. Add flour and cook, stirring, 2 to 3 minutes, allowing flour mixture to brown very lightly. Add paprika and cook, stirring, 30 seconds.

3. Whisk in beef broth, 1 cup water, salt, and pepper. Bring to a boil, whisking until smooth. Reduce heat to low and simmer until sauce is slightly thickened, 30 to 40 minutes.

182 GROUND LAMB AND ORZO–STUFFED PEPPERS

Prep: 15 minutes   Cook: 50 minutes   Serves: 4

4 medium green bell peppers
½ cup orzo (rice-shaped pasta)
1 pound lean ground lamb
1 medium onion, chopped
2 garlic cloves, minced
¼ cup grated Parmesan cheese
1 teaspoon basil

¾ teaspoon salt
¼ teaspoon pepper
1 (16-ounce) can Italian-
   flavored stewed tomatoes,
   with their juice
½ cup dry red wine

1. Preheat oven to 350°. Slice tops off peppers and remove seeds. Stand peppers up in a 9-inch square baking dish.

2. In a medium saucepan of boiling salted water, cook orzo until barely tender, about 5 minutes. Drain well.

3. In a medium bowl, combine ground lamb, orzo, onion, garlic, Parmesan cheese, basil, salt, and pepper. Stuff peppers with lamb mixture, dividing evenly. Mix stewed tomatoes with their juice and wine. Pour over and around peppers. Cover dish with foil.

4. Bake 30 minutes. Remove foil and continue baking, basting occasionally with sauce, until a meat thermometer inserted in center of filling reads 160°, about 15 minutes longer.

183 TURKEY ZUCCHINI BURGERS

Prep: 20 minutes   Cook: 12 minutes   Serves: 6

2 small zucchini (about 6
   ounces), shredded
1 teaspoon salt
1¼ pounds ground turkey
1 scallion, chopped
1 tablespoon mango chutney,
   chopped

1 teaspoon curry powder
¼ teaspoon pepper
   Vegetable cooking spray
¼ cup plain low-fat yogurt

1. In a colander, toss zucchini with ¼ teaspoon salt. Let stand 10 minutes. Rinse well under cold water. One handful at a time, squeeze out excess liquid.

2. In a medium bowl, combine zucchini, ground turkey, scallion, chutney, curry powder, remaining ¾ teaspoon salt, and pepper. Using wet hands, form into 6 burgers about ¾ inch thick.

3. In a large nonstick skillet lightly coated with vegetable cooking spray, cook burgers over medium heat, turning once, until cooked through with no trace of pink in center, but still juicy, about 6 minutes on each side. Top each burger with 1 tablespoon yogurt.

184 YUGOSLAVIAN BEEF SAUSAGES WITH ROASTED EGGPLANT SAUCE

Prep: 20 minutes   Cook: 50 minutes   Serves: 4 to 6

You will have plenty of this tasty eggplant sauce, so slather the extra on slices of crusty bread and serve alongside the sausages.

2 pounds ground round (85% lean)	½ teaspoon pepper
2 garlic cloves, minced	1 medium onion, chopped
2 teaspoons paprika	**Roasted Eggplant Sauce**
2 teaspoons salt	**(recipe follows)**

1. In a medium bowl, combine ground round, garlic, paprika, salt, and pepper. Using about ¼ cup for each, form into 14 sausages about 3½ inches long and 1 inch wide.

2. Build a hot fire in a grill or preheat a broiler with broiler rack 4 inches from source of heat. Grill or broil, turning once, until browned outside but rare and juicy inside, about 4 minutes, or longer if desired. Serve sausages with chopped onion and Roasted Eggplant Sauce.

ROASTED EGGPLANT SAUCE
Makes about 2½ cups

1 head of garlic, unpeeled	¼ cup olive oil
1 medium eggplant (about 1 pound)	1 tablespoon plus 2 teaspoons lemon juice
3 medium ripe tomatoes	½ teaspoon salt
2 medium red bell peppers	¼ teaspoon pepper
1 small onion, chopped	

1. Preheat oven to 375°. Wrap whole garlic head in foil. Pierce eggplant once or twice with tip of a knife.

2. Place whole eggplant, tomatoes, peppers, and wrapped garlic on a foil-lined baking sheet and place in oven. (Each vegetable will be removed as done.) Remove garlic head when it feels soft when squeezed (protect your hand with a kitchen towel), about 25 minutes. Turning peppers once, remove when skins are black all over, about 30 minutes. Do not turn tomatoes, but remove when skins are blackened, about 30 minutes. Turning eggplant once, remove when skin is darkened and eggplant soft, 45 minutes.

3. Cut garlic head in half crosswise and squeeze roasted garlic into a food processor, discarding skins. Add onion. Peel off blackened skins from peppers under cold running water; discard stems and seeds. Add peeled peppers to processor. Halve eggplant and scoop out soft insides; discard skin. Add eggplant to processor. Peel off tomato skins and discard. Add peeled tomatoes to processor.

4. Add olive oil, lemon juice, salt, and pepper. Pulse until vegetables are coarsely chopped. Transfer to a medium bowl, cover, and refrigerate for up to 2 days. Serve sauce at room temperature.

185 THE PRIEST'S EGGPLANTS

Prep: 20 minutes   Stand: 30 minutes   Cook: 1 hour 10 minutes
Serves: 6

In Middle Eastern cuisine, there is a vegetarian stuffed eggplant dish that is so luxurious, it is said even a priest faints wherever it graces a dinner table. Named, therefore, "The Priest Swooned," it is even more toothsome with the addition of lamb. These are made with small (almost mini-sized) Italian eggplants. If you use the long, thin Japanese variety, trim them to be sure they fit into your skillet.

6 small Italian eggplants (about 4 ounces each)	1 (14-ounce) Italian peeled tomatoes, with their juice
2¾ teaspoons salt	½ teaspoon marjoram
3 tablespoons olive oil	¼ teaspoon pepper
1 small onion, chopped, plus 2 large onions, sliced	¾ pound ground lamb or ground round (85% lean)
3 garlic cloves, minced	2 tablespoons chopped parsley

1. Cut off stem and cap from each eggplant. Using a swivel-bladed vegetable peeler, remove 2 lengthwise strips of skin from opposite sides of each eggplant. Cut each eggplant in half lengthwise between peeled areas, so each eggplant half has a strip of peeled area running down the middle. Using a small sharp knife, score flat cut side of each eggplant in a diamond pattern, cutting only ¼ inch deep. In a colander, toss eggplants with 2 teaspoons salt and let stand at least 30 minutes to release bitter juices. Rinse eggplants well under cold running water and drain; pat dry. Scoop out and reserve insides of each eggplant, leaving ¼-inch-thick shells. Coarsely chop eggplant. Set shells aside.

2. In a 12-inch skillet, heat 1 tablespoon olive oil. Add chopped eggplant and cook over medium heat, stirring often, until lightly browned, about 4 minutes. Add chopped onion and cook, stirring often, until softened, about 3 minutes. Add 1 minced garlic clove and cook, stirring, 1 minute. Transfer vegetables to a medium bowl and let cool slightly while preparing sauce.

3. In same skillet, heat remaining 2 tablespoons oil. Add sliced onions and cook over medium heat, stirring often, until quite soft and lightly browned, about 10 minutes. Add remaining 2 minced garlic cloves and cook 1 minute. Add tomatoes with their juice, marjoram, ¼ teaspoon salt, and ⅛ teaspoon pepper. Bring to a boil, breaking up tomatoes in skillet with a spoon. Reduce heat to low and simmer until slightly thickened, about 15 minutes.

4. Meanwhile, add ground lamb, parsley, and remaining ½ teaspoon salt and ⅛ teaspoon pepper to cooled vegetables in bowl. Knead mixture well with your hands. Stuff eggplant shells with meat mixture, dividing evenly. Place stuffed eggplants in a spoke pattern on simmering sauce and cover skillet tightly.

5. Simmer, basting occasionally with sauce, until eggplants are tender, 35 to 40 minutes. Transfer eggplants to a serving platter and cover with foil to keep warm.

6. Increase heat to high and boil sauce, stirring occasionally, until liquid evaporates by half, about 2 minutes. Pour sauce over top of eggplants and serve hot.

186 BEEF AND EGGPLANT PARMESAN
Prep: 20 minutes   Cook: 40 minutes   Serves: 4 to 6

2 medium eggplants (about 2 pounds), cut into ½-inch-thick slices
1½ pounds ground round (85% lean)
1 large onion, chopped
2 garlic cloves, chopped
2 cups tomato sauce
1½ teaspoons oregano
1½ teaspoons basil
½ teaspoon salt
¼ teaspoon pepper
2 cups grated mozzarella cheese
½ cup grated Parmesan cheese

1. Preheat oven to 350°. In a large pot of boiling salted water, cook eggplant slices in batches just until tender, about 2 minutes. Remove slices with a slotted spoon and pat dry with paper towels.

2. In a large skillet, cook ground round, onion, and garlic over medium heat, stirring often to break up lumps of meat, until beef loses its pink color, about 5 minutes. Stir in tomato sauce, oregano, basil, salt, and pepper and bring to a simmer.

3. In a lightly oiled deep 2- to 3-quart casserole, arrange half of eggplant slices in overlapping rows. Spoon half of meat mixture over eggplant and sprinkle on half of mozzarella and Parmesan cheeses; repeat layers.

4. Bake until cheese is melted and casserole is bubbling, about 30 minutes. Let stand 5 minutes before serving.

187 TURKEY-STUFFED TOMATOES
Prep: 15 minutes   Cook: 30 minutes   Serves: 4

Make these in summer, when tomatoes and basil are at their peak, and
serve at cool room temperature as a light lunch or supper.

4 medium ripe tomatoes (about 1½ pounds)	**1 garlic clove, minced**
¾ teaspoon salt	**¾ cup herb-flavored croutons**
½ pound ground turkey or ground chicken	**1 tablespoon fresh basil or** 1 teaspoon dried
1 small onion, finely chopped	**¼ teaspoon pepper**
	1 cup tomato juice

1. Cut tops from tomatoes about ½ inch from tops to make lids. Using a teaspoon, hollow out tomatoes, saving pulp. Coarsely chop tomato pulp. Season insides of tomatoes with ¼ teaspoon salt, turn upside down on paper
towels, and let drain 10 minutes.

2. Meanwhile, in a large nonstick skillet, cook ground turkey, onion, and
garlic over medium heat, stirring often to break up lumps of meat, until turkey loses its pink color, about 5 minutes. Drain off any excess liquid.
Remove from heat and stir in chopped tomato pulp, croutons, basil,
remaining ½ teaspoon salt, and pepper.

3. Stuff mixture into tomato shells and top with tomato lids. Place in a
9-inch square baking dish and pour in tomato juice.

4. Bake, uncovered, until tomatoes are tender but not falling apart, about 25
minutes.

188 BEEF AND SUMMER SQUASH BAKE
Prep: 10 minutes   Cook: 45 minutes   Serves: 4 to 6

1 pound ground round (85% lean)	**1 teaspoon Italian seasoning**
1 small onion, chopped	**½ teaspoon salt**
1 small red bell pepper, chopped	**¼ teaspoon pepper**
1 medium celery rib, chopped	**1 (35-ounce) can peeled Italian** tomatoes, drained and chopped
1 garlic clove, chopped	**¾ cup shredded Cheddar** cheese (3 ounces)
4 medium yellow summer squash (about 1½ pounds), thinly sliced	**¼ cup chopped walnuts**

1. Preheat oven to 375°. In a large, ovenproof skillet or flameproof casserole,
cook ground round, onion, bell pepper, celery, and garlic over medium-
high heat, stirring often to break up lumps of meat, until beef loses its pink
color, about 5 minutes.

2. Add summer squash, Italian seasoning, salt, and pepper. Cook, stirring
often, until squash is crisp-tender, about 5 minutes. Spread tomatoes on top
of squash mixture and cover tightly.

3. Bake 10 minutes. Uncover and bake until liquid in skillet is almost completely evaporated, about 20 minutes. Sprinkle cheese and walnuts over top and bake until cheese melts, about 5 minutes longer.

---

189 AFRICAN ZUCCHINI STUFFED WITH SPICED BEEF

Prep: 20 minutes   Cook: 45 to 55 minutes   Serves: 4 to 6

4 medium zucchini (about 6 ounces each), halved lengthwise	⅓ cup chopped dry-roasted peanuts
1 teaspoon salt	1 tablespoon tomato paste
¼ teaspoon pepper	1½ teaspoons ground ginger
2 tablespoons butter or vegetable oil	1 teaspoon ground cumin
1 medium onion, chopped	1 teaspoon ground allspice
1 garlic clove, minced	½ teaspoon ground coriander
1 pound ground chuck (80% lean) or ground lamb	¼ teaspoon ground cloves
	¾ teaspoon hot pepper sauce
½ cup dry red wine	1 cup tomato puree
	¼ cup peanut butter, preferably natural

1. Preheat oven to 350°. Using a teaspoon, scoop out and reserve insides of zucchini halves, leaving ½-inch-thick shells. Coarsely chop scooped-out zucchini. Sprinkle insides of zucchini shells with ½ teaspoon salt and the pepper; set aside.

2. In a large skillet, melt butter over medium-high heat. Add onion, garlic, and chopped zucchini. Cook, stirring often, until onion is softened, 3 to 5 minutes. Add ground chuck and cook until meat is no longer pink, about 5 minutes. Drain off any fat. Stir in red wine, peanuts, tomato paste, 1 teaspoon ginger, cumin, allspice, coriander, cloves, and ½ teaspoon hot sauce. Cook until liquid evaporates and mixture is thickened, 4 to 5 minutes. Remove from heat and let cool slightly.

3. Stuff zucchini shells with meat mixture. Place stuffed zucchini in a lightly greased 9 x 13-inch baking dish. In a medium bowl, whisk together tomato puree, peanut butter, remaining ½ teaspoon ginger, ½ teaspoon salt, ¼ teaspoon hot sauce, and ½ cup water. Pour over zucchini. Cover with aluminum foil and bake until zucchini are tender, 30 to 40 minutes.

190 ROMANIAN MIXED VEGETABLE STEW WITH VEAL MEATBALLS

Prep: 40 minutes   Stand: 30 minutes   Cook: 3¼ hours
Serves: 8 to 12

1   large eggplant, cut into
    1-inch cubes (about
    2 pounds)
2   medium zucchini, cut into
    1-inch-thick rounds
1   tablespoon plus
    1¾ teaspoons salt
¾   cup olive oil
2   large onions, sliced
2   large carrots, peeled and cut
    into ½-inch-thick rounds
2   medium green bell peppers,
    cut into 1-inch pieces
1   pound fresh mushrooms,
    quartered
1   small head cabbage, cored
    and sliced into ½-inch-
    wide strips
1   pound green beans, cut into
    1-inch pieces

3   large red potatoes (about
    1 pound), sliced ¼ inch
    thick
1   (15-ounce) can Italian peeled
    tomatoes, coarsely
    chopped, juices reserved
3   garlic cloves, chopped
1   tablespoon plus ¾ teaspoon
    thyme
2   teaspoons marjoram
2   bay leaves
½   teaspoon crushed hot red
    pepper
1½ cups fresh bread crumbs
3   eggs
¼   teaspoon fennel seed,
    crushed
¼   teaspoon black pepper
½   cup chopped parsley
3   pounds ground veal

1. In a large colander, toss eggplant and zucchini with 2 teaspoons salt. Let stand 30 minutes. Drain, rinse well under cold water, and rinse again. Pat vegetables dry with paper towels.

2. Preheat oven to 350°. In a very large (8- to 10-quart) flameproof casserole or covered turkey roaster, heat ⅓ cup olive oil over medium-high heat until hot but not smoking. Add eggplant and zucchini and cook, stirring often, until lightly browned, about 10 minutes. Using a slotted spoon, transfer vegetables to a bowl and set aside.

3. Add ⅓ cup olive oil to casserole and reduce heat to medium. Add onions, carrots, bell peppers, and mushrooms. Cook, stirring often, until onions are golden, about 10 minutes. Add cabbage, green beans, potatoes, tomatoes with their juice, and garlic. Cover and cook, stirring often, until cabbage is wilted, about 10 minutes. Stir in 1 tablespoon thyme, marjoram, bay leaves, 2 teaspoons salt, and hot pepper. Cover and bake 1 hour.

4. Meanwhile, in a large bowl, mix bread crumbs, eggs, fennel seed, black pepper, ¼ cup parsley, and remaining ¾ teaspoon salt and ¾ teaspoon thyme until well blended. Add ground veal and knead with your hands until well mixed. Using about 1 tablespoon for each, form veal mixture into meatballs.

5. In a large skillet, heat remaining oil. In batches, cook meatballs, turning often, until browned all over, about 8 minutes per batch.

6. After vegetables have baked 1 hour, add browned meatballs. Bake, uncovered, 30 minutes. Garnish with remaining ¼ cup parsley and serve.

---

191   ARMENIAN SAUSAGE KEBABS WITH ROASTED VEGETABLES
Prep: 15 minutes   Cook: 30 minutes   Serves: 4

1 tablespoon olive oil
1 large onion, sliced, plus
  1 small onion, minced
2 large russet potatoes, sliced
  paper-thin
1 large red bell pepper, cut into
  ½-inch-wide strips
1 large green bell pepper, cut
  into ½-inch-wide strips

4 garlic cloves, minced
1¾ teaspoons salt
½ teaspoon pepper
1 pound lean ground lamb
1 pound ground sirloin
  (90% lean)
1 tablespoon dried mint

1. Preheat oven to 400°. Place oil in a 9 x 13-inch baking dish and tilt to coat inside of dish. In baking dish, toss sliced onion, potatoes, bell peppers, and 2 minced garlic cloves with ¼ teaspoon each salt and pepper. Bake vegetables 15 minutes. With a pancake turner, turn and toss vegetables.

2. Meanwhile, in a medium bowl, knead ground lamb, ground sirloin, minced onion, mint, remaining 2 garlic cloves, 1½ teaspoons salt, and ¼ teaspoon pepper together with your hands until well mixed. Dip your hands in cold water and form meat mixture into 8 thick sausages, about 2 inches wide and 4 inches long. Press 2 sausages lengthwise onto each skewer, with skewer running through middle of sausages, arranging sausages in center of skewer. Suspend skewers, resting on edges of vegetable-filled baking dish, so sausages are hanging above vegetables.

3. Bake until sausages are cooked medium-well done and vegetables are tender, 15 to 20 minutes. Drain off fat from vegetables before serving. (Armenians always cook these sausages medium-well done, about 18 minutes roasting time. If you like your sausages rarer, increase vegetables' first roasting time in step 1 to about 22 minutes. Bake sausages to desired doneness, about 12 minutes for medium-rare.)

Chapter 8

Meals in a Pot: Casseroles, Bakes, and Skillet Suppers

Here's a collection of all those heartwarming, rib-sticking recipes that many of us remember with nostalgia. These are the comforting specialties of tasty home cooking that are making such a comeback on dinner tables, at church socials, and at potluck dinners. All these meals-in-a-pot need are a green salad and some crusty bread to make a complete, satisfying dinner for the whole family.

Recipes in this chapter range from familiar every-day time-savers, like Hamburger Stroganoff, Ground Chicken and Dumplings Skillet Supper, and Cheeseburger Pie, to new ideas and ethnic creations, like Braciola with Italian Vegetable Stuffing, Southwestern Turkey Cornbread Bake, Skillet Spanish Chicken and Rice, and Austrian Pork and Noodle Bake.

When choosing a casserole for baking, consider an enameled cast-iron pot. The heavy material retains heat well, it cooks on top of the stove as well as in the oven, and the casserole can double as a stew, or soup, pot. For a large pot, the five- to six-quart capacity is the most useful. For smaller oven casseroles and bakes, ovenproof glass is an excellent choice.

The skillet recipes in this chapter are for those times when you just don't feel like turning on the oven. While they are essentially carefree dishes, you should look under the lid every now and then to be sure that nothing is scorching. This is particularly true of the pasta-based skillet dinners, which need to be stirred up from the bottom occasionally to prevent burning and sticking.

A well-seasoned cast-iron skillet is just the thing for recipes that call for a trip to the oven after browning the ingredients on top of the stove. Nonstick skillets are excellent for many uses, and they require less fat, but they are rarely provided with ovenproof handles. If you wish to use your nonstick skillet in the oven, wrap the handle in several thicknesses of aluminum foil; this will protect it for temperatures up to 400 degrees.

192   HAMBURGER STROGANOFF
Prep: 10 minutes   Cook: 15 minutes   Serves: 4

2 tablespoons butter or
  vegetable oil
1 medium onion, chopped
½ pound fresh mushrooms,
  sliced
1 pound ground sirloin
  (90% lean) or ground
  round (85% lean)
1 teaspoon Worcestershire
  sauce

¼ teaspoon salt
¼ teaspoon pepper
2 tablespoons flour
1¼ cups beef broth
½ cup sour cream
2 tablespoons chopped fresh
  dill or parsley
  Hot cooked noodles

1. In a large skillet, heat butter. Add onion and cook over medium heat, stirring often, until softened, about 3 minutes. Add mushrooms and cook until mushrooms have given off their liquid and are lightly browned, about 5 minutes. Add ground sirloin and cook, stirring often to break up meat, until meat loses its pink color, about 5 minutes.

2. Add Worcestershire, salt, and pepper. Stir in flour and cook, stirring often, 1 minute. Stir in broth, bring to a simmer, and cook until thickened, about 1 minute.

3. Remove from heat and stir in sour cream. Return skillet to medium heat and cook, stirring constantly, just to warm sour cream through, about 30 seconds. Sprinkle with dill and serve immediately over hot noodles.

193   CREAMY CORN AND BEEF CASSEROLE
Prep: 10 minutes   Cook: 40 minutes   Serves: 6

1 pound ground round
  (85% lean)
1 small onion, chopped
1 (10¾-ounce) can tomato
  soup
2 cups raw elbow macaroni
  (about 8 ounces)

½ teaspoon salt
¼ teaspoon pepper
1 (16-ounce) can creamed
  corn
½ cup shredded Cheddar
  cheese

1. Preheat oven to 350°. In a large skillet, cook ground round and onion over medium-high heat, stirring often to break up lumps of meat, until beef loses its pink color, about 5 minutes. Drain off excess fat.

2. Stir in tomato soup, 1½ cups water, macaroni, salt, and pepper. Bring to a boil, stirring often. Reduce heat to low, partially cover, and simmer until macaroni is barely tender, 6 to 8 minutes. Stir in creamed corn. Pour into a lightly buttered 1½-quart casserole and cover tightly.

3. Bake 15 minutes. Remove cover and sprinkle Cheddar cheese over top. Bake, uncovered, until casserole is bubbling and cheese is melted, about 15 minutes longer.

194 SPOONABLE MUSHROOM-MEAT CASSEROLE
Prep: 10 minutes   Cook: 45 minutes   Serves: 4

1 (10¾-ounce) can reduced-
    sodium cream of
    mushroom soup
1½ cups fresh bread crumbs
1 small onion, minced
1 egg

¼ teaspoon salt
¼ teaspoon pepper
1 pound ground round
    (85% lean)
½ cup milk

1. Preheat oven to 350°. In a large bowl, mix ½ can soup, bread crumbs, onion, egg, salt, and pepper until well blended. Add ground round and mix well. Spread meat mixture evenly into a 9-inch square baking dish.

2. In a small bowl, combine remaining ½ can soup and milk. Pour over top of meat.

3. Bake until topping is lightly browned, about 45 minutes.

195 SPAGHETTI PIE WITH RAGU FILLING
Prep: 20 minutes   Cook: 50 minutes   Serves: 4 to 6

6 ounces spaghetti
½ cup grated Parmesan cheese
2 eggs, beaten
2 tablespoons butter, at room
    temperature
1½ cups part-skim ricotta cheese
1 pound ground pork or
    ground round (85% lean)
1 medium onion, chopped
1 garlic clove, minced

1 cup tomato sauce
1½ teaspoons Italian seasoning
¼ teaspoon crushed fennel
    seed
¼ teaspoon crushed hot red
    pepper
½ cup grated mozzarella
    cheese

1. Preheat oven to 350°. Butter well the inside of a 10-inch pie plate. In a large pot of lightly salted boiling water, cook spaghetti until barely tender, about 8 minutes. Drain well.

2. In a medium bowl, mix hot spaghetti with Parmesan cheese, eggs, and butter until butter melts and egg is beaten. Spread into prepared pie plate, pushing mixture up sides to form a shell. Spoon ricotta cheese onto bottom of shell and spread evenly, leaving a 1-inch border. Cover and refrigerate while making filling.

3. In a large skillet, cook ground pork, onion, and garlic over medium heat, breaking up lumps of meat with a spoon, until pork loses its pink color, about 5 minutes. Stir in tomato sauce, Italian seasoning, fennel seed, and hot pepper. Spread meat filling over ricotta.

4. Bake until spaghetti crust is set, about 30 minutes. Sprinkle mozzarella over top and bake until cheese melts, about 5 minutes. Let stand 5 minutes, then cut into wedges to serve.

196 MEXICALI SKILLET DINNER

Prep: 15 minutes   Cook: 30 minutes   Serves: 6 to 8

2 tablespoons olive oil
1 medium onion, chopped
1 medium green bell pepper, chopped
2 garlic cloves, chopped
1 pound ground chuck (80% lean)
2 cups elbow macaroni (about 12 ounces)
2 tablespoons chili powder, or more to taste
1½ teaspoons salt

1 (35-ounce) can Italian peeled tomatoes, with their juice
1 cup tomato sauce
2 tablespoons tomato paste
1 cup fresh, canned, or thawed frozen corn kernels
¾ cup grated sharp Cheddar cheese
Chopped scallions and/or sliced black olives

1. In a large skillet, heat oil over moderate heat. Add onion, bell pepper, and garlic. Cook, stirring often, until softened, about 5 minutes. Add ground chuck and raw macaroni. Cook, scraping bottom of skillet well and breaking up lumps of meat with a large spoon, until beef loses its pink color, about 5 minutes. Add chili powder and salt. Cook, stirring, 1 minute.

2. Add tomatoes and their juice. Break up tomatoes with a large spoon. Stir in tomato sauce, tomato paste, corn, and 2 cups water. Bring to a boil, reduce heat to low, cover tightly, and simmer until macaroni is tender, stirring often to prevent sticking, about 20 minutes. Sprinkle cheese over top and garnish with scallions and olives, if desired.

197 EASY MEATBALL AND MUSHROOM SKILLET SUPPER

Prep: 10 minutes   Cook: 15 minutes   Serves: 4

½ cup fresh bread crumbs
1 small onion, chopped
1 egg
2 teaspoons Worcestershire sauce
1¾ teaspoons dried dill
½ teaspoon salt
¼ teaspoon pepper
1 pound ground round (85% lean)

2 tablespoons vegetable oil
1 (10¾-ounce) can reduced-sodium cream of mushroom soup
½ cup milk
2 tablespoons dry sherry, dry white wine, or additional milk
Hot cooked egg noodles or rice

1. In a medium bowl, combine bread crumbs, chopped onion, egg, Worcestershire sauce, 1¼ teaspoons dill, salt, and pepper. Stir with a fork until mixed. Add ground round and mix until blended. Form mixture into 12 to 14 meatballs.

2. Heat oil in a large skillet. Add meatballs and cook over medium heat, turning often, until browned all over, about 8 minutes. Drain off any excess fat.

3. Add mushroom soup, milk, remaining ½ teaspoon dill, and sherry to skillet. Bring to a simmer, reduce heat to low, and cover. Cook, stirring occasionally, until meatballs are cooked through, 5 to 7 minutes. Serve hot, with noodles or rice.

---

198   BRACIOLA WITH ITALIAN VEGETABLE STUFFING

Prep: 20 minutes   Cook: 1 hour   Serves: 6 to 8

1 (10-ounce) package frozen chopped spinach, thawed and squeezed dry
1 small onion, finely chopped
1 garlic clove, minced
¾ cup Italian-seasoned bread crumbs
⅓ cup grated Parmesan cheese
1 egg
½ teaspoon salt
¼ teaspoon pepper

1½ pounds ground round (85% lean)
1 (10-ounce) package frozen Italian vegetables in butter sauce, cooked and drained
1 (14-ounce) can stewed Italian-style tomatoes, with their juice
⅓ cup dry red wine

1. Preheat oven to 350°. In a medium bowl, mix spinach, onion, garlic, bread crumbs, Parmesan cheese, egg, salt, and pepper. Add ground round and knead with your hands until well blended.

2. On a lightly moistened piece of wax paper, pat meat mixture evenly into an 8 x 12-inch rectangle. Cover meat with Italian vegetables, leaving a 1-inch border all around.

3. Using wax paper to help lift, roll up meat and press into a thick, compact cylinder about 10 inches long and 4 inches wide. Transfer to a lightly oiled 11 x 7-inch baking dish. Pour stewed tomatoes with their juice and wine over braciola.

4. Bake until a meat thermometer inserted in center of braciola reads 160°, about 1 hour. Let stand 5 minutes. Cut into 1-inch-thick slices and serve with sauce.

199 P.T.A. SUPPER BEEF AND MACARONI CASSEROLE

Prep: 15 minutes   Cook: 50 minutes   Serves: 4 to 6

8 ounces elbow macaroni	¼ teaspoon pepper
1 pound ground chuck (80% lean) or ground round (85% lean)	1 (8-ounce) package cream cheese, softened
1 small onion, chopped	1 cup cottage cheese
2 cups tomato sauce	½ cup sour cream
1 teaspoon celery salt	¼ cup chopped parsley
	2 tablespoons butter

1. Preheat oven to 350°. In a large pot of boiling salted water, cook macaroni until tender, 10 to 12 minutes. Drain well.

2. In a large skillet, cook ground chuck and onion over medium-high heat, stirring often to break up lumps of meat, until beef is no longer pink, about 5 minutes. Drain off excess fat. Stir in tomato sauce, celery salt, and pepper.

3. In a medium bowl, beat together cream cheese, cottage cheese, sour cream, and parsley until smooth.

4. In a buttered, deep, 3-quart casserole, layer half of macaroni, all of cheese mixture, and remaining macaroni. Top macaroni with meat sauce and dot with butter. (Casserole can be prepared up to 1 day ahead, covered, and refrigerated.)

5. Bake until casserole is bubbling, about 45 minutes (or longer if refrigerated).

200 DIME-A-SPOON DINNER NOODLE-ONION BAKE

Prep: 10 minutes   Cook: 50 minutes   Serves: 4

9 ounces corkscrew pasta	1 (10¾-ounce) can cream of mushroom soup
1 pound ground round (85% lean)	1 cup shredded Cheddar cheese (4 ounces)
1 small green bell pepper, chopped	¼ teaspoon pepper
1 (14-ounce) can Italian peeled tomatoes, drained	1 (3-ounce) can French-fried onions

1. In a large saucepan of boiling salted water, cook pasta until just tender, about 9 minutes. Drain well. Return pasta to empty large saucepan.

2. In a large skillet, cook ground round and bell pepper over medium-high heat, stirring often to break up lumps of meat, until beef loses its pink color, about 5 minutes. Drain off excess fat. Add tomatoes and break up with a spoon. Stir in soup, Cheddar cheese, and pepper. Add meat mixture to pasta in saucepan and mix well.

3. In a lightly oiled 2-quart casserole, place half of noodle mixture and sprinkle with half of onions. Spread with remaining noodles and cover.

4. Bake 30 minutes, until casserole is bubbling. Remove cover, sprinkle remaining onions over top, and bake 5 minutes longer.

---

201   SEVEN-LAYER CASSEROLE

Prep: 10 minutes   Cook: 1¼ hours   Serves: 4 to 6

1 cup rice	1 small green bell pepper,
1 cup fresh or thawed frozen	chopped
corn kernels	1 pound ground sirloin
½ teaspoon salt	(90% lean)
½ teaspoon pepper	1 tablespoon chili powder
2 cups tomato sauce	4 strips of bacon
1 small onion, chopped	

1. Preheat oven to 350°. In a lightly greased 2-quart casserole, spread rice in an even layer. Cover with a layer of corn. Season with ¼ teaspoon each salt and pepper.

2. Pour on 1 cup tomato sauce and ½ cup water. Sprinkle chopped onion and bell pepper over sauce. Crumble ground sirloin over vegetables. Season with chili powder and remaining ¼ teaspoon each salt and pepper. Pour on remaining 1 cup tomato sauce and ½ cup water. Arrange bacon over top of casserole.

3. Cover casserole with lid or aluminum foil and bake 1 hour. Uncover and bake until rice is tender, about 15 minutes longer.

---

202   CHEESEBURGER PIE

Prep: 15 minutes   Cook: 35 minutes   Serves: 4 to 6

1 pound ground chuck	1 cup grated sharp Cheddar
(80% lean)	cheese
1 large onion, chopped	1½ cups milk
2 tablespoons ketchup	¾ cup dry buttermilk biscuit
½ teaspoon salt	mix
½ teaspoon pepper	3 eggs
1½ cups frozen hash brown	
potatoes	

1. Preheat oven to 400°. In a large skillet, cook ground chuck and onion over medium heat, stirring often to break up meat, until ground chuck loses its pink color, about 5 minutes. Drain off excess fat. Stir in ketchup, salt, and pepper. Stir in hash browns. Transfer mixture to a greased 10-inch round pie plate. Sprinkle cheese over top.

2. In a medium bowl, whisk together milk, biscuit mix, and eggs. (Batter will be lumpy.) Pour batter over meat mixture. Bake until batter is set, about 30 minutes. Let stand 5 minutes before slicing.

203   MEXICALI MACARONI SUPPER
Prep: 10 minutes   Cook: 30 minutes   Serves: 4 to 6

1   pound ground round (85% lean)
1   medium onion, chopped
1   medium green bell pepper, chopped
2   garlic cloves, minced
2   tablespoons chili powder
1½   teaspoons salt
2   cups elbow macaroni (about 12 ounces)

1   (35-ounce) can tomatoes, coarsely chopped, juices reserved
1   cup tomato sauce
2   tablespoons tomato paste
1   cup canned or thawed frozen corn kernels
¾   cup shredded Monterey Jack cheese

1. In a large nonreactive skillet or flameproof casserole, cook ground round, onion, bell pepper, and garlic over medium heat, stirring often to break up lumps of meat, until beef loses its pink color, about 5 minutes. Add chili powder and salt and cook, stirring, 1 minute.

2. Stir in macaroni, tomatoes and their juice, tomato sauce, tomato paste, corn, and 2 cups water. Bring to a boil, reduce heat to low, cover tightly, and simmer until macaroni is tender, stirring often to prevent sticking, about 25 minutes. Sprinkle cheese over top, cover, and let stand until cheese melts, about 5 minutes.

204   SOUTH-OF-THE-BORDER RICE CASSEROLE
Prep: 10 minutes   Cook: 30 minutes   Serves: 6

1   cup long-grain white rice
1½   pounds ground round (85% lean)
1   medium onion, chopped
1   garlic clove, minced
2   teaspoons chili powder
½   teaspoon ground cumin

¾   teaspoon salt
¼   teaspoon pepper
1   cup tomato sauce
1   cup beef broth
½   cup shredded pepper Jack cheese

1. Preheat oven to 400°. In a medium saucepan of boiling salted water, cook rice until tender, about 10 minutes. Drain well.

2. In a large skillet, cook ground round, onion, and garlic over medium-high heat, stirring often to break up lumps of meat, until beef loses its pink color, about 5 minutes. Drain off excess fat. Add chili powder, cumin, salt, and pepper. Cook, stirring, 1 minute. Stir in tomato sauce, beef broth, and cooked rice. Transfer to a lightly oiled 2-quart casserole. Sprinkle cheese over top.

3. Bake until cheese is melted and casserole is bubbling, about 15 minutes.

205   TEX-MEX BEEF CASSEROLE
Prep: 10 minutes   Cook: 1 hour   Serves: 4 to 6

1¼ cups crushed Cheddar
    cheese–flavored crackers
1 (16-ounce) can creamed corn
1 (14-ounce) can Italian peeled
    tomatoes, drained
1 (4-ounce) can chopped green
    chiles
1 medium onion, chopped
1 medium green bell pepper,
    chopped

2 garlic cloves, minced
3 eggs
½ teaspoon salt
1 tablespoon chili powder
1 pound ground round
    (85% lean)
1 tablespoon butter

1. Preheat oven to 350°. In a large bowl, mix together ¾ cup crushed crackers, corn, tomatoes, chiles, onion, bell pepper, garlic, eggs, salt, and chili powder with a fork until well blended. Add ground round and knead with your hands until mixed. Transfer to a lightly buttered, deep, 3-quart baking dish. Sprinkle remaining ½ cup crackers over top and dot with butter.

2. Bake until center springs back when pressed with a finger, about 1 hour.

206   INDIAN GROUND BEEF AND PEA SAUTE
Prep: 5 minutes   Cook: 25 minutes   Serves: 2 to 4

Keema, a staple of Pakistani cuisine, can have as many variations as the American burger. Try tossing in cooked broccoli spears, chopped green beans, or diced boiled potato. This is a fine recipe for using up leftover vegetables.

1 tablespoon vegetable oil
1 medium onion, chopped
1 pound ground round
    (85% lean) or ground
    sirloin (90% lean)
2 plum tomatoes, chopped
1 tablespoon minced fresh
    ginger

1 garlic clove, minced
2 teaspoons curry powder
1 teaspoon salt
¼ teaspoon pepper
2 teaspoons lemon juice
1 cup frozen peas, thawed
    Hot cooked rice and mango
    chutney

1. Heat oil in a large skillet. Add onion and cook over medium-high heat, stirring often, until lightly browned, about 4 minutes. Add ground round and cook, stirring to break up meat, until beef loses its pink color, about 3 minutes. Add tomatoes, ginger, garlic, curry powder, salt, and pepper. Cook, stirring, 30 seconds.

2. Stir in ½ cup water and lemon juice and bring to a boil. Reduce heat to medium-low and simmer until liquid is evaporated, about 15 minutes. Stir in peas during last 3 minutes of cooking to heat through. Serve with rice and chutney.

207 CURRIED BEEF CASSEROLE WITH APPLE-BANANA CHUTNEY

Prep: 15 minutes   Cook: 1 hour 20 minutes   Serves: 6

South African Dutch settlers learned this recipe from their colonies in Indonesia, so this is a dish that travels well in more ways than one. It is one of my favorite contributions to a potluck buffet. Serve over hot cooked rice.

¾ cup fresh bread crumbs
1 cup milk
4 eggs
1½ pounds lean ground lamb or ground sirloin (90% lean)
2 medium onions, chopped
1 medium green apple, cored and chopped
2 garlic cloves, minced
2 tablespoons curry powder, preferably Madras style

Grated zest and juice of 1 lime
⅓ cup slivered blanched almonds
⅓ cup raisins
¾ teaspoon salt
¼ teaspoon crushed hot red pepper
¾ cup heavy cream
Apple-Banana Chutney (recipe follows)

1. Preheat oven to 325°. Lightly butter inside of a 10-inch deep dish pie plate. In a medium bowl, mix bread crumbs, ¼ cup milk, and 1 egg until blended.

2. In a large skillet, cook ground lamb, onions, and apple over medium-high heat, stirring often to break up lumps of meat, until lamb is no longer pink, about 5 minutes. Drain off excess fat. Add garlic, curry powder, lime zest, and lime juice. Cook, stirring constantly, 1 minute. Remove from heat and stir in almonds and raisins. Season with salt and hot pepper and let cool slightly.

3. Stir cooled meat mixture into soaked bread crumbs. Pack meat filling into prepared pie plate and place on a baking sheet.

4. In a medium bowl, whisk heavy cream with remaining ¾ cup milk and 3 eggs until well blended. Pour egg mixture slowly over top of meat.

5. Bake until custard is set and lightly browned, about 40 minutes. Let stand 5 minutes and serve with Apple-Banana Chutney.

APPLE-BANANA CHUTNEY
Makes about 2½ cups

3 medium green apples, peeled, cored, and cut into ½-inch dice
1 small onion, minced
1 tablespoon grated fresh ginger
1 garlic clove, minced

⅓ cup brown sugar
¼ cup cider vinegar
¼ cup raisins
½ teaspoon cinnamon
¼ teaspoon dry mustard
⅛ teaspoon cayenne
1 medium banana, sliced

1. In a nonreactive heavy medium saucepan, combine all ingredients except banana. Bring to a boil over medium heat, stirring often to dissolve sugar.

2. Reduce heat to low, cover, and simmer 15 minutes. Remove cover and simmer, stirring often, until liquid is almost evaporated, 15 to 20 minutes. Add banana and cook until softened, about 5 minutes. Using a wooden spoon, mash banana into chutney (mixture will be chunky). Let cool completely before serving.

---

208 BEEF AND BEAN CASSEROLE
Prep: 20 minutes   Cook: 45 minutes   Serves: 6 to 8

1 pound ground round
  (85% lean)
2 medium onions, finely
  chopped
3 garlic cloves, minced
1 (16-ounce) can refried beans
¼ cup olive oil
1 fresh jalapeño pepper,
  minced, or 2 tablespoons
  canned chopped green
  chiles

1 tablespoon chili powder
1½ teaspoons ground cumin
2 cups tomato sauce
1 (14-ounce) can Italian peeled
  tomatoes, with their juice
1 dozen corn tortillas
1 cup shredded Cheddar
  cheese (4 ounces)

1. Preheat oven to 350°. In a large skillet, cook ground round, 1 chopped onion, and 1 garlic clove over medium-high heat, stirring often to break up lumps of meat, until beef loses its pink color, about 5 minutes. Stir in refried beans. Transfer mixture to a medium bowl and set aside.

2. In a large skillet, heat 2 tablespoons olive oil over medium heat. Add remaining onion and cook, stirring often, until softened, about 3 minutes. Add remaining garlic, jalapeño pepper, chili powder, and cumin; cook, stirring, 30 seconds. Stir in tomato sauce and tomatoes with juice; break up tomatoes in skillet with a spoon. Bring to a boil, reduce heat to low, and simmer, partially covered, until sauce is slightly thickened, about 20 minutes. Stir ½ cup sauce into meat-bean mixture.

3. One at a time, dip 6 tortillas in simmering sauce until softened. Line bottom of a lightly oiled 9 x 13-inch baking dish with sauced tortillas. Spread meat-bean mixture evenly over tortillas. Repeat dipping procedure with remaining tortillas, arranging on top of meat-bean mixture. Sprinkle shredded Cheddar cheese over top.

4. Bake until casserole is bubbling and cheese melts, about 35 minutes. Let stand 5 minutes before cutting into squares to serve.

209   SIRLOIN STEAK BURGERS WITH MUSHROOM RAGOUT

Prep: 10 minutes   Cook: 15 minutes   Serves: 2 to 3

½ pound fresh mushrooms, sliced
1 medium shallot or scallion, minced
½ cup dry red wine
¼ cup beef broth
1 tablespoon tomato paste

¼ teaspoon thyme
¼ teaspoon pepper
1 pound ground sirloin (90% lean)
¼ teaspoon salt
Vegetable cooking spray

1. In a large nonstick skillet, combine mushrooms, half of the minced shallot, wine, beef broth, ¼ cup water, 1 teaspoon tomato paste, and ⅛ teaspoon each of thyme and pepper. Bring to a boil over medium-high heat. Cook until liquid evaporates to ¼ cup, about 7 minutes. Transfer to a bowl and set mushroom ragout aside. Carefully wipe out skillet with moist paper towels.

2. In a medium bowl, combine ground sirloin, salt, and remaining 2 teaspoons tomato paste and ⅛ teaspoon each thyme and pepper. Form into 3 burgers about 3 inches in diameter.

3. Spray the skillet lightly with vegetable cooking spray and place over medium-high heat 1 minute. Add burgers and cook 2½ minutes on each side for medium-rare. Transfer to a serving dish and cover with foil to keep warm. Pour off any fat from skillet.

4. Return reserved mushroom ragout to skillet. Cook over medium-high heat until reheated, scraping up browned bits on bottom of skillet with a wooden spoon, about 30 seconds. Pour over burgers and serve.

210   ELEANOR AND DICK'S TAMALE PIE

Prep: 20 minutes   Cook: 1 hour 10 minutes   Serves: 4 to 6

1 pound ground round (85% lean)
1 medium onion, chopped
1 medium green bell pepper, chopped
1 2 garlic cloves, minced
2 tablespoons chili powder
1½ teaspoons salt
1 teaspoon oregano
½ teaspoon ground cumin
¼ teaspoon cayenne

1 (28-ounce) can Italian peeled tomatoes, drained and coarsely chopped
1½ cups tomato sauce
1½ cups chopped black olives
1 cup corn kernels, fresh or thawed frozen
1 cup yellow cornmeal, preferably stone-ground
1½ cups shredded Cheddar cheese (6 ounces)

1. Preheat oven to 375°. In a large skillet, cook ground round, onion, bell pepper, and garlic over medium-high heat, stirring often to break up lumps of meat, until beef loses its pink color, about 5 minutes.

2. Add chili powder, 1 teaspoon salt, oregano, cumin, and cayenne. Cook, stirring, 1 minute. Add tomatoes, tomato sauce, olives, and corn. Bring to a boil, reduce heat to medium-low, and simmer until thickened, 15 to 20 minutes. Spread filling evenly in a lightly oiled 9-inch square baking dish.

3. In a medium saucepan, bring 2 cups water and remaining ½ teaspoon salt to a boil over high heat. Gradually whisk in cornmeal, reduce heat to low, and cook, whisking constantly, until thick and smooth, about 1 minute. Spread warm cornmeal evenly over filling.

4. Bake 30 minutes. Sprinkle Cheddar cheese over top and continue baking until topping is set and golden brown, about 10 minutes longer.

---

211 BEEF, SPINACH, AND RICE TORTINO
Prep: 20 minutes   Cook: 50 minutes   Serves: 6 to 8

This layered Italian torte can be a successful appetizer served in thin slices, but I love it as the centerpiece of a Sunday supper with a big green salad and lots of red wine.

1 tablespoon butter, softened	¾ teaspoon salt
1 tablespoon dried bread crumbs	⅜ teaspoon pepper
1 pound ground round (85% lean) or ground sirloin (90% lean)	1 cup ricotta cheese
	3 eggs
	4 cups cooked rice
1 medium onion, chopped	½ cup grated Parmesan cheese
1 garlic clove, chopped	1 (10-ounce) package frozen chopped spinach, thawed and squeezed dry
1 cup tomato sauce	
2 teaspoons Italian seasoning	Tomato sauce, as accompaniment

1. Preheat oven to 350°. Coat inside of an 8½-inch round springform pan with softened butter. Dust inside of pan with crumbs, tilting to coat completely.

2. In a large skillet, cook ground round, onion, and garlic over medium-high heat, stirring often, until beef loses all trace of pink, about 5 minutes. Drain off excess fat. Stir in tomato sauce, Italian seasoning, ½ teaspoon salt, and ¼ teaspoon pepper. Beat in ricotta cheese and 1 egg until well blended.

3. In a small bowl, beat remaining 2 eggs lightly. In a large bowl, combine rice, Parmesan cheese, spinach, beaten eggs, and remaining ¼ teaspoon salt and ⅛ teaspoon pepper. Mix until well blended.

4. Spread half of rice mixture evenly in prepared pan. Pour in meat mixture and spread smooth. Top with remaining rice mixture and spread evenly. Cove pan tightly with foil.

5. Bake 30 minutes. Remove foil and bake until top of tortino is lightly browned, about 15 minutes longer. Let stand 10 minutes before cutting into wedges. Pass a bowl of hot tomato sauce on the side.

212 JEAN'S SANTA FE CASSEROLE
Prep: 10 minutes   Cook: 35 minutes   Serves: 4

- 1 pound ground round (85% lean)
- 1 medium onion, chopped
- 1 small green bell pepper, chopped
- 1 garlic clove, minced
- 1 (16-ounce) can hominy, drained and rinsed
- 1 (13½-ounce) jar tamales, unwrapped and chopped

- 1 (10¾-ounce) can cream of chicken soup
- 1 (4-ounce) can chopped green chiles
- 1 (3½-ounce) can chopped black olives, drained
- 2 teaspoons chili powder
- 1 cup crushed tortilla chips

1. Preheat oven to 350°. In a large skillet, cook ground round, onion, bell pepper, and garlic over medium-high heat, stirring often to break up lumps of meat, until beef loses its pink color, about 5 minutes.

2. In a lightly oiled 2-quart casserole, combine meat mixture, hominy, chopped tamales, soup, chiles, olives, and chili powder. Sprinkle crushed tortilla chips over top.

3. Bake until casserole is bubbling, about 30 minutes.

213 JUDY'S PIZZA PIE SUPREME
Prep: 10 minutes   Cook: 35 minutes   Serves: 4 to 6

This recipe will only work with dry nondairy creamer. Plain instant milk won't do it—I've tried.

- 1¼ pounds ground round (85% lean)
- ½ cup dry nondairy creamer
- ½ cup dried Italian-flavored bread crumbs
- 1¼ teaspoons garlic salt
- ¼ teaspoon pepper
- 1 cup shredded Cheddar cheese (4 ounces)

- 1 (6-ounce) can tomato paste
- 1 (4-ounce) can sliced mushrooms, liquid reserved
- 1 small onion finely chopped
- 1 teaspoon oregano
- ⅓ cup grated Parmesan cheese

1. Preheat oven to 350°. In a medium bowl, combine ground round, 1 cup water, creamer, bread crumbs, garlic salt, and pepper. Press mixture evenly into a 9-inch pie pan to form a shell.

2. In a medium bowl, combine Cheddar cheese, tomato paste, mushrooms with their liquid, onion, and oregano. Spoon mixture into meat shell. Sprinkle Parmesan cheese over top.

3. Bake until top is browned and meat shell is cooked through, about 35 minutes. Let stand 5 minutes. Drain off excess fat and cut into wedges to serve.

214 MEAT AND POTATOES PIE
Prep: 10 minutes   Cook: 45 minutes   Serves: 4

1 (1.15-ounce) package dry
  onion soup mix
½ cup dried bread crumbs
¼ cup tomato juice
¼ cup ketchup
1 egg
1 pound ground round
  (85% lean)
3 large russet potatoes (about
  1½ pounds), peeled and
  cut into 2-inch chunks

6 ounces cream cheese,
  softened
About ⅓ cup milk
¾ teaspoon salt
¼ teaspoon pepper
1 tablespoon chopped fresh
  chives or parsley

1. Preheat oven to 350°. In a medium bowl, combine soup mix, bread crumbs, tomato juice, ketchup, and egg. Add ground round and mix well. Pat into a thick shell in a 9-inch round pie plate.

2. Bake meat shell until cooked through, about 35 minutes. Let stand 5 minutes, then pour off excess fat.

3. Meanwhile, in a large saucepan of boiling salted water, cook potatoes until tender when pierced with tip of a sharp knife, about 12 minutes. Drain well.

4. In a medium bowl, mash warm potatoes with cream cheese, ⅓ cup milk, salt, and pepper. Add 1 to 2 tablespoons more milk, if necessary, to thin. Heap potatoes in center of meat pie, sprinkle with chives, and cut into wedges to serve.

---

215 QUICK CHILI BEEF CUPS
Prep: 5 minutes   Cook: 25 minutes   Serves: 4 to 6

1 small onion, finely chopped
1 small green bell pepper,
  finely chopped
⅓ cup plus 2 tablespoons chili
  sauce
⅓ cup rolled oats

1 egg
1 teaspoon chili powder
1 teaspoon garlic salt
1 pound ground round
  (85% lean)

1. Preheat oven to 375°. In a medium bowl, mix onion, bell pepper, ⅓ cup chili sauce, oats, egg, chili powder, and garlic salt. Add ground round and knead with your hands until blended. Divide meat mixture evenly among 6 muffin cups (about 2¾ inches in diameter and 1¼ inches deep) and smooth tops.

2. Bake 15 minutes. Spread 1 teaspoon remaining chili sauce over top of each chili beef cup. Bake until a meat thermometer inserted in center of a chili cup reads 165°, 10 to 15 minutes longer.

216   SKILLET SPANISH CHICKEN AND RICE
Prep: 10 minutes   Cook: 40 minutes   Serves: 4 to 5

1 tablespoon olive oil
1 pound ground chicken
1 medium onion, chopped
1 medium green bell pepper, chopped
2 celery ribs, chopped
2 garlic cloves, chopped
1 cup converted rice
½ cup reduced-sodium chicken broth

1 (28-ounce) can Italian peeled tomatoes, with their juice
1 teaspoon paprika
1½ teaspoons salt
½ teaspoon pepper
¼ teaspoon saffron threads, crushed
½ cup sliced pimiento-stuffed green olives

1. In a large skillet or flameproof casserole, heat olive oil. Add chicken, onion, bell pepper, celery, and garlic. Cook over medium heat, stirring often to break up lumps of meat, until chicken has lost its pink color, about 4 minutes.

2. Stir in rice, tomatoes with their juice, paprika, salt, pepper, and saffron. Bring to a simmer, breaking up tomatoes in skillet with a spoon. Reduce heat to low, cover tightly, and simmer until rice is tender, about 30 minutes. Stir in olives.

217   CHICKEN CHOW MEIN CASSEROLE
Prep: 15 minutes   Cook: 35 minutes   Serves: 4 to 6

Anyone who grew up in the Fifties will recognize the flavors in this casserole, updated to use ground chicken and spiked with a dash of sherry.

1 tablespoon vegetable oil
1½ pounds ground chicken or turkey
1 medium onion, chopped
2 celery ribs, sliced
1 small green bell pepper, chopped
1 (10¾-ounce) can cream of mushroom soup
1 (10¾-ounce) can cream of chicken soup

1 (8-ounce) can chopped water chestnuts, drained
2 tablespoons dry sherry
1 tablespoon soy sauce
¼ teaspoon pepper
2 cups cooked rice
1½ cups crispy chow mein noodles

1. Preheat oven to 350°. Heat oil in a large skillet. Add ground chicken, onion, celery, and bell pepper. Cook over medium heat, stirring often to break up lumps of meat, until chicken is no longer pink, about 5 minutes.

2. In a large bowl, combine chicken mixture, cream of mushroom soup, cream of chicken soup, water chestnuts, sherry, soy sauce, pepper, and ¼ cup water. Stir in rice. Transfer to a lightly buttered, deep, 2-quart casserole. Sprinkle noodles over top.

3. Bake casserole until bubbling, about 30 minutes.

218   CHICKEN CACCIATORE PIE
Prep: 10 minutes   Cook: 40 minutes   Serves: 4 to 6

1 (16-ounce) can Italian-
   flavored stewed tomatoes
1 small onion, chopped
1 small green bell pepper,
   chopped
1 garlic clove, minced
½ cup fresh bread crumbs
1 egg

1¼ teaspoons salt
1 teaspoon Italian seasoning
¼ teaspoon pepper
1½ pounds ground chicken
½ cup grated mozzarella
   cheese
3 tablespoons grated
   Parmesan cheese

1. Preheat oven to 350°. Drain stewed tomatoes in a sieve over a bowl, reserving ⅓ cup juice. Set stewed tomatoes aside.

2. In a medium bowl, combine reserved tomato juice, onion, bell pepper, garlic, bread crumbs, egg, salt, Italian seasoning, and pepper. Add ground chicken and mix well. With wet hands, pat mixture evenly into a lightly oiled 10-inch pie plate, pushing up sides to form a shell.

3. Bake 25 minutes. Drain off excess liquid. Sprinkle mozzarella over bottom of shell, then add a layer of stewed tomatoes. Sprinkle Parmesan over tomatoes.

4. Bake until chicken shell is cooked through, about 15 minutes. Let stand 5 minutes. Drain off excess liquid, then cut into wedges to serve.

219   GROUND CHICKEN AND DUMPLINGS SKILLET SUPPER
Prep: 5 minutes   Cook: 25 minutes   Serves: 4 to 6

1½ pounds ground chicken
1 small onion, chopped
1 (10-ounce) package frozen
   mixed vegetables, thawed
3 tablespoons flour
2 cups reduced-sodium
   chicken broth

¼ cup chopped parsley
¾ teaspoon poultry seasoning
½ teaspoon salt
¼ teaspoon pepper
1 cup dry buttermilk biscuit
   mix
⅓ cup milk

1. In a large skillet, cook ground chicken and onion over medium heat, stirring often to break up lumps of meat, until chicken loses its pink color, about 5 minutes. Drain off excess liquid.

2. Stir in mixed vegetables. Sprinkle on flour and cook, stirring, 1 minute. Add chicken broth, 2 tablespoons parsley, poultry seasoning, salt, and pepper. Bring to a simmer.

3. In a medium bowl, stir together biscuit mix, milk, and remaining 2 tablespoons parsley until a soft dough forms. Drop dough by heaping tablespoons on top of simmering mixture. Cook, uncovered, 10 minutes. Cover tightly and cook until dumplings are cooked through, about 10 minutes longer. Serve directly from skillet.

220 CHILEAN CHICKEN CASSEROLE WITH SPOONBREAD TOPPING

Prep: 20 minutes   Cook: 45 minutes   Serves: 4 to 6

2 pounds ground chicken
1 medium onion, chopped
1 garlic, minced
1 (14-ounce) can Italian peeled tomatoes, drained
1½ teaspoons salt
1½ teaspoons ground cumin
1 teaspoon paprika
¼ teaspoon crushed hot red pepper
½ cup sliced ripe olives

¼ cup raisins
2 hard-boiled eggs, sliced
2 cups fresh, canned, or thawed frozen corn kernels
1 tablespoon flour
1 tablespoon milk
2 tablespoons butter
2 eggs
1 teaspoon sugar

1. In a large skillet, cook chicken, onion, and garlic over medium heat, stirring often to break up lumps of meat, until chicken loses its pink color, about 5 minutes. Drain off excess liquid. Stir in tomatoes, salt, cumin, paprika, and hot pepper. Cook, breaking up tomatoes in skillet with a spoon, 2 minutes. Stir in olives and raisins.

2. In a round 1½-quart baking dish or soufflé dish, spread half of chicken mixture. Arrange hard-boiled eggs on top and cover with remaining chicken mixture.

3. In a blender, process corn, flour, and milk until smooth. In a small saucepan, melt butter over low heat; stir in corn mixture. Cook, stirring constantly, until thickened, about 2 minutes.

4. In a small bowl, whisk eggs. Gradually whisk hot corn mixture into eggs. Spread corn topping evenly over chicken and sprinkle sugar evenly over top. Bake until topping is golden brown and set, 30 to 40 minutes.

221 CHICKEN TAMALE PIE IN HOMINY GRITS SHELL

Prep: 15 minutes   Cook: 1¼ hours   Serves: 4 to 6

1 tablespoon olive oil
1 pound ground chicken
1 small onion, chopped
1 small green bell pepper, chopped
2 garlic cloves, minced
1 tablespoon chili powder
1 (14-ounce) can peeled Italian tomatoes, chopped, juices reserved

1 cup tomato sauce
½ teaspoon salt
¾ cup hominy grits (not instant)
½ cup shredded Cheddar cheese
2 tablespoons butter
¼ teaspoon garlic salt
1 egg, beaten

1. Preheat oven to 350°. In a large skillet, heat olive oil. Add ground chicken, chopped onion, bell pepper, and garlic. Cook over medium heat, stirring often to break up lumps, until chicken loses its pink color, about 5 minutes. Add chili powder and cook, stirring, 1 minute. Add tomatoes with their juice, tomato sauce, and salt. Bring to a simmer, reduce heat to medium-low, and simmer until thickened, about 30 minutes. Remove from heat and let cool.

2. Meanwhile, in a medium saucepan, bring 3½ cups water to a boil over high heat. Gradually stir grits into water. Reduce heat to low and simmer, uncovered, stirring often, until very thick, about 20 minutes. Stir in Cheddar cheese, butter, and garlic salt. Spread grits mixture evenly into a lightly buttered 10-inch pie plate to make a thick shell.

3. Stir the egg into the cooled chicken chili, then spoon chili into grits shell. Bake until grits shell is lightly browned, 15 to 20 minutes.

222 SLOPPY TOMS

Prep: 10 minutes   Cook: 10 minutes   Serves: 4

1 tablespoon vegetable oil
1 small onion, chopped
1 small green bell pepper, chopped
1 celery rib, chopped
1 pound ground turkey

¾ cup chili sauce
1 teaspoon Worcestershire sauce
½ teaspoon garlic salt
¼ teaspoon pepper
4 hamburger buns, toasted

1. In a large skillet, heat oil over medium heat. Add onion, bell pepper, and celery and cook, stirring often, until vegetables are softened, about 4 minutes.

2. Add turkey and cook, stirring often to break up lumps of meat, until turkey loses its pink color, about 3 minutes.

3. Add chili sauce, Worcestershire, garlic salt, and pepper. Cook, stirring often, until thickened, 1 to 2 minutes. Serve on toasted hamburger buns.

223 UPSIDE-DOWN PIZZA PIE WITH BUTTERMILK BISCUIT CRUST

Prep: 15 minutes   Cook: 25 minutes   Serves: 4 to 6

½ pound ground turkey
½ pound sweet Italian turkey
   sausage, casings
   removed, crumbled
1 medium onion, chopped
1 medium zucchini, cut into
   ½-inch dice
1 garlic clove, minced
1 cup tomato sauce

2 teaspoons Italian seasoning
¼ teaspoon crushed hot red
   pepper
1 cup shredded mozzarella
   cheese (4 ounces)
1 cup dry buttermilk biscuit
   mix
⅓ cup grated Parmesan cheese
   About ⅓ cup milk

1. Preheat oven to 425°. In a large ovenproof skillet, cook ground turkey, turkey sausage, onion, zucchini, and garlic over medium-high heat, stirring often to break up lumps of meat, until turkey loses its pink color, about 5 minutes.

2. Add tomato sauce, Italian seasoning, and hot pepper. Bring to a simmer, remove from heat, and stir in ½ cup mozzarella.

3. In a medium bowl, combine biscuit mix and Parmesan cheese. Add just enough milk to form a soft dough. On a lightly floured work surface, roll out to a 9-inch circle. Place dough over filling in skillet and sprinkle remaining ½ cup mozzarella cheese on top.

4. Bake until crust is golden brown, about 20 minutes. Cut into wedges and spoon out crust and filling directly from skillet.

224 STUFFING-STUFFED TURKEY PIE

Prep: 10 minutes   Cook: 45 minutes   Serves: 4 to 6

1 (7-ounce) package dry herb-
   seasoned stuffing mix
¼ cup milk
1 egg
1 teaspoon salt
¼ teaspoon pepper
1½ pounds ground turkey
1 tablespoon butter

1 small onion, chopped
1 medium celery rib, chopped
1 medium Granny Smith
   apple, peeled and
   chopped
½ cup reduced-sodium
   chicken broth

1. Preheat oven to 350°. Crush ½ cup stuffing; reserve remaining stuffing. In a medium bowl, combine crushed stuffing, milk, egg, salt, and pepper. Add ground turkey and mix well. Spread turkey mixture evenly in a 9-inch pie plate.

2. In a medium skillet, melt butter. Add onion, celery, and apple and cook over medium heat, stirring often, until onion is softened, about 4 minutes. Add chicken broth and bring to a boil.

3. In a medium bowl, combine remaining stuffing and broth mixture. Mix until moistened evenly. Spoon stuffing into turkey shell.

4. Bake until stuffing is browned and turkey shell is cooked through, about 40 minutes. Let stand 5 minutes. Drain off excess liquid and cut into wedges to serve.

---

225 POTATO PIE WITH TURKEY RAGU FILLING
Prep: 30 minutes   Cook: 1¼ hours   Serves: 6 to 8

1½	pounds red potatoes, peeled	1 medium onion, chopped
¼	cup grated Parmesan cheese	1 garlic clove, minced
3	tablespoons butter	1 cup tomato sauce
1	teaspoon salt	1 teaspoon Italian seasoning
½	teaspoon pepper	1 egg
¼	cup dried bread crumbs	¼ cup shredded mozzarella
1½	pounds ground turkey	cheese

1. Preheat oven to 350°. In a large saucepan of boiling salted water, cook potatoes until tender when pierced with the point of a sharp knife, about 20 minutes. Drain well. Mash potatoes with Parmesan cheese, 2 tablespoons butter, ½ teaspoon salt, and ¼ teaspoon pepper.

2. Coat inside of a 9-inch pie plate with remaining 1 tablespoon butter. Add bread crumbs and shake pie plate to coat well. Spread mashed potatoes evenly in prepared pan to form a thick shell. Bake pie shell until beginning to brown, about 20 minutes.

3. Meanwhile, in a large skillet, cook ground turkey, onion, and garlic over medium-high heat, stirring often to break up lumps of meat, until turkey loses its pink color, about 5 minutes. Drain off excess liquid. Stir in tomato sauce, Italian seasoning, and remaining ½ teaspoon salt and ¼ teaspoon pepper. Bring to a simmer, reduce heat to low, and simmer until thickened, about 15 minutes.

4. In a medium bowl, beat egg. Gradually stir all of turkey mixture into egg. Mound turkey mixture in potato shell. Bake until filling is hot and shell is golden brown, 15 to 20 minutes. Sprinkle mozzarella over top and return to oven until cheese melts, 1 to 2 minutes. Let stand 5 minutes before cutting into wedges to serve.

226   TURKEY TORTILLA CASSEROLE
Prep: 15 minutes   Cook: 40 minutes   Serves: 6 to 8

1½ pounds ground turkey
1 medium onion, chopped
1 garlic clove, minced
2 scallions, chopped
½ teaspoon ground cumin
1 (10¾-ounce) can cream of
   mushroom soup
1½ cups tomato salsa
1 (4-ounce) can diced green
   chiles

1 (3½-ounce) can sliced black
   olives, drained
12 corn tortillas, torn into
   2-inch pieces
1 cup shredded Cheddar
   cheese (4 ounces)
1 cup shredded Monterey Jack
   cheese (4 ounces)
½ cup reduced-sodium
   chicken broth

1. Preheat oven to 350°. In a large skillet, cook ground turkey, onion, and garlic over medium-high heat, stirring often to break up lumps of meat, until turkey loses its pink color, about 5 minutes. Stir in scallions and cumin.

2. In a medium bowl, whisk together soup, salsa, chiles, and olives. In a lightly oiled 9 x 13-inch baking dish, layer half of tortillas. Top with half of turkey mixture, then half of soup mixture. Sprinkle on ½ cup each Cheddar and Jack cheeses. Repeat layers.

3. Bake casserole until bubbling, about 35 minutes. Let stand 5 minutes before cutting into squares to serve.

227   SOUTHWESTERN TURKEY CORNBREAD BAKE
Prep: 10 minutes   Cook: 30 minutes   Serves: 4

1 tablespoon olive oil
1 pound ground turkey
1 medium onion, chopped
1 (10-ounce) can mild
   enchilada sauce
1 (11-ounce) can Mexicorn
   (whole kernel corn with
   red and green peppers),
   drained
1 cup shredded Cheddar
   cheese (4 ounces)

½ cup flour
2 tablespoons yellow
   cornmeal
¾ teaspoon baking powder
¼ teaspoon salt
½ cup milk
1 egg
1 tablespoon vegetable oil

1. Preheat oven to 400°. In a large ovenproof skillet, heat olive oil. Add ground turkey and onion and cook over medium-high heat, stirring often to break up lumps of meat, until turkey loses its pink color, about 5 minutes. Stir in enchilada sauce and Mexicorn. Bring to a simmer. Sprinkle ½ cup Cheddar cheese over turkey mixture.

2. In a medium bowl, whisk together flour, cornmeal, baking powder, and salt. In a small bowl, whisk together milk, egg, and vegetable oil. Whisk liquids into flour mixture just until smooth. Stir in remaining ½ cup cheese. Pour batter evenly over meat mixture, leaving a 1-inch border around edges.

3. Bake 20 minutes, or until light golden brown. Cut into wedges to serve.

---

228 TRANSYLVANIAN PORK AND SAUERKRAUT BAKE

Prep: 30 minutes   Cook: 1 hour 50 minutes   Serves: 8

2 pounds sauerkraut, fresh or bottled, not canned
½ cup converted rice
6 slices of bacon, cut into 1-inch pieces
1 pound kielbasa or other smoked sausage, sliced 1 inch thick
1 pound ground pork
2 medium onions, chopped

2 garlic cloves, minced
2 teaspoons paprika
2 teaspoons caraway seeds
1¼ teaspoons salt
½ teaspoon pepper
1 cup sour cream
1 (14-ounce) can Italian peeled tomatoes, cut up, juices reserved

1. Preheat oven to 350°. In a large bowl, soak sauerkraut in cold water to cover 10 minutes. Drain, rinse well under cold water, and drain again. One handful at a time, squeeze out excess liquid from sauerkraut.

2. In a medium saucepan of lightly salted boiling water, cook rice 10 minutes. Drain, rinse under cold water, and drain again; set aside.

3. In a large skillet, cook bacon and kielbasa over medium-high heat, turning often, until bacon is crisp, about 5 minutes. With a slotted spoon, transfer bacon and kielbasa to paper towels to drain. Pour off all but 1 tablespoon fat from skillet.

4. Add ground pork, onions, and garlic to skillet and cook, stirring often to break up lumps of meat, until pork loses its pink color, about 5 minutes. Pour off excess fat. Add paprika, caraway seeds, salt, and pepper. Cook, stirring, 1 minute; remove from heat.

5. In a lightly oiled, deep 2-quart casserole, spread a third of sauerkraut. Layer on half of pork mixture, half of rice, and then ½ cup sour cream. Top with half of remaining sauerkraut, then repeat layers of pork, rice, and sour cream. Cover with remaining sauerkraut. Pour cut-up tomatoes with juice over all.

6. Cover tightly and bake 1 hour. Uncover and bake until casserole is bubbling, about 30 minutes. Let stand 10 minutes before serving.

229   AUSTRIAN PORK AND NOODLE BAKE
Prep: 20 minutes   Cook: 1 hour   Serves: 6 to 8

1 pound wide egg noodles	½ teaspoon pepper
5 tablespoons butter	1 cup sour cream
3 medium onions, chopped	5 eggs
1½ pounds ground pork	¼ cup chopped parsley
2 garlic cloves, minced	2 tablespoons poppy seeds
1½ teaspoons salt	¾ cup fresh bread crumbs

1. In a large saucepan of boiling salted water, cook noodles until just tender, about 8 minutes. Drain well.

2. Preheat oven to 350°. In a large skillet or flameproof casserole, melt 3 tablespoons butter over medium-high heat. Add onions, and cook, stirring often, until lightly browned, 8 to 10 minutes. Add ground pork and garlic and cook, stirring often to break up lumps of meat, until pork loses its pink color, about 5 minutes. Drain off excess fat. Stir in 1 teaspoon salt and ¼ teaspoon pepper.

3. In a large bowl, whisk together sour cream, eggs, parsley, poppy seeds, remaining ½ teaspoon salt, and ¼ teaspoon pepper. Add noodles and pork mixture, and stir and toss to mix. Spread evenly in a well-buttered 9 x 13-inch baking dish. Sprinkle bread crumbs over top and dot with remaining 2 tablespoons butter.

4. Bake until center is set and top is browned, about 45 minutes. Let stand 5 minutes before cutting into squares to serve.

230   RIVIERA CASSEROLE
Prep: 15 minutes   Cook: 50 minutes   Serves: 6 to 8

¾ cup converted rice	4 medium zucchini, cut into
1½ pounds ground pork	½-inch-thick slices
1 garlic clove, minced	1 large onion, sliced
1¼ teaspoons salt	⅛ teaspoon black pepper
½ teaspoon marjoram	½ cup grated Parmesan cheese
¼ teaspoon fennel seed	1 (28-ounce) can Italian peeled
¼ teaspoon crushed hot red	tomatoes, with their juice
pepper	1 teaspoon basil

1. In a medium saucepan of boiling salted water, cook rice 10 minutes. Drain, rinse under cold water, and drain again.

2. In a large skillet, cook ground pork and garlic over medium-high heat, stirring often to break up lumps of meat, until pork loses its pink color, about 5 minutes. Season with ¾ teaspoon salt, marjoram, fennel, and hot pepper. Using a slotted spoon, transfer meat mixture to a bowl, leaving fat in skillet.

3. In same skillet, cook zucchini and onion with remaining ½ teaspoon salt and black pepper over medium-high heat, stirring often, until crisp-tender, about 5 minutes.

4. In a lightly oiled 9 x 13-inch baking dish, layer half of pork, half of rice, half of zucchini and onions, and ¼ cup Parmesan cheese. Continue layering with remaining pork, rice, and zucchini.

5. In a medium bowl, combine tomatoes with their juice and basil, breaking up tomatoes well with a spoon. Pour tomato mixture over casserole and sprinkle remaining ¼ cup Parmesan cheese over top.

6. Bake until casserole is bubbling, about 30 minutes. Let stand 5 minutes before serving.

---

231 VEAL ROLLS WITH HERBED PORK STUFFING

Prep: 15 minutes   Cook: 15 minutes   Serves: 4

8 thinly sliced veal scallops (about 1 pound)	½ teaspoon salt
¾ pound ground pork	¼ teaspoon pepper
¾ cup fresh bread crumbs	3 tablespoons olive oil
⅓ cup grated Parmesan cheese	½ cup dry Marsala
2 tablespoons minced onion	½ cup beef broth
2 tablespoons chopped fresh basil or 1 teaspoon dried	1 tablespoon lemon juice
1 garlic clove, minced	3 tablespoons cold butter, cut into 3 pieces

1. Pound veal scallops between 2 sheets of moistened wax paper until evenly flattened ¼-inch thick.

2. In a medium bowl, combine ground pork, bread crumbs, Parmesan cheese, onion, basil, garlic, ¼ teaspoon salt, and ⅛ teaspoon pepper. Place 3 tablespoons pork mixture in center of each cutlet. Fold in sides and roll up into a cylinder. Fasten each roll lengthwise with a wooden toothpick. Season veal rolls with remaining ¼ teaspoon salt and ⅛ teaspoon pepper.

3. In a large skillet, heat olive oil. Add veal rolls in batches if necessary, and cook over medium-high heat, turning often, until lightly browned, about 6 minutes. Drain off excess fat.

4. Add Marsala, beef broth, and lemon juice. Bring to a boil; reduce heat to low, and simmer, covered, until veal rolls are cooked through, about 10 minutes. Transfer veal rolls to a heated serving platter and cover with foil to keep warm.

5. Off heat, whisk butter into sauce, 1 piece at a time. Pour sauce over veal rolls and serve.

232   PORK AND PEPPER FRITTATA
Prep: 10 minutes   Cook: 14 to 16 minutes   Serves: 6

1 tablespoon olive oil	¾ teaspoon salt
1 medium onion, sliced	⅛ teaspoon crushed hot red
1 medium red bell pepper,	pepper
chopped	6 eggs
½ pound ground pork	¼ teaspoon black pepper
1 garlic clove, minced	3 tablespoons grated
1 teaspoon basil	Parmesan cheese

1. Arrange a broiling rack about 6 inches from source of heat and preheat broiler. In a 9-inch flameproof nonstick or well-seasoned cast-iron skillet, heat oil over medium heat. Add onion and pepper and cook, stirring often, until onion is lightly browned, about 5 minutes. Add ground pork and garlic. Cook, stirring often to break up lumps of meat, until pork loses its pink color, about 5 minutes. Drain off excess fat. Stir in basil, ½ teaspoon salt, and hot pepper.

2. In a medium bowl, whisk eggs with remaining ¼ teaspoon salt, and black pepper until foamy. Pour eggs into skillet, and reduce heat to medium-low. With a spatula, lift up cooked portion of eggs, tilting pan to allow uncooked eggs to run underneath. Continue cooking in this manner until eggs are mostly set, but top is still shiny, about 3 minutes.

3. Sprinkle Parmesan cheese over top of frittata. Broil until frittata is puffed and golden brown, 1 to 2 minutes.

233   ROMAN HOLIDAY SKILLET SUPPER
Prep: 10 minutes   Cook: 40 minutes   Serves: 4 to 6

1 pound ground pork	¼ teaspoon sage
1 medium onion, chopped	¼ teaspoon salt
1 garlic clove, minced	¼ teaspoon crushed hot red
8 ounces penne or other	pepper
tubular pasta	1 (19-ounce) can cannellini
1 (13½-ounce) jar marinara	beans, drained and rinsed
sauce	1 cup shredded mozzarella
1¾ cups beef broth	cheese (4 ounces)
¼ teaspoon fennel seed	

1. In a 12-inch skillet, cook ground pork, onion, and garlic over medium-high heat, stirring often, until pork loses all traces of pink, about 5 minutes. Drain off excess fat.

2. Stir in penne, marinara sauce, beef broth, fennel, sage, salt, hot pepper, and ½ cup water. Bring to a boil, reduce heat to low, and cover skillet tightly.

3. Simmer, stirring often to avoid scorching, until penne is tender and liquid is almost evaporated, 25 to 30 minutes. Stir in cannellini beans and sprinkle mozzarella over top. Cover and cook until cheese is melted and beans are heated through, about 3 minutes.

---

234 ROMANIAN GROUND VEAL AND POTATO CASSEROLE

Prep: 15 minutes   Cook: 1 hour   Serves: 6 to 8

1¾ teaspoons salt
½ teaspoon pepper
3 to 5 tablespoons vegetable oil
4 pounds russet potatoes, peeled and sliced ¼-inch thick
2 pounds ground veal
2 large onions, chopped
1 large green bell pepper, chopped
2 garlic cloves, minced

3 tablespoons flour
½ cup dry white wine
2 teaspoons thyme
¼ teaspoon fennel seed, crushed
4 eggs
⅓ cup chopped parsley
3 tablespoons butter, softened
2 tablespoons fresh bread crumbs
1 cup heavy cream
½ cup grated Parmesan cheese

1. In a small bowl, mix together 1 teaspoon salt and ¼ teaspoon pepper. In a large skillet, heat 3 tablespoons oil. In 3 batches, cook potato slices over medium-high heat, sprinkling each batch with a third of salt and pepper mixture and turning often until potatoes are lightly browned and opaque, about 5 minutes per batch. Add additional oil as needed. Transfer potatoes to a paper towel–lined baking sheet to drain.

2. Preheat oven to 400°. In a large skillet, cook ground veal, onions, pepper, and garlic over medium-high heat, stirring often to break up meat, until veal loses its pink color, about 5 minutes. Stir in flour. Cook, stirring without browning, 1 to 2 minutes. Stir in wine, thyme, fennel, and remaining ¾ teaspoon salt and ¼ teaspoon pepper. Bring to a simmer, reduce heat to medium-low, and simmer, stirring often, until sauce thickens, about 3 minutes; let cool slightly. In a small bowl, lightly beat 2 eggs with a fork. Gradually beat in about 1 cup of veal mixture and return to skillet. Stir in parsley.

3. Using 1 tablespoon butter, grease 9 x 13-inch baking dish. Dust with bread crumbs to coat. Arrange a third of potatoes, overlapping slightly, in baking dish; cover with half of veal filling. Top with half of remaining potatoes. Layer on remaining veal filling and then remaining potatoes. Dot top of potatoes with 2 tablespoons butter.

4. Bake, uncovered, 30 minutes. In a medium bowl, whisk together cream, remaining 2 eggs, and Parmesan cheese. Pour cream mixture over casserole and bake until top is set and deep golden brown, 15 to 20 minutes. Let casserole stand 10 minutes before serving.

235 VEAL CRESPELLE PARMIGIANA
Prep: 40 minutes   Stand: 30 minutes   Cook: 2 hours   Serves: 6

1 pound ground veal
1 small onion, finely chopped
⅓ cup dry white wine
¼ cup heavy cream
1 (28-ounce) can Italian peeled tomatoes, drained
1 teaspoon basil
¾ teaspoon salt
¼ teaspoon pepper
1 cup fresh or thawed frozen peas

½ cup grated Parmesan cheese
2 tablespoons bread crumbs
4 tablespoons butter
¼ cup flour
2 cups milk
¼ teaspoon grated nutmeg
Quick Crepes (recipe follows)

1. In a medium saucepan, cook ground veal and onion over medium heat, stirring often to break up lumps of meat, until veal loses its pink color, about 5 minutes.

2. Add wine, increase heat to high, and boil until wine has almost evaporated, about 5 minutes. Add cream and boil until cream has evaporated to about 1 tablespoon, about 5 minutes. Add tomatoes, basil, ¼ teaspoon salt, and pepper. Bring to a boil, breaking up tomatoes in pan with a large spoon. Reduce heat to low and simmer until sauce is thickened, about 1 hour. Remove from heat and stir in peas, ¼ cup Parmesan cheese, and bread crumbs.

3. In a heavy medium saucepan, melt butter over medium-low heat. Whisk in flour and cook, stirring, 2 minutes without letting mixture brown. Whisk in milk, remaining ½ teaspoon salt, and nutmeg. Bring to a boil, whisking until smooth and thick. Reduce heat to low and simmer, stirring often, 5 minutes. Remove from heat and whisk in remaining ¼ cup Parmesan cheese.

4. Preheat oven to 350°. Lightly butter a 9 x 13-inch baking dish. Spread a thin layer of Parmesan sauce over bottom of dish. Place about ¼ cup of veal filling across center of 1 crepe, roll up, and transfer to baking dish. Repeat procedure with remaining crepes and filling. Spread remaining sauce over filled crepes.

5. Bake until top is lightly browned and sauce is bubbling, about 35 minutes. Let stand 5 minutes before serving.

QUICK CREPES
Makes about 12 crepes

1 cup instant-blending flour, such as Wondra
1 egg

½ teaspoon salt
1½ cups milk
Vegetable cooking spray

1. In a blender, combine flour, egg, and salt. With machine on, add milk in a stream. Blend until smooth, scraping down sides of blender jar if necessary, about 30 seconds. Let stand until batter is slightly thickened, about 30 minutes.

2. Spray an 8-inch nonstick skillet with vegetable cooking spray and heat over medium-high heat. Pour about ¼ cup batter into skillet and quickly swirl so batter coats bottom of skillet. Cook until underside of crepe is lightly browned, about 1 minute. Turn and cook other side until lightly browned, about 1 minute. Transfer crepe to a plate. Repeat procedure with remaining batter, spraying skillet with vegetable cooking spray each time before adding batter to skillet. Stack cooked crepes, separating them with sheets of wax paper. (Crepes can be prepared up to 1 day ahead, wrapped tightly in plastic, and refrigerated for up to 2 days or frozen for up to 1 month. Defrost thoroughly before using.)

236 VEAL, BROCCOLI, AND PASTA CASSEROLE

Prep: 15 minutes   Cook: 1 hour   Serves: 4 to 6

1 bunch of broccoli, cut into florets	1½ cups milk
12 ounces ziti or other tubular pasta	1 teaspoon salt
	¼ teaspoon crushed hot red pepper
3 tablespoons butter	⅛ teaspoon grated nutmeg
1 pound ground veal	1 cup shredded Cheddar cheese (4 ounces)
1 small onion, chopped	
2 garlic cloves, minced	1 cup fresh bread crumbs
3 tablespoons flour	3 tablespoons grated Parmesan cheese
1 teaspoon thyme	
1½ cups reduced-sodium chicken broth	

1. Preheat oven to 375°. In a large saucepan of boiling salted water, cook broccoli over high heat until crisp-tender, about 3 minutes. Using a large skimmer or a slotted spoon, transfer broccoli to a colander. Rinse under cold running water and drain well. Place broccoli in a buttered, deep, 3-quart casserole.

2. In same saucepan of boiling salted water, cook ziti over high heat until barely tender, about 9 minutes. Drain, rinse under cold water, and drain again. Add to broccoli in casserole.

3. In a large skillet, heat 2 tablespoons butter. Add ground veal, onion, and garlic and cook over medium-high heat, stirring often to break up lumps of meat, until veal loses its pink color, about 5 minutes. Sprinkle on flour and thyme. Cook without browning, stirring often, 2 minutes. Stir in chicken broth, milk, salt, hot pepper, and nutmeg. Bring to a boil, whisking until thick. Reduce heat to low and cook, stirring often, 3 minutes. Remove from heat, add Cheddar cheese, and stir until melted. Add veal-cheese sauce to casserole and toss to combine. Sprinkle bread crumbs and Parmesan cheese over top and dot with remaining butter.

4. Bake until casserole is bubbling and top is golden brown, about 30 minutes.

237 SWEDISH LAMB AND POTATO PUDDING
Prep: 15 minutes   Cook: 1 hour 35 minutes   Serves: 4 to 6

3 medium russet potatoes
(about 1½ pounds),
peeled and cut into 1-inch
chunks
1½ pounds lean ground lamb
1 small onion, finely chopped
3 tablespoons chopped fresh
dill or 2 teaspoons dried

2 tablespoons flour
1 egg
¼ teaspoon grated nutmeg
2 teaspoons salt
½ teaspoon pepper
1 cup heavy cream
2 tablespoons butter, cut up
¼ cup fresh bread crumbs

1. In a large saucepan of boiling salted water, cook potatoes until just tender when pierced with tip of a sharp knife, about 15 minutes. Drain well and mash until smooth.

2. Preheat oven to 300°. In a large bowl, combine mashed potatoes, ground lamb, onion, dill, flour, egg, nutmeg, salt, and pepper. Gradually stir in heavy cream until absorbed.

3. Generously coat inside of a 1½-quart casserole with 1 tablespoon butter. Dust inside with 2 tablespoons bread crumbs; shake out excess. Transfer meat mixture to prepared casserole. Sprinkle remaining 2 tablespoons bread crumbs over top of casserole and dot with remaining butter.

4. Bake until a meat thermometer inserted in center of pudding reads 160°, about 1 hour 20 minutes. Let stand 10 minutes before spooning out to serve.

238 MRS. SOUERS' SLUMGULLION
Prep: 10 minutes   Cook: 18 to 21 minutes   Serves: 4

8 ounces wide egg noodles
1 pound ground round
(85% lean)
1 medium onion, chopped
1 medium green bell pepper,
chopped

1 garlic clove, minced
1 (32-ounce) can tomato-
vegetable juice,
such as V-8
1 cup sour cream

1. In a large pot of boiling salted water, partially cook egg noodles until just softened, about 5 minutes. Drain well.

2. In a large skillet, cook ground round, onion, bell pepper, and garlic over medium-high heat, stirring often to break up lumps of meat, until beef loses its pink color, about 5 minutes. Drain off excess fat. Add tomato-vegetable juice and drained noodles.

3. Bring to a boil, reduce heat to low, cover, and simmer, stirring often, until noodles are tender and liquid is almost completely absorbed, 7 to 10 minutes. Stir in sour cream and cook, without allowing to boil, just until heated through, about 1 minute.

239 LAMB AND OKRA SUPPER
Prep: 10 minutes   Cook: 40 minutes   Serves: 4

2 tablespoons vegetable oil
1 medium onion, chopped
1 medium green bell pepper, chopped
1 medium celery rib, chopped
1 garlic clove, minced
1 pound lean ground lamb
1 teaspoon thyme
1 teaspoon oregano
½ teaspoon basil
1 teaspoon salt
⅛ teaspoon cayenne

1 bay leaf
1 (35-ounce) can Italian peeled tomatoes, coarsely chopped, juices reserved
1 tablespoon Worcestershire sauce
1 (10-ounce) package frozen cut okra, thawed
Hot cooked rice
2 scallions, chopped
¼ cup chopped roasted peanuts

1. In a large skillet, heat oil. Add onion, bell pepper, celery, and garlic. Cook over medium heat, stirring, until onion is softened, about 5 minutes. Add ground lamb and increase heat to medium-high. Cook, stirring often to break up lumps of meat, until lamb loses its pink color, about 5 minutes. Drain off excess fat.

2. Season lamb mixture with thyme, oregano, basil, salt, and cayenne. Add bay leaf and cook, stirring, 1 minute. Add tomatoes with their juice and Worcestershire. Bring to a boil, reduce heat to low, and simmer, uncovered, stirring occasionally, 20 minutes.

3. Add okra and cook 10 minutes longer, or until thickened. Discard bay leaf. Serve over bowls of hot rice, garnished with scallions and peanuts.

240 LAMB PILAF
Prep: 10 minutes   Cook: 20 minutes   Serves: 4 to 6

1 pound lean ground lamb
1 medium onion, chopped
1 garlic clove, minced
1½ cups converted rice
¼ cup pine nuts (pignoli)
1 (13¾-ounce) can beef broth

¼ cup chopped parsley
½ teaspoon salt
¼ teaspoon ground allspice
¼ teaspoon pepper
¼ cup grated Parmesan cheese

1. In a large skillet, cook ground lamb, onion, and garlic over medium-high heat, stirring often to break up lumps of meat, until lamb loses its pink color, about 5 minutes. Stir in rice and pine nuts. Cook, stirring, until rice turns opaque, about 2 minutes.

2. Stir in beef broth, parsley, salt, allspice, pepper, and ¾ cup water. Bring to a boil, reduce heat to low, cover, and simmer until rice is tender and liquid is absorbed, about 15 minutes. Sprinkle Parmesan cheese over top.

241 OLD WORLD MOUSSAKA

Prep: 20 minutes   Stand: 1 hour   Cook: 1½ hours   Serves: 8

Eggplant slices are broiled rather than fried here to make a lighter dish. The contemporary-sounding, golden brown yogurt topping is an authentic touch.

2 **medium eggplants (about 2 pounds)**	1 **(6-ounce) can tomato paste**
2 **teaspoons salt**	½ **cup dry red wine**
¼ **cup olive oil**	2 **teaspoons oregano**
2 **pounds lean ground lamb**	¼ **teaspoon ground allspice**
1 **medium onion, chopped**	¼ **teaspoon pepper**
2 **garlic cloves, minced**	½ **cup grated Parmesan cheese**
1 **(28-ounce) can Italian peeled tomatoes, with their juice**	2 **tablespoons bread crumbs**
	2 **cups plain low-fat yogurt**
	4 **eggs**

1. Cut eggplant crosswise into ¼-inch-thick slices. Sprinkle slices lightly with salt. Place in a large colander and let stand 1 hour. Rinse well and pat dry with paper towels.

2. Position a broiler rack about 4 inches from source of heat and preheat broiler. Brush each side of eggplant slices with olive oil. In batches, broil slices, turning once, until lightly browned, about 4 minutes per side.

3. Meanwhile, in a large Dutch oven, cook ground lamb, onion, and garlic over medium-high heat, stirring often to break up lumps of meat, until lamb loses its pink color, about 5 minutes. Drain off excess fat.

4. Add tomatoes with their juice, tomato paste, red wine, oregano, allspice, and pepper; break up tomatoes with a large spoon. Bring to a boil, reduce heat to low, and simmer, stirring often, until thickened, about 30 minutes. Remove from heat and stir in ¼ cup Parmesan cheese

5. Preheat oven to 350°. Sprinkle bread crumbs over bottom of a lightly oiled 9 x 13-inch baking dish. Arrange a layer of overlapping eggplant slices in bottom of dish. Cover with lamb mixture. Top with remaining eggplant slices. In a small bowl, whisk together yogurt and eggs. Spread yogurt mixture evenly over eggplant and sprinkle remaining ¼ cup Parmesan cheese on top.

6. Bake until yogurt topping is set and golden brown, about 45 minutes. Let stand 10 minutes before cutting into squares to serve.

242 PROVENÇAL SKILLET SUPPER
Prep: 10 minutes   Cook: 35 minutes   Serves: 6 to 8

1 pound lean ground lamb or
    ground round (85% lean)
1 medium onion, chopped
1 garlic clove, minced
10 ounces linguine, preferably
    spinach linguine, broken
    into 1½-inch lengths
    (2½ cups)
1 (28-ounce) can Italian peeled
    tomatoes, with their juice
2 medium zucchini, sliced
    into ¼-inch rounds

1 cup tomato sauce
½ teaspoon basil
½ teaspoon thyme
½ teaspoon rosemary
¼ teaspoon salt
¼ teaspoon pepper
½ cup pitted black olives,
    chopped
Grated Parmesan cheese

1. In a nonreactive 12-inch skillet or flameproof casserole, cook ground lamb, onion, and garlic over medium-high heat, stirring often to break up lumps of meat, until lamb is no longer pink, about 5 minutes. Drain off excess fat.

2. Stir in linguine, tomatoes with their juice, zucchini, tomato sauce, basil, thyme, rosemary, salt, pepper, and 1½ cups water. Bring to a simmer, reduce heat to low, and cover. Cook, stirring often to avoid scorching, until linguine is tender, about 25 minutes. Sprinkle with olives and pass a bowl of grated Parmesan cheese on the side.

Chapter 9

Dinner Against the Clock

One of the most important reasons for ground meat's enduring popularity is its talent for making flavorful meals fast. Bring home a pound of ground meat, and there is very little fussing: no marinating or braising to tenderize, no trimming of extraneous fat and bones, no pounding to a proper thickness. Ground meats can be pan-fried, broiled, baked, simmered, microwaved, or grilled—whatever suits your fancy and your schedule.

All of the recipes in this chapter can be prepared in 20 minutes or less, including preparation. Even though they are short in cooking time, they are long on flavor, and many are complete one-dish meals.

Gingery Beef Fried Rice utilizes leftover rice, ground round, fresh ginger, and vegetables to whip up supper in a flash. Teacher's Thai Beef Salad is refreshing and light, with the tartness of lime juice and zing of hot pepper. Chicken Burgers au Poivre, with its quick Cognac sauce, is a speedy dish suitable for entertaining. And Crunchy Chinese Chicken in Lettuce Cups is as good as anything you could order from a take-out restaurant

Did you know how stir-frying originated? As Chinese cooks of the past had very little fuel available, they devised dishes that cooked quickly in a burst of heat. Stir-frying gave doubly successful results, not only producing tasty dishes, but conserving valuable energy. This chapter has its share of stir-fry recipes, such as Ground Chicken Chop Suey and Gingery Beef Fried Rice, to use when cooking against the clock.

243 GINGERY BEEF FRIED RICE

Prep: 10 minutes   Cook: 6 minutes   Serves: 2 to 4

Here's another opportunity to recycle leftovers. Be sure that your leftover rice is cold, or the grains won't separate properly.

2 tablespoons soy sauce	1 medium carrot, finely
½ teaspoon sugar	chopped
¼ teaspoon salt	1 celery rib, finely chopped
¼ teaspoon pepper	1 scallion, chopped
2 tablespoons vegetable oil	1 teaspoon minced fresh
2 eggs, well beaten	ginger
½ pound ground round	1 garlic clove, minced
(85% lean)	2 cups cold cooked rice

1. In a small bowl, combine soy sauce, sugar, salt, and pepper; set aside. In a large skillet, heat oil. Add eggs and cook over medium heat, stirring constantly, until eggs are soft-set, about 45 seconds. Transfer eggs to a bowl and set aside.

2. Add ground round, carrot, celery, and scallion to skillet and cook over medium heat, stirring often to break up lumps of meat, until beef loses its pink color, about 3 minutes. Add ginger and garlic and cook, stirring often, 1 minute. Drain off excess fat.

3. Increase heat to high, add rice, and stir-fry until heated through, about 1 minute. Add soy sauce mixture and eggs and stir-fry 30 seconds longer.

244 LITTLE JOE'S SPECIAL

Prep: 10 minutes   Cook: 10 minutes   Serves: 4

1 tablespoon olive oil	4 eggs
1 small onion, chopped	½ teaspoon basil
1 pound ground round	½ teaspoon salt
(85% lean)	¼ teaspoon hot pepper sauce
1 garlic clove, minced	¼ cup grated Parmesan cheese
1 (10-ounce) package frozen	
chopped spinach, thawed	
and squeezed dry	

1. In a large nonstick skillet, heat olive oil. Add onion and cook over medium-high heat, stirring often, until onion is lightly browned, about 3 minutes.

2. Add ground round and garlic. Cook, stirring often to break up lumps of meat, until beef loses its pink color, about 5 minutes. Add spinach and cook, stirring often, 1 minute. Reduce heat to medium.

3. In a medium bowl, beat eggs, basil, salt, and hot sauce. Add egg mixture to skillet and cook, stirring often, until eggs are set, about 1 minute longer. Sprinkle cheese over top and serve immediately.

245 TEACHER'S THAI BEEF SALAD
Prep: 10 minutes   Cook: 5 minutes   Serves: 3

1 pound ground sirloin
   (90% lean)
1 teaspoon grated fresh ginger
1 garlic clove, minced
3 tablespoons lime or lemon
   juice
2 tablespoons Asian fish sauce
   (See Note)
¼ teaspoon crushed hot red
   pepper

6 red leaf or romaine lettuce
   leaves
1 small red onion, thinly
   sliced
1 scallion, chopped
3 tablespoons chopped fresh
   cilantro or parsley

1. In a large nonstick skillet, cook ground sirloin, ginger, and garlic over medium-high heat, stirring often to break up lumps of meat, until beef loses its pink color, about 5 minutes.

2. Stir in lime juice, fish sauce, and hot pepper. Bring to a boil and cook until liquid is evaporated by half, about 1 minute.

3. Arrange lettuce on a round serving dish. Mound hot beef mixture in center. Garnish with sliced red onion, chopped scallion, and cilantro.

NOTE: *Fish sauce is available in Asian markets and in many supermarkets. It is called nuoc mam in Vietnam, nam pla in Thailand, and pastis in Indonesia. If unavailable, substitute a mixture of equal parts soy sauce, Worcestershire sauce, and water.*

246 BEEF AND POTATO PANCAKES
Prep: 10 minutes   Cook: 10 minutes   Serves: 4 to 6

1 pound ground round
   (85% lean)
2 medium russet potatoes
   (about ¾ pound), peeled
   and grated
1 small onion, grated
1 egg

2 tablespoons flour
1 teaspoon salt
½ teaspoon rosemary
¼ teaspoon pepper
2 tablespoons vegetable oil
   Quick Mushroom Sauce
   (page 183)

1. In a medium bowl, combine ground round, grated potatoes, onion, egg, flour, salt, rosemary, and pepper.

2. In a 12-inch skillet or on a griddle, heat oil over medium-high heat. Form meat mixture into 6 patties about ½ inch thick. Place patties in skillet and cook, turning once, until crispy brown on outside and cooked through, about 5 minutes per side. (Adjust heat to avoid burning.)

3. Transfer pancakes to paper towels to drain briefly, then serve with Quick Mushroom Sauce.

247 DR. SALISBURY'S STEAK
Prep: 10 minutes   Cook: 8 minutes   Serves: 4

Dr. J. H. Salisbury became famous espousing the fortifying qualities of broiled ground meat. His name lives on wherever this highbrow version of the hamburger is served. Allow a half hour to prepare the gravy, or make it ahead and reheat it just before serving.

1 **small onion, finely chopped**	½ **teaspoon pepper**
1 **garlic clove, minced**	1½ **pounds ground sirloin**
½ **cup fresh bread crumbs**	**(90% lean)**
¼ **cup milk**	½ **cup flour**
1 **tablespoon Worcestershire**	**Quick Brown Gravy (recipe**
sauce	**follows)**
1¼ **teaspoons salt**	

1. Position a broiler rack about 4 inches from source of heat and preheat broiler. In a medium bowl, combine onion, garlic, bread crumbs, milk, Worcestershire sauce, salt, and pepper. Add ground sirloin and mix well. Form into 4 oval patties about 4½ inches long, 3 inches wide, and 1 inch thick.

2. Place flour on a plate. Dredge ovals in flour, shaking off excess.

3. Broil, turning once, until browned on both sides, about 8 minutes for rare, or longer if desired. Serve with Quick Brown Gravy.

QUICK BROWN GRAVY
Makes about 2 cups

This is an excellent gravy to make when you want a little something extra for your meatloaf and mashed potatoes, but are without any pan drippings.

2 **tablespoons butter**	1 **teaspoon tomato paste**
1 **small onion, chopped**	¼ **teaspoon liquid gravy**
1 **small carrot, chopped**	**seasoning**
1 **small celery rib, chopped**	¼ **teaspoon salt**
2 **tablespoons flour**	¼ **teaspoon pepper**
2 **cups beef broth**	

1. In a small saucepan, melt butter. Add onion, carrot, and celery. Cover and cook over medium heat, stirring occasionally, until vegetables are softened, about 5 minutes. Sprinkle on flour and cook uncovered, stirring, until flour is lightly browned, about 2 to 3 minutes.

2. Stir in beef broth, tomato paste, and gravy seasoning. Bring to a boil, reduce heat to low, and simmer until thickened, about 20 minutes. Strain to remove vegetables and season with salt and pepper.

248 GLASNOST BEEF CUTLETS WITH QUICK MUSHROOM SAUCE

Prep: 5 minutes   Cook: 7 to 9 minutes   Serves: 4

1½ cups fresh bread crumbs	1 small onion, minced
1 egg	⅓ cup ice water
¼ cup milk	1 tablespoon butter
1 tablespoon chopped fresh dill or 1 teaspoon dried	1 tablespoon vegetable oil Quick Mushroom Sauce
½ teaspoon salt	(optional, recipe follows)
¼ teaspoon pepper	
1 pound ground round (85% lean) or ground sirloin (90% lean)	

1. In a medium bowl, stir together ½ cup bread crumbs, egg, milk, dill, salt, and pepper with a fork until mixed. Add ground round, onion, and ice water. Knead with your hands until well blended. Form into 4 ovals about 4 inches long, 2 inches wide, and 1 inch thick.

2. Place remaining bread crumbs on a plate. Coat meat ovals with bread crumbs, pressing crumbs gently to adhere.

3. In a large skillet, melt butter in oil over medium-high heat. Add cutlets and cook, turning once, 6 to 8 minutes for rare to medium-rare, or longer if desired. Adjust heat if necessary to avoid burning crumbs. Transfer cutlets to paper towels to drain briefly before serving hot with cold Quick Mushroom Sauce, if desired.

QUICK MUSHROOM SAUCE

Makes about 1 cup

½ pound fresh mushrooms, sliced	¼ cup sour cream or plain low-fat yogurt, at room temperature
2 scallions, chopped	⅛ teaspoon salt
1½ teaspoons chopped fresh dill or ½ teaspoon dried	⅛ teaspoon pepper
1 tablespoon lemon juice	

1. In a medium saucepan of lightly salted boiling water, cook mushrooms 1 minute. Drain well.

2. In a medium bowl, combine warm mushrooms with remaining ingredients and serve.

249 PAN-FRIED SIRLOIN BURGERS WITH GORGONZOLA SAUCE

Prep: 5 minutes   Cook: 15 minutes   Serves: 4

1⅓ pounds ground sirloin
    (90% lean)
1 teaspoon salt
¼ teaspoon pepper
2 tablespoons vegetable oil
1 tablespoon butter
1 shallot, minced, or
    1 tablespoon minced red
    onion

¼ cup dry red wine
1 cup heavy cream
¼ cup crumbled Gorgonzola
    or other blue cheese
2 tablespoons chopped
    parsley

1. In a medium bowl, combine ground sirloin, salt, and pepper. Form into 4 burgers about 1 inch thick.

2. In a large skillet, heat oil. Add burgers and cook over medium-high heat, turning once, until browned outside but still pink and juicy inside, 8 to 12 minutes for rare to medium-rare, or longer if desired. Transfer burgers to a plate and cover with foil to keep warm. Pour off any fat from skillet.

3. Reduce heat to low, add butter to skillet, and melt. Add shallot and cook, stirring, until softened, about 30 seconds. Add red wine, increase heat to high, and boil until reduced to 2 tablespoons, about 2 minutes. Add cream and boil until reduced to about ½ cup. Remove from heat and whisk in Gorgonzola until melted. Pour sauce over burgers and serve, garnished with chopped parsley.

250 QUICK BEEF AND GARLIC SAUSAGES

Prep: 5 minutes   Cook: 5 minutes   Serves: 4

This Romanian recipe makes the most from simple ingredients. The addition of baking soda to the meat mixture assures a fluffy texture.

¼ teaspoon baking soda
¼ cup beef broth
1 pound ground chuck
    (80% lean) or ground
    round (85% lean)
2 garlic cloves, crushed

¾ teaspoon salt
¼ teaspoon thyme
⅛ teaspoon ground allspice
⅛ teaspoon ground cloves
⅛ teaspoon pepper

1. In a small bowl, stir baking soda into beef broth until dissolved. In a medium bowl, combine ground chuck, crushed garlic, salt, broth mixture, thyme, allspice, cloves, and pepper. Knead with your hands until well blended. With hands rinsed in cold water, form mixture into 8 compact sausages about 3 inches long and 1½ inches thick. (If desired, cover and refrigerate until ready to serve, up to 24 hours.)

2. Position a broiler rack 4 inches away from source of heat and preheat broiler. Broil sausages, turning once, until outside is lightly browned, about 5 minutes for medium-rare, or longer if desired. (Sausages can also be cooked on an outdoor grill.)

---

251 EGG FOO-TATA WITH CHINESE BROWN SAUCE

Prep: 10 minutes   Cook: 10 minutes   Serves: 2 to 4

½ pound ground chuck
(80% lean) or ground lean
pork
¼ pound fresh mushrooms,
sliced
2 scallions, chopped
1 celery rib, chopped
1 cup fresh bean sprouts

1 tablespoon soy sauce
¼ teaspoon salt
¼ teaspoon pepper
5 eggs, well beaten
Chinese Brown Sauce
(recipe follows)

1. Position a broiler rack 6 inches from source of heat and preheat broiler. In a large flameproof nonstick or well-seasoned cast-iron skillet, cook ground chuck, mushrooms, scallions, and celery over medium heat, stirring often to break up lumps of meat, until beef loses its pink color, about 3 minutes.

2. Stir in bean sprouts, soy sauce, salt, and pepper. Pour in beaten eggs and reduce heat to medium-low. As eggs cook, lift up cooked portion with a spatula and tilt pan to let uncooked eggs run underneath. Cook until eggs are mostly set, but the top is still shiny, about 3 minutes.

3. Place skillet under broiler and cook until top of eggs is firm, 1 to 2 minutes. Serve from skillet, cut into wedges, with a bowl of Chinese Brown Sauce passed on the side.

CHINESE BROWN SAUCE
Makes about 1 cup

2½ teaspoons cornstarch
⅔ cup beef stock or canned
broth
1 tablespoon soy sauce

1 tablespoon dry sherry
¼ teaspoon brown sugar
¼ teaspoon salt

In a small bowl, dissolve cornstarch in 1 tablespoon cold water. In a small saucepan, combine cornstarch mixture, stock, soy sauce, sherry, brown sugar, and salt. Cook over low heat, stirring often, until mixture boils and thickens, about 2 minutes.

252 PASTA FRITTATA
Prep: 5 minutes   Cook: 15 minutes   Serves: 4 to 6

⅔ cup ziti or other tubular
   pasta
½ pound ground round
   (85% lean)
½ cup marinara sauce
5 eggs

1 teaspoon Italian seasoning
¾ teaspoon salt
¼ teaspoon pepper
3 tablespoons grated
   Parmesan cheese

1. In a medium saucepan of boiling salted water, cook ziti until tender but still firm, about 8 minutes. Drain well.

2. Position a broiler rack about 6 inches from source of heat and preheat broiler. In a 9-inch flameproof nonstick or well-seasoned cast-iron skillet, cook ground round over medium-high heat, stirring often to break up lumps of meat, until beef loses its pink color, about 3 minutes. Stir in cooked pasta and marinara sauce and bring to a simmer.

3. In a medium bowl, whisk eggs with Italian seasoning, salt, and pepper until foamy. Pour into skillet. With a spatula, lift up cooked portion of eggs, tilting pan to allow uncooked eggs to run underneath. Continue cooking in this manner until eggs are mostly set but top is still shiny, about 2 minutes.

3. Sprinkle Parmesan cheese over top of frittata. Broil until frittata is puffed and golden brown, 1 to 2 minutes. Allow frittata to stand a few minutes before serving directly from skillet.

253 DEWEY'S VEALETTE BURGERS
Prep: 10 minutes   Chill: 15 minutes   Cook: 10 minutes   Serves: 4

Whenever I'm in Woodstock, New York, I make a pilgrimage to Dewey's Coffee Shop for their down-home interpretation of Veal Cordon Bleu. Here's my version of their version.

1 pound ground veal
1 teaspoon salt
¼ teaspoon pepper
1 egg
3 tablespoons vegetable oil
1¼ cups fresh bread crumbs
4 thin slices boiled ham

4 thin slices Swiss cheese
4 hamburger rolls
   Sliced tomatoes, shredded
   lettuce, and Russian
   dressing or mayonnaise

1. In a medium bowl, mix ground veal, salt, and pepper. Form into 4 thin patties about ¾ inch thick.

2. In a shallow bowl, beat egg with 1 tablespoon oil. Place bread crumbs on a plate. Dip patties in egg mixture, then coat with bread crumbs. Refrigerate patties 15 minutes to set coating.

3. In a large skillet, heat remaining 2 tablespoons oil over medium heat. Add patties and cook until bottoms are golden brown, about 5 minutes. Turn and cook 4 minutes. Top each patty with 1 slice of ham and 1 slice of Swiss cheese (trimmed to fit, if necessary). Cover skillet and cook until cheese is melted and patties are medium-well done, 1 to 2 minutes. (Adjust heat as necessary to avoid burning crust.) Serve on buns with sliced tomatoes, lettuce, and Russian dressing.

254   BROCCOLI-CHEDDAR FRITTATA WITH GROUND PORK

Prep: 10 minutes   Cook: 10 minutes   Serves: 4

1 tablespoon olive oil	½ teaspoon oregano
1 small onion, chopped	½ teaspoon salt
1 pound ground pork	¼ teaspoon crushed hot red
1 garlic clove, minced	pepper
1 (10-ounce) package frozen	¼ cup shredded Cheddar
chopped broccoli, thawed	cheese
4 eggs	

1. In a large nonstick or well-seasoned cast-iron skillet, heat olive oil. Add onion and cook over medium-high heat, stirring often, until onion is lightly browned, about 3 minutes.

2. Add ground pork and garlic. Cook, stirring often to break up lumps of meat, until pork loses its pink color, about 5 minutes. Tilt skillet and drain off all but 1 tablespoon fat. Add broccoli and cook, stirring often, 1 minute. Reduce heat to medium.

3. In a medium bowl, beat eggs with oregano, salt, and hot pepper. Add to skillet and cook, stirring often, until eggs are set, about 1 minute longer. Sprinkle Cheddar cheese over top and serve.

255   TEXAS-FRIED CHICKEN BURGERS
Prep: 5 minutes   Cook: 10 minutes   Serves: 4

1 egg	½ cup flour
1¼ teaspoons salt	1 tablespoon butter
½ teaspoon pepper	2 tablespoons vegetable oil
1¼ pounds ground chicken	1 cup tomato salsa

1. In a medium bowl, beat together egg, 1 teaspoon salt, and ¼ teaspoon pepper with a fork until well blended. Add ground chicken and mix just until combined. Form into 4 patties about ¾ inch thick.

2. On a plate, mix together flour with remaining ¼ teaspoon each salt and pepper. Dredge patties in seasoned flour.

3. In a large skillet, melt butter in oil over medium heat. Add burgers and cook, turning once, until golden brown on both sides and meat springs back when touched lightly in center, about 10 minutes; chicken should be white throughout but still juicy. Transfer burgers to a paper towel–lined plate to drain. Serve immediately with salsa on the side.

Variation: **TEXAS-FRIED CHICKEN BURGERS WITH MILK GRAVY**

After cooking burgers, transfer to paper towel–lined plate to drain and cover with foil to keep warm. Sprinkle 2 tablespoons flour into fat in skillet and cook over medium-low heat, whisking, until lightly browned, 2 to 3 minutes. Whisk in 1½ cups milk and ⅛ teaspoon hot pepper sauce, bring to a simmer, and cook until thickened, about 1 minute. Season gravy with salt and pepper to taste and serve immediately with chicken burgers. If serving gravy, omit tomato salsa.

256   CHICKEN BURGERS AU POIVRE
Prep: 5 minutes   Cook: 12 minutes   Serves: 4

1 pound ground chicken	1 tablespoon chopped scallions
2 teaspoons Worcestershire sauce	¼ cup reduced-sodium chicken broth
¼ teaspoon salt	¼ cup Cognac or brandy
1 teaspoon coarsely cracked pepper	1 tablespoon chopped fresh chives or parsley
2 teaspoons vegetable oil	
2 teaspoons butter	

1. In a medium bowl, combine ground chicken, Worcestershire sauce, and salt; mix well. Using wet hands, form into 4 burgers about 1 inch thick. Sprinkle pepper over both sides of patties.

2. In a large nonstick skillet, heat oil. Add burgers and cook over medium heat, turning once, until browned on both sides and the meat bounces back when pressed in center, 8 to 10 minutes. Transfer to a plate and cover with foil to keep warm.

3. Add butter to pan and melt. Add scallions and cook until softened, about 30 seconds. Add broth and boil, scraping up browned bits from bottom of pan with a wooden spoon. Carefully add Cognac. Averting your face, light Cognac with a match, let flames subside, and cook until liquid is evaporated to ¼ cup, about 1 minute. Pour sauce over burgers and garnish with chives.

---

257 CRUNCHY CHINESE CHICKEN IN LETTUCE CUPS

Prep: 10 minutes   Cook: 10 minutes   Serves: 4

3 tablespoons soy sauce	2 teaspoons minced fresh ginger
2 tablespoons dry sherry	1 garlic clove, minced
2 teaspoons rice vinegar	1 small red bell pepper, cut into ¼-inch dice
2 teaspoons Asian sesame oil	1 medium celery rib, cut into ¼-inch dice
1½ teaspoons sugar	1 jalapeño pepper, seeded and minced
1 teaspoon salt	1 scallion, chopped
¼ teaspoon crushed hot red pepper	⅓ cup roasted peanuts
1 tablespoon cornstarch	12 iceberg lettuce leaves
1 pound ground chicken	
¼ cup vegetable oil	

1. In a small bowl, combine 2 tablespoons soy sauce, 1 tablespoon sherry, rice vinegar, 1 teaspoon sesame oil, sugar, salt, and hot pepper. Add 2 teaspoons cornstarch and stir to dissolve; set sauce aside.

2. In a medium bowl, combine ground chicken, remaining 1 tablespoon each soy sauce and sherry, and 1 teaspoon each sesame oil and cornstarch. Mix to blend well.

3. In a wok or large skillet, heat 2 tablespoons oil over high heat. Add ginger and garlic and stir-fry until fragrant, about 30 seconds. Add bell pepper, celery, and jalapeño pepper and stir-fry until crisp-tender, about 1 minute. Transfer vegetables to a plate.

4. Add remaining 2 tablespoons oil to wok. Add ground chicken mixture and stir-fry, breaking up mixture with a spoon, until chicken loses its pink color, about 3 minutes.

5. Return vegetables to wok. Stir reserved sauce and add to pan. Cook, stirring, until sauce is thickened, about 1 minute. Stir in scallion and peanuts.

6. Spoon chicken mixture into center of a round platter. Arrange lettuce leaves around chicken. To eat, spoon chicken mixture into center of a lettuce leaf, fold in sides, roll up into a cylinder, and eat with your fingers.

258   GROUND CHICKEN CHOP SUEY
Prep: 10 minutes   Cook: 7 minutes   Serves: 4

1 tablespoon plus 2 teaspoons
  dry sherry
4 teaspoons soy sauce
4 teaspoons cornstarch
1⅓ pounds ground chicken
1 cup reduced-sodium
  chicken broth
2 tablespoons vegetable oil
1 celery rib, sliced ¼ inch
  thick

1 medium carrot, sliced
  ¼ inch thick
1 cup fresh bean sprouts
2 scallions, chopped
1 teaspoon minced ginger
1 garlic clove, minced
  Hot cooked rice

1. In a medium bowl, combine 1 tablespoon sherry and 2 teaspoons each soy sauce and cornstarch. Stir until cornstarch dissolves. Add ground chicken and mix well. In a small bowl, dissolve remaining 2 teaspoons cornstarch in broth. Stir in remaining 2 teaspoons soy sauce and set sauce aside.

2. In a wok or large skillet, heat 1 tablespoon vegetable oil over high heat. Add celery, carrot, and bean sprouts. Stir-fry until vegetables are crisptender, about 1 minute. Transfer vegetables to a plate.

3. Add remaining 1 tablespoon oil to skillet and heat. Add scallions, ginger, and garlic. Stir-fry until fragrant, about 15 seconds. Add chicken mixture and stir-fry, breaking up lumps, until chicken loses its pink color, about 3 minutes.

4. Return vegetables to skillet. Stir sauce and pour into skillet. Cook, stirring, until mixture boils and thickens, about 1 minute. Serve immediately over hot cooked rice.

Chapter 10

Microwaved Ground Meats

The microwave oven has made an indelible impression on the way many Americans eat. With this in mind, this chapter offers ground meat recipes that illustrate how the microwave can be used at its best.

Remember that the amount of wattage in each microwave affects the microwave's strength. For example, a recipe cooked in a 500-watt oven will take longer to cook than in a more powerful 700-watt oven. So you may have to adjust your cooking times slightly. Also, it is recommended that your microwave oven have its own independent, unshared outlet, so it can draw full power. (Try not to have your refrigerator and microwave on the same outlet.) These recipes were tested in a 700-watt microwave.

There are certain things that the microwave does very well, and in record time. Baking potatoes in a flash is a microwave specialty. A baked potato, topped with a satisfying, meaty stuffing, is one of my favorite quick, after-work meals. I can never decide between making Budapest Potatoes with Veal Goulash Stuffing or Acapulco Potatoes with Chicken Salsa Topping.

If you want to try adapting your favorite meatloaf recipe to the microwave, try Glazed Meat Ring, Texas Style, or Meat and Vegetable Pie as blueprints. Since microwaving can cook a dish unevenly (even if you use a carousel), forming the meat mixture in a ring or disc assures that the dish will cook more evenly than in the traditional loaf shape.

Saucy ground meat dishes with a good deal of liquid, such as Easy Microwave Italian Meat Sauce or Kinder, Gentler Chili, are particularly well-adapted to the microwave. Because microwaving sometimes causes herbs to act unpredictably, I like to adjust the seasonings at the end of the cooking time.

259 MICROWAVE LASAGNE

Prep: 15 minutes   Cook: 1 hour   Stand: 15 to 20 minutes
Serves: 3 to 5

When you have a lasagne craving, but you're not cooking for a crowd, try this scaled-down, timesaving recipe. The noodles aren't boiled first—they cook right in the pan!

1 pound ground round (85% lean) or ground sirloin (90% lean)
1 (28-ounce) jar marinara sauce
¾ cup dry red wine
1 (15-ounce) container part-skim ricotta cheese

½ cup grated Parmesan cheese
1 cup grated mozzarella cheese (4 ounces)
2 eggs
1 teaspoon Italian seasoning
¼ cup chopped parsley
9 uncooked lasagne noodles (about 7 ounces)

1. In a 2-quart microwave-safe bowl, microwave ground round with ½ cup marinara sauce, uncovered, on High, stirring halfway through to break up lumps of meat, until beef has lost its pink color, about 5 minutes. Stir in remaining sauce and red wine. Cover bowl with microwave-safe plastic wrap and microwave on High until boiling, about 5 minutes. Set meat sauce aside.

2. In a medium bowl, stir together ricotta, Parmesan, mozzarella, eggs, Italian seasoning, and parsley until well mixed; set cheese mixture aside.

3. In an 11 x 7-inch microwave-safe baking dish (a 2-quart Pyrex dish works well), place a third of the hot meat sauce. Arrange 3 uncooked lasagne noodles in dish, pressing into sauce. Spread half of cheese mixture over noodles. Cover cheese mixture with 3 more noodles and top noodles with half of remaining sauce. Layer on remaining cheese mixture and top with last 3 noodles and remaining sauce. Cover dish with microwave-safe plastic wrap.

4. Microwave on High 10 minutes, then cook on Medium-High 35 to 40 minutes, until noodles are almost tender. Let lasagne stand at room temperature, still covered with plastic wrap, until noodles are cooked through, 15 to 20 minutes.

260 SUPERFAST CHILI PASTA PIE
Prep: 20 minutes   Cook: 18 minutes   Serves: 4 to 6

6 ounces ziti	1 garlic clove, minced
½ cup grated Parmesan cheese	1 cup tomato sauce
1 tablespoon butter	1 tablespoon chili powder
1 pound ground round	½ teaspoon salt
(85% lean)	⅛ teaspoon crushed hot red
1 medium onion, chopped	pepper
1 small green bell pepper,	1 cup shredded sharp
chopped	Cheddar cheese

1. In a large pot of boiling salted water, cook ziti until barely tender, about 10 minutes. Drain well. In a large bowl, combine hot ziti, Parmesan cheese, and butter. Spread mixture into a lightly buttered 10-inch glass pie plate; set aside.

2. Meanwhile, in a 2-quart microwave-safe bowl, combine ground round, onion, bell pepper, and garlic. Cover tightly with microwave-safe plastic wrap and microwave on High, stirring once to break up lumps of meat, until beef loses its pink color, about 5 minutes. Stir in tomato sauce, chili powder, salt, and hot pepper. Microwave, uncovered, on High until bubbling, about 1 minute.

3. Leaving a ½-inch border around edges, sprinkle ¾ cup cheese over pasta shell. Spoon chili filling over cheese; sprinkle chili with remaining ¼ cup cheese. Microwave on High until cheese melts, 1 to 2 minutes. Cover plate with foil and let stand 3 minutes to complete cooking.

261 EASY MICROWAVE ITALIAN MEAT SAUCE
Prep: 10 minutes   Cook: 27 minutes   Makes: About 3 cups (enough for 1½ pounds of cooked pasta)

1 medium onion, chopped	1 (28-ounce) can crushed
2 garlic cloves, minced	tomatoes
3 tablespoons olive oil	2 cups tomato sauce
1½ pounds ground chuck	1½ teaspoons basil
(80% lean) or ground	1 teaspoon oregano
round (85% lean)	¼ teaspoon pepper

1. In a 2-quart glass or ceramic bowl, combine onion, garlic, and oil. Cover tightly with microwave-safe plastic wrap and cook on High, stirring once, until onion is softened, about 4 minutes.

2. Add ground chuck and cook, uncovered, on High, stirring and breaking up lumps twice, until meat has lost its pink color, about 8 minutes.

3. Add tomatoes, tomato sauce, basil, oregano, and pepper. Microwave, uncovered, on High, stirring twice, until sauce has thickened slightly, about 15 minutes.

262   GLAZED MEAT RING, TEXAS STYLE
Prep: 15 minutes   Cook: 15 minutes   Serves: 4 to 6

1 medium onion, finely chopped	½ teaspoon pepper
1 small green bell pepper, finely chopped	1 pound ground round (85% lean)
1 garlic clove, minced	1 pound ground pork
1 cup fresh bread crumbs	¼ cup chili sauce
⅓ cup milk	2 teaspoons corn syrup
2 eggs	1½ teaspoons Worcestershire sauce
2 teaspoons salt	

1. In a large bowl, combine onion, bell pepper, garlic, bread crumbs, milk, eggs, salt, and pepper. Add ground round and ground pork and knead with your hands until well mixed.

2. Place a microwave-safe custard cup in center of a 10-inch glass pie plate. Molding around custard cup, form meat mixture into a ring about 1½ inches high.

3. In a small bowl, combine chili sauce, corn syrup, Worcestershire sauce, and ¼ cup water. Brush chili sauce mixture over top of meat ring.

4. Cover pie plate with wax paper. Microwave on High until a meat thermometer inserted in center of meat ring reads 150°, about 15 minutes. Let stand, covered, until temperature rises to 160°, about 5 minutes. Drain off excess liquid before serving.

263   KINDER, GENTLER CHILI
Prep: 10 minutes   Cook: 15 minutes   Serves: 4

While kids love chili, they often can't handle assertive spices, so I use this recipe when I'm serving youngsters. (Cook fresh chopped jalapeños along with the beef, and add more chili powder to boost the heat factor if you like it hot.)

1 pound ground sirloin (90% lean)	1 (14½-ounce) can stewed tomatoes, undrained
1 medium onion, minced	2 tablespoons tomato paste
1 garlic clove, minced	2 teaspoons chili powder
1 (16-ounce) can Mexican-style corn or kidney beans, drained	1 teaspoon salt
	¼ teaspoon pepper

1. In a 2-quart microwave-safe bowl, place ground sirloin. Cover tightly with microwave-safe plastic wrap. Microwave on High 3 minutes. Add onion and garlic, stirring to break up meat. Cover and microwave on High until beef loses its pink color, about 3 minutes.

2. Stir in corn, tomatoes, tomato paste, chili powder, salt, and pepper. Microwave, uncovered, on High until thickened, about 8 minutes.

264 SAVORY STUFFED PEPPERS
Prep: 10 minutes   Cook: 8 minutes   Serves: 4

4 medium green bell peppers
1 small onion, finely chopped
½ cup saltine cracker crumbs
⅓ cup ketchup
¾ teaspoon garlic salt
½ teaspoon thyme
½ teaspoon Italian seasoning

⅛ teaspoon crushed hot red pepper
1¼ pounds ground round (85% lean)
1 (14½-ounce) can stewed tomatoes, with their juice

1. Slice tops off peppers and remove seeds. Stand peppers up in a 9-inch square microwave-safe dish.

2. In a medium bowl, combine onion, cracker crumbs, ketchup, garlic salt, thyme, Italian seasoning, and hot pepper. Add ground round and mix well.

3. Stuff peppers with meat mixture, dividing evenly. Pour stewed tomatoes with their juice around peppers. Cover tightly with microwave-safe plastic wrap.

4. Microwave on Medium-High until a meat thermometer inserted in center of meat mixture reads 150°, about 8 minutes. Let stand, covered, until temperature rises to 160°, about 5 minutes.

265 BUDAPEST POTATOES WITH VEAL GOULASH STUFFING
Prep: 10 minutes   Cook: 24 to 31 minutes   Serves: 4

4 large russet potatoes (8 to 10 ounces each)
1 pound ground veal
1 medium onion, chopped
1 tablespoon flour
½ cup beef broth

1 tablespoon tomato paste
2 teaspoons paprika
¼ teaspoon salt
⅛ teaspoon pepper
2 teaspoons sour cream or plain low-fat yogurt

1. Scrub potatoes under cold running water but do not dry. Pierce potatoes once in center with a fork. Wrap each potato in a microwave-safe paper towel. Arrange potatoes in a circle and microwave on High just until potatoes pierce easily in centers with a fork, 18 to 22 minutes. Let stand 5 minutes, still wrapped in paper towels, to complete cooking.

2. Meanwhile, in a 2-quart microwave-safe bowl, combine ground veal and onion. Cover tightly with microwave-safe plastic wrap. Microwave on High, stirring once to break up lumps of meat, until veal has lost its pink color, 5 minutes. Drain off excess fat. Stir in flour.

3. Stir in beef broth, tomato paste, paprika, salt, and pepper. Microwave on High, uncovered, until thickened, about 1 minute. Off heat, stir in sour cream.

4. Cut potatoes in half lengthwise. Fluff with a fork. Arrange potatoes on individual dinner plates and spoon veal stuffing on top.

266 DRUNKEN PICADILLO IN ACORN SQUASH
Prep: 15 minutes   Cook: 35 minutes   Serves: 4

¼ cup raisins
2 tablespoons dark rum
2 acorn squash (about
   1½ pounds each)
1 pound ground round
   (85% lean)
1 small onion, chopped
1 small red or green bell
   pepper, chopped
1 garlic clove, minced

1 (14-ounce) can Italian peeled
   tomatoes, drained
¼ cup chopped pimiento-
   stuffed green olives
½ teaspoon oregano
¼ teaspoon thyme
½ teaspoon salt
¼ teaspoon crushed hot red
   pepper
2 tablespoons chopped fresh
   cilantro or parsley

1. In a small microwave-safe bowl, microwave raisins and rum on High for 45 seconds. Pierce each squash several times with a long-pronged meat fork. Place in a microwave-safe baking dish, and microwave on High 10 minutes. Turn squash over. Continue to cook 7 to 10 minutes longer, until soft to the touch. Cover loosely with foil and set aside.

2. In a 2-quart microwave-safe bowl, combine ground round, onion, bell pepper, and garlic. Cover tightly with microwave-safe plastic wrap and microwave on High, stirring once, until meat loses its pink color, about 5 minutes. Add tomatoes and break up in bowl with a spoon. Stir in raisins with rum, olives, oregano, thyme, salt, and hot pepper. Microwave on High, stirring occasionally, until liquid is evaporated, about 10 minutes.

3. Cut each squash in half lengthwise and remove seeds. Trim a thin slice off bottoms of squash halves so they stand flat. Spoon filling into each acorn squash, garnish with cilantro, and serve.

267 MEAT AND VEGETABLE PIE
Prep: 15 minutes   Cook: 25 minutes   Serves: 4

1 pound ground round
   (85% lean)
1 medium onion, chopped
1 medium russet potato,
   grated
1 medium carrot, grated

1 small bell pepper, chopped
¾ cup dried bread crumbs
1 cup tomato sauce
1 egg
1¼ teaspoons garlic salt
½ teaspoon pepper

1. In a medium bowl, combine ground round, onion, potato, carrot, bell pepper, bread crumbs, ½ cup tomato sauce, egg, garlic salt, and pepper.

2. In a 10-inch glass pie plate, pat meat mixture into a thick, flat disc. Spread remaining tomato sauce over top.

3. Cover pie plate with wax paper. Microwave on High until a meat thermometer inserted 2 inches from edge of pie reads about 150°, 25 minutes. Let stand, covered, until temperature rises to 160°, about 5 minutes.

268 ACAPULCO POTATOES WITH CHICKEN SALSA TOPPING

Prep: 10 minutes   Cook: 27 to 31 minutes   Serves: 4

4 large russet potatoes, 8 to 10 ounces each	1½ cups tomato salsa
1 pound ground chicken	½ teaspoon salt
	¼ cup sour cream

1. Scrub potatoes under cold running water but do not dry. Pierce each potato once in center with a fork. Wrap each potato in a microwave-safe paper towel. Arrange potatoes in a circle and microwave on High just until potatoes pierce easily in centers with a fork, 18 to 22 minutes. Let stand 5 minutes, still wrapped in paper towels, to complete cooking.

2. Meanwhile, place ground chicken in a 2-quart microwave-safe bowl and cover tightly with plastic wrap. Cook on High, stirring once to break up meat, until it has lost its pink color, about 5 minutes. Drain off excess liquid. Stir in salsa and salt and cook on High, stirring once, until hot, about 4 minutes.

3. Cut potatoes in half lengthwise. Fluff with a fork. Arrange potatoes on individual dinner plates, spoon chicken mixture over top, and garnish with a dollop of sour cream.

269 MICROWAVE ZUCCHINI-BEEF BAKE

Prep: 15 minutes   Cook: 20 minutes   Serves: 4

This is a microwave version of food writer Irene Rothschild's recipe.

2 tablespoons olive oil	1 cup tomato sauce
3 medium zucchini, sliced ½ inch thick	½ teaspoon salt
1 pound ground sirloin (90% lean)	¼ teaspoon cinnamon
	¼ teaspoon pepper
1 small onion, chopped	½ cup low-fat cottage cheese
1 garlic clove, minced	1 egg
	¼ cup grated Parmesan cheese

1. In a large skillet, heat oil over medium-high heat. Add zucchini slices and cook, turning often, until lightly browned, about 5 minutes. Transfer zucchini slices to paper towels to drain briefly. Arrange overlapping slices in a microwave-safe 9-inch square baking dish.

2. In a 2-quart microwave-safe bowl, place ground sirloin, onion, and garlic. Cover tightly with microwave-safe plastic wrap. Microwave on High, stirring once to break up lumps of meat, until beef loses its pink color, about 6 minutes. Drain off excess fat. Stir in tomato sauce, salt, cinnamon and pepper. Pour meat filling over zucchini.

3. In a small bowl, combine cottage cheese and egg. Spread mixture over meat filling and sprinkle with Parmesan cheese. Cover with wax paper. Cook on Medium-High until cheese topping is set, about 8 minutes. Let stand 5 minutes to complete cooking.

270 INSTANT TURKEY STROGANOFF
Prep: 5 minutes   Cook: 12 minutes   Serves: 4

1 pound ground turkey
1 medium onion, finely
  chopped
1 tablespoon flour
1 (10¾-ounce) can cream of
  mushroom soup
1 (4-ounce) can mushroom
  stems and pieces, drained

2 tablespoons dry sherry
¼ cup sour cream
¼ teaspoon paprika
⅛ teaspoon pepper
  Hot cooked noodles

1. In a 2-quart microwave-safe casserole with a lid, combine ground turkey and onion. Cover with lid and microwave on High, stirring once, until meat loses its pink color, about 5 minutes. Stir in flour. Cook on High, uncovered, 1 minute.

2. Stir in mushroom soup, mushrooms, and sherry. Cover with lid and cook on High, stirring once, until bubbling, about 5 minutes. Stir in sour cream, paprika, and pepper. Cover with lid and cook on Medium just until sour cream is heated through, about 1 minute. Do not let boil after adding sour cream. Serve stroganoff over hot cooked noodles.

271 GINGER TURKEY MEATBALLS
Prep: 20 minutes   Cook: 15 minutes   Makes: About 32 meatballs

Pop batches of these tasty meatballs into the microwave for a speedy hors d'oeuvres.

1¼ pounds ground turkey
½ cup chopped water
  chestnuts
⅓ cup finely chopped
  crystallized ginger

3 tablespoons soy sauce
½ teaspoon salt
¼ teaspoon pepper
1 tablespoon molasses

1. In a medium bowl, mix ground turkey, water chestnuts, crystallized ginger, 1 tablespoon soy sauce, salt, and pepper. Using about 1 tablespoon for each, form turkey mixture into meatballs. (Dip hands in cold water to prevent sticking.) Refrigerate meatballs until shortly before serving.

2. In a small bowl, combine remaining 2 tablespoons soy sauce with molasses.

3. Cook turkey meatballs in batches. In a 10-inch glass pie plate, arrange about 12 meatballs in a circle. Brush with some soy-molasses mixture. Microwave on Medium-High 3 minutes. Turn meatballs, brush again, and cook just until meat is cooked through, about 4 minutes.

Chapter 11

Meat in the Morning: Breakfast and Brunch Specialties

There's nothing like a big, hearty breakfast to put zest into the morning, especially when its a meaty treat sizzling on the stove, its savory aroma wafting through the kitchen. Many of us consider breakfast to be the most special of meals, as it is normally shared with only our closest, most intimate acquaintances.

A brunch is a wonderful way to entertain. Since the cooking schedule can be tight, a brunch menu should be carefully planned, so you can enjoy your company without spending all morning in the kitchen. Make-ahead dishes are the order of the day. A *strata*, an Italian custard casserole with layers of meat and bread, is a perfect example of this genre. This delectable dish (of which this chapter offers many variations) is easily prepared the night before, and refrigerated overnight, then popped into the oven the next day. Served with fresh baked muffins and a colorful fruit salad, it makes a beautiful brunch entree.

There are many times when you want to serve an out-of-the-ordinary breakfast dish but you don't want to fuss. Recipes like Herbed Breakfast Patties and Denver Breakfast Pie may be quick and easy, but they are satisfying enough for a lumberjack.

---

272 LUMBERJACK RED FLANNEL HASH
Prep: 10 minutes   Cook: 15 minutes   Serves: 4

1 **pound ground round** (85% lean)	¼ **teaspoon pepper**
1 **medium onion, chopped**	3 **tablespoons vegetable oil**
1 **(8-ounce) can whole beets, drained and chopped**	2 **cups frozen hash brown potatoes**
1 **teaspoon salt**	**Quick Brown Gravy (page 182)**

1. In a large skillet, cook ground round and onion over medium-high heat, stirring often to break up meat, until beef loses its pink color, about 5 minutes. Stir in beets, salt, and pepper. With a slotted spoon, transfer meat mixture to a plate. Pour any fat or juices out of skillet.

2. In same skillet, heat oil over medium heat. Add potatoes and place meat mixture on top. Cover and cook, stirring occasionally, until potatoes are browned, about 10 minutes. Remove cover during last 2 minutes of cooking to allow potatoes to crisp. Serve with Quick Brown Gravy.

273   CHRISTMAS BREAKFAST CASSEROLE
Prep: 15 minutes   Chill: 2 hours   Cook: 1 hour 5 minutes   Serves: 6

Made in a jiffy the night before if you like, this casserole patiently waits to be baked for an extra-special holiday brunch.

1 pound ground pork	4 eggs
1 small onion, chopped	2 cups milk
1 garlic clove, minced	¼ teaspoon black pepper
1 teaspoon salt	4 cups Italian or French bread,
½ teaspoon Italian seasoning	cut into 1-inch cubes
¼ teaspoon fennel seed,	1½ cups shredded Cheddar
crushed	cheese (6 ounces)
¼ teaspoon crushed hot red	
pepper	

1. Preheat oven to 350°. In a large skillet, cook ground pork, onion, and garlic over medium-high heat, stirring often to break up meat, until pork loses its pink color, about 5 minutes. Stir in ¾ teaspoon salt, Italian seasoning, fennel seed, and hot pepper.

2. In a medium bowl, whisk together eggs, milk, remaining ¼ teaspoon salt, and black pepper.

3. In a lightly buttered 9 x 13-inch baking dish, spread 2 cups bread cubes. Cover with pork mixture. Spread remaining 2 cups bread cubes over pork mixture, then sprinkle on Cheddar cheese. Pour egg mixture over all, cover with plastic wrap, and refrigerate at least 2 hours or overnight.

4. Bake until egg mixture is set and top is browned, 50 to 60 minutes. Let stand 5 minutes before cutting into squares to serve.

274   TURKEY HASHED HASH
Prep: 5 minutes   Cook: 10 minutes   Serves: 4

¼ cup vegetable oil	1 teaspoon poultry seasoning
1¼ pounds ground turkey	1 teaspoon salt
1 small onion, chopped	¼ teaspoon pepper
1 small green bell pepper,	2 cups frozen hash brown
chopped	potatoes

1. In a large skillet, heat 1 tablespoon oil. Add ground turkey, onion, and bell pepper and cook over medium heat, stirring often to break up lumps of meat, until turkey has lost its pink color, about 5 minutes. Stir in poultry seasoning, salt, and pepper and transfer mixture to a plate.

2. Heat remaining 3 tablespoons oil in same skillet over medium-high heat. Add hash brown potatoes and cook until bottom starts to brown, about 1 minute. Add turkey mixture and cook, turning often, until potatoes are browned, about 5 minutes.

275 SPANISH BEEF AND POTATO TORTILLA

Prep: 20 minutes   Cook: 45 minutes   Serves: 4 to 8

In Spain, a *tortilla* is not a thin pancake as it is in Latin America, but a plump omelette stuffed with any number of toothsome fillings. Here is one of my favorite combinations. Since it can be made ahead and served at room temperature, it makes a great brunch or buffet dish.

1 pound ground round (85% lean)	¾ teaspoon hot pepper sauce
1 garlic clove, minced	2 tablespoons olive oil
1 teaspoon paprika	1 pound russet potatoes, sliced paper-thin
8 eggs	1 large onion, sliced
⅓ cup milk	1 cup shredded Monterey Jack cheese (4 ounces)
1 teaspoon rosemary	
1½ teaspoons salt	

1. Preheat oven to 350°. In a 9-inch ovenproof skillet, preferably nonstick, cook ground round, garlic, and paprika, stirring often to break up lumps of meat, until beef loses its pink color, about 5 minutes. Drain off any excess fat. Set beef mixture aside.

2. In a medium bowl, whisk eggs, milk, rosemary, ¾ teaspoon salt, and hot sauce until well blended.

3. Heat olive oil in skillet. Add potatoes and cook over medium-high heat, stirring often, until potatoes are slightly softened, about 10 minutes. Add onion and cook, stirring often, until potatoes are lightly browned and onion is softened, about 5 minutes. Stir in beef mixture and Monterey Jack cheese.

4. Reduce heat to medium and add seasoned eggs. Using a rubber spatula, lift up cooked portion of eggs to allow uncooked portion to flow underneath, tilting pan as necessary. Cook until eggs are partially set, about 3 minutes.

5. Transfer skillet to oven and bake until eggs are set, 15 to 20 minutes. Let stand 5 minutes before cutting into wedges. Serve warm or at room temperature.

NOTE: *If the handle of your skillet is not heatproof, wrap with aluminum foil.*

276   CHICKEN PATTIES WITH CHUNKY CREOLE SAUCE

Prep: 15 minutes   Cook: 40 minutes   Serves: 4

1⅓ pounds ground chicken	1 egg
1 scallion, minced	½ cup flour
1 teaspoon white wine Worcestershire sauce	1¼ cups fresh bread crumbs
½ teaspoon garlic salt	2 tablespoons vegetable oil
⅛ teaspoon cayenne	Chunky Creole Sauce (recipe follows)
⅛ teaspoon pepper	Hot cooked rice

1. In a medium bowl, mix together ground chicken, scallion, Worcestershire sauce, garlic salt, cayenne, and pepper until well blended. With wet hands, form into 4 patties about 3½ inches in diameter.

2. In a medium bowl, beat egg with 1 tablespoon water. On 2 separate plates, place flour and bread crumbs. One at a time, dredge each patty in flour, dip in egg, and coat with crumbs.

3. In a large skillet, heat oil over medium heat. Add chicken patties and cook, turning once, until golden brown on both sides and cooked through, about 6 minutes per side. (Adjust heat to avoid burning crust. Never cook chicken patties less than medium-well done.)

4. Serve patties with hot Chunky Creole Sauce, spooning extra sauce over hot rice.

CHUNKY CREOLE SAUCE
Makes about 2 cups

1 tablespoon butter	1 teaspoon white wine Worcestershire sauce
1 celery rib, chopped	½ teaspoon thyme
1 scallion, chopped	½ teaspoon basil
1 garlic clove, minced	¼ teaspoon cayenne
1 tablespoon flour	
1 (15-ounce) can stewed tomatoes, with their juice	

1. In a medium saucepan, melt butter over medium heat. Add celery, scallion, and garlic. Cook, partially covered, stirring often, until celery is slightly softened, about 5 minutes.

2. Add flour and cook, stirring, 1 minute. Stir in stewed tomatoes with their juice, Worcestershire sauce, thyme, basil, and cayenne. Bring to a boil, reduce heat to low, and simmer until thickened, about 20 minutes.

277   CHICKEN AND ZUCCHINI FRITTATA
Prep: 15 minutes   Cook: 15 minutes   Serves: 4 to 6

2 tablespoons olive oil
2 small zucchini (about ½ pound), cut into ¼-inch-thick rounds
1 small red onion, sliced
1 pound ground chicken
1 garlic clove, minced
1 teaspoon salt

½ teaspoon crushed hot red pepper
6 eggs
2 tablespoons chopped fresh basil or ¾ teaspoon dried
¼ cup shredded Cheddar cheese

1. Position a broiler rack about 6 inches from source of heat and preheat broiler. In a 9-inch ovenproof skillet, heat olive oil over medium-high heat. Add zucchini and onion. Cook, turning often, until zucchini is lightly browned and onion is softened, about 5 minutes. With a slotted spoon, transfer vegetables to a plate.

2. Reduce heat to medium. Add ground chicken and garlic and cook, stirring often to break up lumps of meat, until chicken loses its pink color, about 5 minutes. Season with ½ teaspoon salt and ¼ teaspoon hot pepper. Stir in reserved vegetables.

3. In a medium bowl, whisk eggs, basil, and remaining ½ teaspoon salt and ¼ teaspoon hot pepper until foamy. Pour eggs into skillet. With a spatula, lift up cooked portion of eggs, tilting pan to allow uncooked eggs to run underneath. Continue cooking in this manner until eggs are mostly set but top is still shiny, about 1 minute.

4. Sprinkle Cheddar cheese over top. Broil until frittata is puffed and golden brown, 1 to 2 minutes.

278   SAUSAGE AND HASH BROWN BREAKFAST PIE
Prep: 10 minutes   Cook: 45 minutes   Serves: 4 to 6

Herbed Breakfast Patties (page 208)
16 ounces frozen hash brown potatoes, thawed

2 tablespoons butter, melted
½ cup shredded Cheddar cheese

1. Preheat oven to 350°. Form a shell by spreading Herbed Breakfast Patties mixture evenly in bottom and up sides of a 9-inch pie plate.

2. Place potatoes in shell and drizzle on melted butter.

3. Bake 40 minutes, or until sausage is cooked through. Top with cheese and bake 5 minutes longer, until cheese melts. Tilt pan to drain off excess fat and cut into wedges to serve.

279   TURKEY AND CHILE PUFF
Prep: 15 minutes   Cook: 35 minutes   Serves: 4 to 6

1   pound ground turkey
1   small onion, chopped
1   garlic clove, minced
¾   teaspoon salt
¼   teaspoon pepper
3   (4-ounce) cans whole mild
    green chiles, rinsed and
    drained

6   eggs
¾   cup flour
¾   teaspoon baking powder
½   cup milk
⅛   teaspoon cayenne
¾   cup shredded sharp
    Cheddar cheese

1. Preheat oven to 350°. In a large skillet, cook ground turkey, onion, and garlic over medium-high heat, stirring often to break up lumps of meat, until turkey loses its pink color, about 5 minutes. Drain off excess liquid. Season with ½ teaspoon salt and pepper. Spread turkey mixture evenly over bottom of a lightly oiled 9-inch square baking dish. Arrange whole chiles over turkey.

2. In a blender or food processor, combine eggs, flour, baking powder, milk, remaining ¼ teaspoon salt, and cayenne; process until smooth. Pour batter over chiles and sprinkle Cheddar cheese over all.

3. Bake until batter is puffed and set, 25 to 30 minutes. Serve immediately.

280   BAKED TURKEY AND WILD RICE HASH
Prep: 10 minutes   Cook: 1 hour 40 minutes   Serves: 6 to 8

5½   cups chicken stock or
    reduced-sodium canned
    broth
1½   teaspoons salt
1½   cups wild rice (about
    12 ounces)
1½   pounds ground turkey
2   medium onions, chopped
1   pound fresh mushrooms,
    thinly sliced

1   teaspoon thyme
½   teaspoon poultry seasoning
½   teaspoon pepper
4   tablespoons butter
⅓   cup flour
1½   cups half-and-half
½   cup sliced almonds

1. In a large saucepan, bring 4 cups chicken stock and ¼ teaspoon salt to a boil. Add wild rice and return to boil. Reduce heat to low, cover tightly, and simmer until rice is just tender, about 45 minutes. Drain rice, if necessary. (Rice can be cooked up to a day ahead.)

2. Preheat oven to 350°. In a large skillet, cook ground turkey, onions, and mushrooms over medium heat, stirring often to break up lumps of meat, until turkey loses its pink color, about 6 minutes. Drain off excess liquid. Stir in thyme, poultry seasoning, ½ teaspoon salt, and ¼ teaspoon pepper.

3. In a medium saucepan, melt butter over medium-low heat. Whisk in flour and cook, stirring constantly, 2 minutes without letting mixture brown. Whisk in half-and-half and remaining 1½ cups chicken stock, ¾ teaspoon salt, and ¼ teaspoon pepper. Bring to a boil, whisking constantly until thickened. Reduce heat to low and simmer, whisking often, 3 minutes.

4. Spread wild rice evenly over bottom of a lightly buttered 9 x 13-inch baking dish. Cover with turkey mixture. Spread sauce over turkey.

5. Bake 30 minutes. Sprinkle almonds over top and bake until hash is bubbling and almonds are browned, 10 to 15 minutes longer.

---

281   CHICKEN AND SPINACH FILO PIE
Prep: 30 minutes   Cook: 1 hour 10 minutes   Serves: 8 to 12

1 stick (4 ounces) butter
⅓ cup flour
1½ cups milk
1 cup reduced-sodium chicken broth
1 teaspoon salt
¼ teaspoon pepper
⅛ teaspoon grated nutmeg
2 eggs
1½ pounds ground chicken

1 medium onion, chopped
1 garlic clove, minced
2 (10-ounce) packages frozen chopped spinach, thawed and squeezed dry
2 teaspoons savory
1 teaspoon oregano
6 tablespoons olive oil
16 sheets of filo dough
¾ cup grated Parmesan cheese

1. In a heavy medium saucepan, melt ½ stick butter over medium-low heat. Whisk in flour and cook, stirring, about 2 minutes without letting mixture brown. Whisk in milk and broth and bring to a boil, whisking until smooth and thickened. Reduce heat to low and simmer, whisking often, 3 minutes. Season with ¼ teaspoon salt, pepper, and nutmeg. In a medium bowl, beat eggs until blended. Gradually whisk hot sauce into eggs.

2. In a large skillet, cook ground chicken, onion, and garlic over medium heat, stirring often to break up lumps of meat, until chicken loses its pink color, about 5 minutes. Drain off excess liquid. Blend in spinach, savory, oregano, and remaining ¾ teaspoon salt. Stir in sauce.

3. Preheat oven to 350°. In a small saucepan, melt remaining ½ stick butter in olive oil over low heat; set aside next to work area. Open and stack filo sheets and cover with a damp towel.

4. Layer 8 filo sheets in a lightly buttered 9 x 13-inch pan, brushing each sheet with butter mixture and folding edges in to fit pan.

5. Spread chicken mixture evenly in pan and sprinkle with Parmesan cheese. Layer remaining filo sheets over filling, brushing each sheet with butter mixture and letting excess hang over edges of pan. Tuck edges into baking pan. Brush top with remaining butter mixture.

6. Bake until top of dough is golden brown and filling is heated through, 50 to 60 minutes. Let stand 10 minutes before cutting into squares to serve.

282 PORK AND APPLE PANCAKES
Prep: 10 minutes   Cook: 8 minutes   Makes: 16 pancakes

¾ pound ground pork
2 medium Granny Smith
    apples, cored and thinly
    sliced
¼ teaspoon sage
¼ teaspoon salt

2 cups dry buttermilk
    biscuit mix
1 cup milk
2 eggs
    Vegetable oil, for griddle
    Applesauce or maple syrup

1. Preheat oven to 200°. In a large skillet, cook ground pork and apple slices over medium-high heat, stirring often to break up lumps of meat, until pork loses its pink color, about 5 minutes. Drain off excess fat. Stir in sage and salt. Let meat mixture cool until tepid.

2. In a medium bowl, whisk biscuit mix, milk, and eggs until smooth. Stir in tepid pork and apple mixture.

3. Heat a large skillet or griddle over high heat. Skillet or griddle is hot enough to cook pancakes when a sprinkle of water forms droplets that "dance" on skillet's surface. Lightly grease skillet or griddle with vegetable oil.

4. In batches, using about 3 tablespoons batter for each pancake, pour batter onto hot skillet. Cook until edges of pancakes are dry, about 2 minutes. With a small metal spatula, turn pancakes and cook until undersides are browned and pancakes are cooked through, about 1 minute. Transfer cooked pancakes to a baking sheet and keep warm in oven. Repeat procedure with remaining batter. Serve pancakes hot with applesauce or maple syrup.

---

283 FETTUCCINE AND CHICKEN CASSEROLE
Prep: 20 minutes   Cook: 1¼ hours   Serves: 6 to 8

8 ounces fettuccine
1 pound ground chicken
1 medium onion, chopped
2 tablespoons flour
1½ cups milk, scalded
1 cup shredded Cheddar
    cheese (4 ounces)
1 cup grated Parmesan cheese
    (4 ounces)

1 stick (4 ounces) butter, cut
    up, at room temperature
¼ cup chopped parsley
⅛ teaspoon grated nutmeg
¾ teaspoon salt
¼ teaspoon hot pepper sauce
6 eggs, separated

1. In a large saucepan of boiling salted water, cook fettuccine until just tender, about 9 minutes. Drain, rinse under cold water, and drain again.

2. Meanwhile, in a large skillet over medium heat, cook ground chicken and onion, stirring often to break up lumps of meat, until chicken loses its pink color, about 5 minutes. Drain off any liquid. Stir in flour.

3. In a large bowl, combine fettuccine, chicken mixture, scalded milk, Cheddar cheese, Parmesan cheese, butter, parsley, nutmeg, salt, and hot sauce. Toss to mix. Let stand until tepid, about 15 minutes. Stir egg yolks gently but thoroughly into fettuccine mixture.

4. Preheat oven to 350°. Beat egg whites just until stiff peaks form. Stir a fourth of beaten whites into fettuccine mixture. Gently fold in remaining egg whites. Transfer to a lightly buttered 3-quart casserole about 3 inches deep.

5. Bake until custard is set and top is puffed and deep golden brown, about 1 hour. Let stand 5 minutes before serving.

---

284 TURKEY, MUSHROOM, AND SWISS CHEESE STRATA

Prep: 20 minutes   Chill: 2 hours   Cook: 1 hour   Serves: 8 to 12

1½ pounds ground turkey	½ pound boiled ham, cut into ½-inch cubes
1 medium onion, chopped	
½ pound fresh mushrooms, sliced	5 eggs
	2¼ cups milk
½ cup dry white wine	12 to 16 slices whole-wheat bread, cut into ½-inch cubes
1½ teaspoons tarragon	
1 teaspoon salt	
½ teaspoon pepper	3 cups shredded Swiss cheese

1. Preheat oven to 350°. In a large skillet, cook ground turkey, onion, and mushrooms over medium-high heat, stirring often to break up lumps of meat, until turkey loses its pink color, about 5 minutes. Add wine, tarragon, ½ teaspoon salt, and ¼ teaspoon pepper. Cook until liquid is almost evaporated, about 2 minutes. Stir in diced ham.

2. In a medium bowl, whisk together eggs, milk, and remaining ½ teaspoon salt and ¼ teaspoon pepper.

3. In a lightly buttered 9 x 13-inch baking dish, place enough bread cubes to cover bottom. Cover with turkey mixture, then sprinkle on 1½ cups cheese. Top with remaining bread cubes. Sprinkle remaining cheese over bread. Pour egg mixture over all, cover with plastic wrap, and refrigerate for at least 2 hours or overnight.

4. Bake until egg mixture is set and top is browned, 50 to 60 minutes. Let stand 5 minutes before cutting into squares to serve.

285   DENVER BREAKFAST PIE
Prep: 5 minutes   Cook: 17 minutes   Serves: 4 to 6

2¼ cups dry buttermilk biscuit mix	½ teaspoon sage
⅔ cup milk	½ teaspoon thyme
1 pound ground pork	½ teaspoon pepper
1 small onion, chopped	5 eggs
1 small red bell pepper, chopped	2 tablespoons chopped parsley
1 teaspoon salt	Tomato salsa

1. Preheat oven to 450°. In a medium bowl, stir biscuit mix with milk until a soft dough forms. With floured hands, press dough evenly into a lightly buttered 9-inch pie plate, pushing dough up sides to form a shell.

2. Bake until lightly browned, about 10 minutes. (Biscuit will lose its shell shape.) Protecting your hands with a clean kitchen towel, press biscuit against pie plate to re-form shell.

3. Meanwhile, in a large skillet, cook ground pork, onion, and bell pepper over medium-high heat, stirring often to break up lumps of meat, until pork loses its pink color, about 5 minutes. Pour off excess fat. Stir in ¾ teaspoon salt, sage, thyme, and ¼ teaspoon pepper.

4. In a medium bowl, whisk eggs, parsley, and remaining ¼ teaspoon each salt and pepper until blended. Pour into skillet and stir until eggs are scrambled to desired doneness. Pour egg mixture into hot biscuit shell. Cut into wedges to serve. Pass a bowl of salsa on the side.

286   HERBED BREAKFAST PATTIES
Prep: 5 minutes   Cook: 12 minutes   Serves: 6

1 pound ground pork	¼ teaspoon ground allspice
¾ teaspoon salt	⅛ teaspoon ground ginger
1 teaspoon ground sage	⅛ teaspoon ground coriander
¼ teaspoon pepper	⅛ teaspoon cayenne
¼ teaspoon thyme	1 tablespoon vegetable oil
¼ teaspoon marjoram	

1. In a medium bowl, combine all ingredients except oil. Form into 6 patties about ½ inch thick.

2. In a large skillet, heat oil. Add patties and cook over medium-high heat, turning once, until browned outside and cooked through, 10 to 12 minutes.

Chapter 12

Pizzas, Tacos, Sandwiches, and Such

Here's what I call the "fun foods" chapter, a collection of meaty goodies that seem to be at their best when you toss away the plate and eat them right out of your hands. For years, I have joked with my best friend about his habit of eating pizza with a fork and knife—I'm sorry, but it just doesn't taste the same.

Ever-popular pizza pops up in quite a few surprising guises. The Lebanese Lamb Pizzas, without a smidgen of cheese, are exotic and intriguingly spiced. Folded over into half-moon shapes, Pork and Broccoli Calzones made a great supper with a green salad. Favorite pizza ingredients are rolled into Stuffed Pizza Bread that scored a 10½ with my friends. I even included some Tortilla Salsa Pizzas, made in a snap with flour tortillas, ground meat, and bottled salsa.

Of course, many Mexican foods fit into this "let-the-good-times-roll" category. With very little effort, you can turn my basic recipe for Mexican Meat Filling into a variety of spicy taste teasers. Who can resist quesadillas, burritos, tacos, and tostadas? I learned how to make these South-of-the-border specialties while I was a student in Guadalajara in Mexico. While my experimenting with the original recipes over the years may have altered the authenticity slightly, I can tell you that they are *muy sabrosos* (delicious).

Kids love to eat sandwiches. For them, you'll find a number of "sloppy" ground meat fillings that always garner requests for seconds.

---

287 SLOPPY JOES
Prep: 10 minutes   Cook: 40 minutes   Serves: 8

1 **pound ground round**	1 **cup beef broth**
(85% lean)	¾ **teaspoon celery salt**
1 **small onion, chopped**	¼ **teaspoon pepper**
1 **celery rib, chopped**	8 **hamburger buns, toasted**
1 **cup ketchup**	

1. In a large skillet, cook ground round, onion, and celery over medium heat, stirring often to break up lumps of meat, until beef loses its pink color, about 5 minutes.

2. Stir in ketchup, broth, celery salt, and pepper. Bring to a boil, reduce heat to low, partially cover, and simmer, stirring often, until thickened, about 35 minutes. Serve on toasted hamburger buns.

288   SLOPPY JOSÉS
Prep: 10 minutes   Cook: 30 minutes   Serves: 8

1 pound ground round
   (85% lean)
1 small onion, chopped
1 small green bell pepper,
   chopped
1 jalapeño pepper, seeded
   and chopped, or
   2 tablespoons canned
   chopped green chiles
1 garlic clove, minced

1 tablespoon chili powder
1 cup tomato sauce
1 cup tomato juice
½ teaspoon salt
1 (16-ounce) can kidney
   beans, drained
8 hamburger buns, toasted
1 cup shredded Cheddar
   cheese (4 ounces)

1. In a large skillet, cook ground round, onion, bell pepper, jalapeño pepper, and garlic over medium heat, stirring often to break up lumps of meat, until beef loses its pink color, about 5 minutes. Drain off excess fat. Add chili powder and cook, stirring, 1 minute.

2. Stir in tomato sauce, tomato juice, and salt. Bring to a boil, reduce heat, cover partially, and simmer, stirring often, until thickened, about 20 minutes. Add kidney beans and cook until beans are heated through, about 5 minutes.

3. Serve on toasted hamburger buns. Pass a bowl of grated Cheddar cheese for sprinkling on top.

289   SLOPPY GIUSEPPES
Prep: 10 minutes   Cook: 25 minutes   Serves: 12

1 pound ground round
   (85% lean)
1 pound hot Italian sausage,
   removed from casing and
   crumbled
1 small onion, chopped
1 small green bell pepper,
   chopped

¼ pound fresh mushrooms,
   sliced
1 garlic clove, minced
1 cup tomato sauce
½ teaspoon oregano
¼ teaspoon sugar
¼ cup grated Parmesan cheese
12 Italian rolls, toasted

1. In a large skillet or flameproof casserole, cook ground round, sausage, onion, bell pepper, mushrooms, and garlic over medium heat, stirring often to break up lumps, until meat loses its pink color, about 6 minutes.

2. Stir in tomato sauce, oregano, sugar, and ⅓ cup water. Bring to a boil, reduce heat to low, partially cover, and simmer, stirring often, until thickened, 20 to 25 minutes. Stir in Parmesan cheese. Serve on toasted Italian rolls.

290 CALIFORNIA-STYLE BURRITOS

Prep: 10 minutes   Cook: 5 minutes   Makes: 10 burritos

8 (10-inch) flour tortillas
1 (16-ounce) can refried beans
2 cups Mexican Meat Filling, (page 212)
1 large avocado, diced
⅔ cup tomato salsa

⅔ cup sour cream
2 cups shredded sharp Cheddar cheese
2 cups shredded iceberg lettuce

1. Preheat oven to 425°. Wrap tortillas in aluminum foil and bake until heated through, 10 to 15 minutes. Reduce oven temperature to 200°. Or place tortillas between 2 double layers of moistened paper towels and microwave on High about 2 minutes, until heated through.

2. In separate medium saucepans, cook beans and meat filling over medium-low heat, stirring often, until heated through. For each burrito, spread 1 warm tortilla with about 3 tablespoons refried beans, leaving a 2-inch border around edges. Place about 3 tablespoons meat filling in center of beans and top with 1 tablespoon each avocado, salsa, and sour cream. Sprinkle a scant ¼ cup each shredded cheese and lettuce over each. Fold in sides of tortilla, then fold up bottom edge and roll up like a cigar. Keep burritos warm in oven while making remainder. Serve immediately.

291 LAMB-STUFFED SUPPER PITAS

Prep: 15 minutes   Cook: 17 minutes   Serves: 4

4 pita breads, partially opened
1 pound lean ground lamb or ground sirloin (90% lean)
1 medium zucchini, cut into ½-inch dice
1 small onion, minced
1 garlic clove, minced
1 (10-ounce) package chopped frozen spinach, thawed and squeezed dry

1 teaspoon oregano
1 teaspoon salt
¼ teaspoon pepper
¼ cup grated Parmesan cheese
2 medium ripe tomatoes, diced
¼ cup plain low-fat yogurt

1. Preheat oven to 400°. Stack pitas, wrap in foil, and bake until heated through, about 10 minutes.

2. Meanwhile, in a large skillet, cook ground lamb, zucchini, onion, and garlic over medium-high heat, stirring often to break up lumps of meat, until lamb loses its pink color, about 5 minutes. Add spinach, oregano, salt, and pepper. Cook, mixing well, until heated through, about 2 minutes. Remove from heat and stir in cheese.

3. Spoon lamb filling into pitas. Top with diced tomatoes and a dollop of yogurt.

292   PEPPERY BEEF PIZZA

Prep: 10 minutes   Cook: 20 minutes   Serves: 6

1 pound prepared pizza
    dough or frozen white
    bread dough, thawed
1½ cups shredded mozzarella
    cheese (6 ounces)
3 medium plum tomatoes, cut
    crosswise into ½-inch
    slices
¾ pound ground sirloin
    (90% lean)
1 small red bell pepper, cut
    lengthwise into ½-inch
    strips

1 small yellow bell pepper,
    cut lengthwise into
    ½-inch strips
1 small red onion, thinly
    sliced
2 garlic cloves, minced
¼ teaspoon crushed hot red
    pepper
2 tablespoons grated
    Parmesan cheese
1 tablespoon olive oil
2 tablespoons chopped fresh
    basil or parsley

1. Preheat oven to 500° if using pizza dough or 475° if using bread dough. On a lightly floured work surface, roll out dough to a 12-inch circle and transfer to a pizza pan.

2. Sprinkle 1 cup mozzarella cheese evenly over dough, leaving a 1-inch border all around. Arrange tomatoes over cheese. Crumble ground sirloin over tomatoes. Top with red and yellow peppers, red onion, garlic, and hot pepper. Sprinkle Parmesan cheese and remaining ½ cup mozzarella over pizza. Drizzle olive oil over top.

3. Bake 15 to 20 minutes, until crust is golden and pizza is cooked through. Sprinkle on basil just before serving.

293   MEXICAN MEAT FILLING

Prep: 5 minutes   Cook: 10 minutes   Makes: 2 cups

Make a double batch of this spicy filling to store in the freezer. It is the basis for a whole *fiesta* of quick and easy dishes and can be an invaluable stash when you need to make dinner *muy pronto!*

1 pound ground chuck
    (80% lean) or ground
    round (85% lean)
1 medium onion, chopped
2 garlic cloves, minced
1 small fresh chile pepper,
    seeded and minced, or
    ⅛ teaspoon cayenne

2 tablespoons chili powder
½ teaspoon ground cumin
¾ teaspoon salt
1 cup tomato sauce

In a large skillet, cook ground chuck, onion, garlic, and chile pepper over medium-high heat, stirring often, until meat is no longer pink, about 5 minutes. Add chili powder, cumin, and salt and cook 1 minute. Add tomato sauce and cook, stirring often, until thickened, about 5 minutes.

294 HOT ITALIAN HERO
Prep: 20 minutes   Cook: 40 minutes   Serves: 8

1 (2-pound) round loaf of
  Italian or French bread,
  unsliced
1 pound ground round
  (85% lean)
1 pound hot Italian sausage,
  casings removed
1 large onion, chopped

1 medium green bell pepper,
  chopped
2 garlic cloves, minced
1 cup tomato sauce
1 cup sliced black olives
1½ teaspoons Italian seasoning
1½ cups shredded mozzarella
  cheese (6 ounces)

1. Preheat oven to 350°. Slice top off bread loaf. Pull out soft inside (and reserve for another use, such as bread crumbs), leaving a 1-inch-thick shell. Set aside.

2. In a large skillet, cook ground round, sausage, onion, bell pepper, and garlic over medium-high heat, stirring often to break up lumps, until meat loses its pink color, about 7 minutes.

3. Add tomato sauce, sliced olives, and Italian seasoning. Cook, stirring, until heated through, about 2 minutes. Stir in cheese.

4. Spoon meat filling into bread shell; replace top of loaf. Wrap tightly in aluminum foil. Bake 30 to 35 minutes, or until heated through. For ease in cutting, remove top of loaf and separately cut top and bottom into 8 wedges. Replace top wedges to serve.

295 BEEF AND CHEDDAR QUESADILLAS
Prep: 10 minutes   Cook: 10 minutes   Serves: 5

10 (8-inch) flour tortillas
2 tablespoons vegetable oil
2 cups Mexican Meat Filling
  (page 212)
1⅔ cups shredded sharp
  Cheddar cheese (about
  6 ounces)

⅔ cup tomato salsa
⅓ cup sour cream (optional)
2 avocados, sliced

1. Preheat oven to 325°. Lightly brush 1 tortilla with oil and place on a baking sheet. Spread a heaping ⅓ cup meat filling over tortilla. Sprinkle on ⅓ cup shredded cheese. Brush another tortilla with oil; place on top of filled tortilla. Repeat procedure with remaining pairs of tortillas and filling. (You may overlap quesadillas to fit onto baking sheets.)

2. Bake until cheese has melted and quesadillas are heated through, about 8 minutes. Transfer quesadillas to plates. Top each quesadilla with 2 tablespoons salsa and 1 tablespoon sour cream, if desired. Arrange avocado slices on tops in a spoke pattern. Using a pizza wheel or sharp knife, cut quesadillas into wedges and serve hot.

296   LEBANESE LAMB PIZZAS

Prep: 20 minutes   Rising Time: 1½ hours
Cook: 15 minutes   Makes: 6 pizzas

2 tablespoons olive oil
¼ cup pine nuts (pignoli)
1 pound lean ground lamb
1 medium onion, chopped
1 small Italian frying pepper
   or green bell pepper,
   chopped
2 garlic cloves, minced
¼ cup chopped parsley
¼ cup tomato paste

2 tablespoons lemon juice
1 teaspoon dried mint
1¼ teaspoons salt
½ teaspoon ground allspice
½ teaspoon paprika
¼ teaspoon pepper
⅛ teaspoon cayenne
1 pound prepared pizza
   dough or frozen bread
   dough, thawed

1. Position racks in bottom third and center of oven and preheat to 500°. Heat oil in a large skillet. Add pine nuts and cook over medium heat, stirring often, until lightly browned, 1 to 2 minutes. With a slotted spoon, transfer pine nuts to paper towels to drain.

2. In a large bowl, combine ground lamb, onion, Italian pepper, garlic, parsley, tomato paste, lemon juice, mint, salt, allspice, paprika, pepper, and cayenne. Knead with your hands until well mixed.

3. Divide pizza dough into 6 balls. On a lightly floured surface, roll out 1 ball to a 5- to 6-inch round. Transfer round to a baking sheet. Spread a sixth of lamb mixture over dough, leaving a 1-inch border around edges. Sprinkle top with about 2 teaspoons browned pine nuts. Repeat procedure with remaining dough, filling, and pine nuts, arranging pizzas on 2 baking sheets.

4. Bake 12 to 15 minutes, switching positions of sheets halfway through baking times, until crusts are golden brown.

297   BEEF TACOS

Prep: 10 minutes   Cook: 5 minutes   Makes: 6 tacos

2 cups Mexican Meat Filling
   (page 212)
6 taco shells
1½ cups shredded iceberg
   lettuce
2 medium tomatoes, seeded
   and chopped

1 cup shredded sharp
   Cheddar cheese
   (4 ounces)
Bottled taco sauce

1. In a medium saucepan, cook meat filling over medium-low heat, stirring often, until hot, about 5 minutes. Transfer filling to a warm bowl.

2. On a large platter, arrange taco shells, shredded lettuce, tomatoes, and grated cheese. Set out filling and a bowl of taco sauce. Allow guests to fill their own taco shells and add garnishes as desired.

298   BEEF TOSTADAS
Prep: 10 minutes   Cook: 5 minutes   Serves: 4

¼ cup vegetable oil
4 corn tortillas
1 (16-ounce) can refried beans
2 cups Mexican Meat Filling
(page 212)

2 cups shredded iceberg
lettuce
1 cup grated sharp Cheddar
cheese
1½ cups tomato salsa

1. In a large skillet, heat oil over medium-high heat until very hot but not smoking. One at a time, cook tortillas, turning once, until crisp, about 45 seconds. With tongs, transfer tortillas to a paper towel–lined baking sheet and let drain.

2. In separate medium saucepans, cook beans and meat filling over medium-low heat, stirring often, until hot. Spread each tortilla with ½ cup refried beans. Top each with about ½ cup each shredded lettuce and meat filling. Sprinkle grated cheese over tostadas, then top each with a dollop of salsa.

---

299   STUFFED PIZZA BREAD
Prep: 30 minutes   Cook: 50 minutes   Serves: 8

1 pound ground pork
1 small onion, finely chopped
1 garlic clove, minced
2 tablespoons tomato paste
1 teaspoon Italian seasoning
¼ teaspoon fennel seed,
crushed
¾ teaspoon salt

¼ teaspoon crushed hot red
pepper
½ cup shredded mozzarella
cheese
1 pound prepared pizza
dough or frozen bread
dough, thawed
1 tablespoon olive oil

1. In a large skillet, cook ground pork, onion, and garlic over medium-high heat, stirring often to break up lumps of meat, until pork loses its pink color, about 5 minutes. Drain off excess fat. Remove from heat and stir in tomato paste, Italian seasoning, fennel seed, salt, and hot pepper. Let filling cool completely; then stir in mozzarella cheese.

2. Preheat oven to 400°. On a floured work surface, roll out dough to a 10 x 14-inch rectangle. Spread cooled filling on dough, leaving a 1-inch border on all sides. Starting at a long side, roll up dough tightly. Pinch seams shut and fold short ends under roll. With a sharp knife, make three 1-inch slashes on top of loaf, cutting through to filling. Place bread on a large baking sheet and brush lightly with olive oil.

3. Bake pizza bread until loaf is golden brown and bottom sounds hollow when tapped with your knuckle, 35 to 45 minutes. Let bread cool completely before slicing.

300 CHICKEN ENCHILADAS WITH GREEN SAUCE

Prep: 15 minutes   Cook: 35 minutes   Serves: 6 to 10

Canned tomatillos are available in many supermarkets. If you can't find them, substitute 3 cups of bottled green salsa for the homemade version below.

2 **pounds ground chicken**	¼ **cup vegetable oil**
1 **small onion, finely chopped**	12 **corn tortillas**
1 **cup sour cream**	1½ **cups shredded Monterey**
1 **teaspoon salt**	**Jack cheese (about**
½ **teaspoon pepper**	**6 ounces)**
Tomatillo Tomato Salsa	
(recipe follows)	

1. Preheat oven to 350°. In a large skillet, cook ground chicken and onion over medium heat, stirring often to break up lumps, until chicken loses its pink color, about 5 minutes. Drain off excess liquid. Stir in ⅓ cup sour cream, salt, and pepper. Transfer to a medium bowl and let cool slightly.

2. Stir remaining ⅔ cup sour cream into Tomatillo Salsa. Spread a thin layer of salsa mixture in bottom of a lightly oiled 9 x 13-inch baking dish; pour about ½ cup onto a plate.

3 In a medium nonstick skillet, heat 1 teaspoon oil over medium-high heat. One at a time, place a tortilla in the hot oil. Cook, turning once, just until tortilla is softened and pliable, about 15 seconds per side. With tongs, pick up tortilla and dip tortilla in salsa mixture on plate, turning to coat both sides. Place about ⅓ cup filling down center of tortilla, roll up, and transfer to prepared baking dish. Repeat procedure with remaining tortillas, filling, and sauce. As necessary, add more oil to skillet and salsa to plate. Pour remaining sauce over top of enchiladas and sprinkle Monterey Jack cheese over top.

4. Bake until enchiladas are bubbling and cheese is melted, about 25 minutes.

TOMATILLO TOMATO SALSA
Makes about 2½ cups

3 **(11-ounce) cans tomatillos**	2 **jalapeño peppers, seeded**
(Mexican green	¼ **cup packed cilantro leaves**
tomatoes), rinsed and	¼ **teaspoon salt**
drained (see Note)	⅛ **teaspoon sugar**
1 **small onion, chopped**	2 **tablespoons vegetable oil**
3 **garlic cloves**	

1. In a food processor or blender, combine tomatillos, onion, garlic, jalapeño peppers, cilantro, salt, and sugar. Puree until smooth.

2 In a large skillet, heat oil. Add tomatillo puree and simmer over medium-low heat, stirring often, until slightly thickened, about 5 minutes.

NOTE: *If fresh tomatillos are available, 2½ pounds can be substituted for canned. Remove husks and simmer until barely tender in salted water, about 6 minutes. Do not overcook tomatillos or they will burst.*

---

301   PIZZA RUSTICA
Prep: 15 minutes   Cook: 1 hour   Serves: 6 to 10

Without a doubt, this is one of my most popular buffet dishes—layers of Italian cheese, thick meaty tomato sauce, and roasted peppers in a flaky double crust. It's a knife-and-fork pizza, just for my friend Patrick.

- 1 pound ground pork
- 1 medium onion, chopped
- 1 garlic clove, minced
- 1¼ cups tomato puree
- 1 (3-ounce) can tomato paste
- 1½ teaspoons basil
- ¾ teaspoon salt
- ¼ teaspoon crushed hot red pepper
- ½ cup chopped pitted Mediterranean black olives
- 5 eggs

- 1 (15-ounce) container part-skim ricotta cheese
- 1 cup grated Parmesan cheese (about 4 ounces)
- ¼ cup chopped parsley
- ¼ teaspoon black pepper
- 1 (17½-ounce) package frozen puff pastry, thawed
- ½ pound part-skim mozzarella cheese, sliced
- 1 (12-ounce) jar roasted red peppers, drained

1. In a large skillet, cook ground pork, onion, and garlic over medium heat, stirring often to break up lumps, until meat loses its pink color, about 5 minutes. Stir in tomato puree, tomato paste, basil, ½ teaspoon salt, and hot pepper. Bring to a simmer, stirring often. Add olives.

2. In a large bowl, beat 4 eggs lightly with a fork. Add ricotta, Parmesan cheese, parsley, remaining ¼ teaspoon salt, and black pepper. Mix to blend well.

3. Preheat oven to 400°. On a lightly floured work surface, roll 1 sheet of puff pastry ⅛ inch thick. Cut into a 12-inch circle. Ease pastry circle into a 10-inch pie plate, letting excess hang over sides. Roll out remaining sheet of pastry and cut into an 11-inch circle and set aside.

4. Line bottom of pastry with half of cheese mixture and top with half of mozzarella. Spread half of tomato sauce over cheese. Arrange half of peppers over sauce. Repeat layers. Cover with pastry circle. Press edges of pastry together to seal, fold over to form a seam, and crimp. In a decorative manner, cut four 1-inch slashes in top to allow steam to escape.

5. In a small bowl, beat remaining egg. Brush pastry with some of beaten egg. Place pie plate on a baking sheet and bake until golden brown, about 45 minutes. Let stand at least 20 minutes before cutting into wedges to serve.

302   PORK AND BROCCOLI CALZONES
Prep: 20 minutes   Cook: 20 minutes   Makes: 4 calzones

½ pound ground pork
1 small onion, minced
1 garlic clove, minced
1 teaspoon basil
½ teaspoon sage
¼ teaspoon fennel seed, crushed
¾ teaspoon salt
¼ teaspoon crushed hot red pepper

1 (10-ounce) package frozen chopped broccoli, thawed
1 cup low-fat ricotta cheese
½ cup shredded mozzarella cheese
⅓ cup grated Parmesan cheese
1 pound prepared pizza dough or frozen bread dough, thawed
1 tablespoon olive oil

1. Preheat oven to 500°. In a large skillet, cook ground pork, onion, and garlic over medium-high heat, stirring often to break up lumps of meat, until pork loses its pink color, about 5 minutes. Drain off excess fat. Stir in basil, sage, fennel, salt, and hot pepper. Remove from heat and let cool slightly. Stir in broccoli, ricotta, mozzarella, and Parmesan.

2. Divide dough into 4 balls. On a lightly floured work surface, roll out 1 ball to a 9-inch circle. Place a fourth of filling in center of dough, leaving a 1-inch border. Fold dough over in half to enclose filling in a half-moon shape. Pinch edges of dough sealed, then flute. Brush top of dough lightly with olive oil. Transfer to a baking sheet. Repeat procedure with remaining dough and filling, placing calzones on 2 baking sheets.

3. Bake until calzones are golden brown, 12 to 15 minutes. Serve hot.

303   TORTILLA SALSA PIZZAS
Prep: 10 minutes   Cook: 15 minutes   Serves: 4

1 pound ground chicken
1 small onion, chopped
1 garlic clove, minced
2 teaspoons chili powder
4 (7- or 8-inch) flour tortillas

2 tablespoons olive oil
¾ cup tomato salsa
1 cup shredded Monterey Jack cheese (4 ounces)

1. Preheat oven to 400°. In a large skillet, cook ground chicken, onion, and garlic over medium-high heat, stirring often to break up lumps of meat, until chicken loses its pink color, about 5 minutes. Drain off excess liquid. Stir in chili powder.

2. Place tortillas flat on 2 large baking sheets and brush lightly with olive oil. Bake 3 to 4 minutes, or until crisp.

3. Spread 2 tablespoons salsa over each tortilla. Spoon a fourth of chicken mixture over each. Sprinkle on cheese and dot with remaining salsa.

4. Bake until cheese is melted and tortillas are browned, about 6 minutes. Serve 1 per person, each cut into 4 wedges.

304 MACHO MEATBALL HEROES
Prep: 15 minutes   Cook: 1 hour   Serves: 6 to 8

½ cup fresh bread crumbs
¼ cup milk
1 egg
2½ teaspoons Italian seasoning
¼ teaspoon salt
½ teaspoon crushed hot red
    pepper
1 pound ground round
    (85% lean)
¾ pound ground pork

¼ cup olive oil
1 medium onion, minced
1 garlic clove, minced
1 (28-ounce) can peeled Italian
    tomatoes with added
    puree, chopped
1 cup tomato sauce
6 individual Italian rolls,
    sliced lengthwise
    Grated Parmesan cheese

1. In a medium bowl, combine bread crumbs, milk, egg, 1 teaspoon Italian seasoning, salt, and ¼ teaspoon hot pepper. Mix with a fork to combine. Add ground round and ground pork and mix until blended. Using about 1 tablespoon for each, form meat mixture into 18 meatballs.

2. In a large skillet or flameproof casserole, heat oil over medium heat. In batches, if necessary, add meatballs and cook, turning, until browned and crusty all over, about 8 minutes per batch. With a slotted spoon, transfer meatballs to a plate and set aside. Discard all but 2 tablespoons of fat from skillet.

3. Add onion to skillet and cook, stirring often, until softened, about 3 minutes. Add garlic and cook, stirring, 1 minute. Add tomatoes with their puree, tomato sauce, and remaining 1½ teaspoons Italian seasoning and ¼ teaspoon hot pepper. Reduce heat to low, partially cover, and simmer 30 minutes. Return meatballs to skillet and cook, uncovered, 15 minutes.

4. Pull out soft insides from rolls, leaving shells about ¾ inch thick. (Save insides for another use, such as making bread crumbs.) Place 3 meatballs in the bottom of each roll, spoon about ¼ cup tomato sauce over meatballs, and replace tops of rolls. Pass bowls of remaining tomato sauce and Parmesan cheese on the side.

305   PENNSYLVANIA BBQ

Prep: 10 minutes   Cook: 1 hour 40 minutes   Serves: 8

My elegant friend Irene Rothschild is quite accomplished in the kitchen, as her cookbooks and cooking students testify. But when she has a bunch of kids to serve, she offers this rendition of a homespun Pennsylvania favorite.

2   pounds ground chuck
    (80% lean)
1   medium onion, chopped
1   small bell pepper, chopped
1   celery rib, chopped
2   garlic cloves, chopped
3   cups tomato sauce

½   cup ketchup
2   tablespoons vinegar
2   tablespoons brown sugar
1   tablespoon salt
1   tablespoon pepper
12   hamburger buns, toasted

1. In a large nonreactive saucepan or flameproof casserole, cook ground chuck, onion, bell pepper, celery, and garlic over medium-high heat, stirring often to break up lumps of meat, until beef loses its pink color, about 8 minutes. Drain off excess fat.

2. Stir in tomato sauce, ketchup, vinegar, brown sugar, salt, and pepper. Bring to a boil, reduce heat to low, cover, and simmer, stirring occasionally, until thickened, about 1½ hours. Serve on toasted hamburger buns.

Chapter 13

It's a Wrap: Savory Pastries

Juicy, well-seasoned meat filling surrounded by a flaky crust—what a mouthwatering image! If the thought of a steaming savory pastry makes your eyes glaze over, don't worry, you're far from alone. In fact, in researching recipes for this book, it was intriguing to find how many countries boasted pastry-wrapped ground meats to be sliced and served on a plate with a fork or individually to eat out of hand. Here you'll find spicy meat and potato pies from the Bayou Country in Louisiana, deep-dish beef and mushroom pie from Russia, Grecian chicken and spinach filo pies, pork and cabbage strudel from Hungary, peppery chicken turnovers from Chile, and Marrakesh Lamb Turnovers from Morocco.

Some of these pastries make excellent hors d'oeuvres. Chinese Curried Beef Turnovers, the three piroshki recipes, and Spicy Lamb Samosas are perfect cocktail party fare, particularly because they can be made ahead, frozen unbaked, and cooked at the last minute to pass around steaming hot. Simply place the unbaked pastries on a baking sheet and freeze them, uncovered, until firm. Then individually wrap the pastries in aluminum foil. (Small pastries can be loosely stacked in an airtight container to be stored in the freezer, if used within two weeks.) When ready to cook, unwrap and bake at the temperature in the recipe, allowing an extra 10 or 15 minutes for the frozen pastry to cook through.

It's important that pastries brown evenly in the oven. If you are baking two sheets at a time, you'll find the top sheet always browns quickest, as the hot air rises and collects in the top part of the oven. In order to get the whole batch finished at the same time and to ensure even browning, switch the positions of the two baking sheets from top to bottom halfway during the baking.

306   SPICY CAJUN PORK PIES

Prep: 30 minutes   Cook: 35 minutes   Makes: 10 pies

2 tablespoons butter or
vegetable oil
1 medium onion, finely
chopped
2 celery ribs, finely chopped
2 scallions, chopped
1 medium green bell pepper,
finely chopped
1 pound ground pork
1 teaspoon garlic salt
1 teaspoon paprika

1 teaspoon thyme
1 teaspoon basil
¼ teaspoon black pepper
⅛ teaspoon crushed hot red
pepper
1 cup tomato sauce
Flaky Pastry Dough
(page 228)
1 egg, beaten with 1 teaspoon
milk to make a glaze

1. Preheat oven to 400°. In a large skillet, melt butter over medium heat. Add onion, celery, scallions, and bell pepper. Cook, stirring often, until softened, about 5 minutes. Add ground pork, garlic salt, paprika, thyme, basil, black pepper, and hot pepper. Cook, stirring often, until meat is no longer pink, about 5 minutes. Add tomato sauce and cook, stirring often, until thickened, about 3 minutes. Remove from heat and let filling cool completely.

2. On a lightly floured surface, roll out dough ⅛ inch thick. Using a 6-inch saucer as a guide, cut out 10 circles, gathering up dough scraps and rerolling as necessary. Place about ⅓ cup cooled filling on lower half of dough circle. Brush edge of dough with some egg glaze and fold dough in half to enclose filling. Press edges together and seal with tines of a fork. Pierce top of dough with fork to allow steam to escape. Repeat with remaining dough and filling.

3. Lightly brush pies with egg glaze. Bake until golden brown, about 20 minutes, switching positions of racks from top to bottom halfway through baking time. Serve hot, warm, or at room temperature.

---

307   DILLED BEEF PIROSHKI

*Prep: 1 hour   Cook: 20 to 25 minutes   Serves: 10 to 20 as an
appetizer; makes 40 piroshki*

1 pound ground round
(85% lean)
2 medium onions, chopped
1 garlic clove, minced
2 hard-boiled eggs, chopped
3 tablespoons sour cream or
plain low-fat yogurt

1 tablespoon chopped fresh
dill or 1 teaspoon dried
½ teaspoon salt
¼ teaspoon pepper
4 (7½-ounce) cans buttermilk
biscuits
1 egg, well beaten

1. In a large skillet, cook ground round, onions, and garlic over medium-high heat, stirring often to break up lumps of meat, until beef has lost its pink color, about 5 minutes. Drain off excess fat. Off heat, stir in hard-boiled eggs, sour cream, dill, salt, and pepper; let filling cool completely.

2. Preheat oven to 400°. One can at a time, separate biscuits. On a lightly floured surface, roll out each biscuit to a 3½-inch circle. Place about 1 tablespoon cooled filling in the center of each circle. Fold circles in half to enclose filling and pinch edges shut. Press edges with a fork to seal closed. Place filled piroshki on ungreased baking sheets. Repeat procedure with remaining dough and filling. (Gather up dough scraps, knead together, and reroll as necessary.)

3. Just before baking, brush tops of piroshki with beaten egg. Bake piroshki, in batches if necessary, 15 to 20 minutes, until golden brown. Keep unbaked piroshki batches covered with clean kitchen towels. Serve hot or warm. (Baked piroshki can be tightly wrapped and frozen for up to 1 month. Defrost and reheat in 350° oven 15 minutes.)

---

308 BALTIC PIROG PIE

Prep: 10 minutes   Cook: 1 hour   Serves: 6 to 8

3 medium carrots, cut into ¼-inch dice	2 teaspoons dried dill
1½ pounds ground round (85% lean)	1½ teaspoons salt
	¼ teaspoon pepper
2 medium onions, finely chopped	2 tablespoons flour
	1 cup sour cream
½ pound fresh mushrooms, quartered	Sour Cream Pastry (page 237)
	1 egg, beaten

1. In a medium saucepan of boiling salted water, cook carrots 2 minutes, or until crisp-tender. Drain, rinse under cold water, and drain again.

2. In a large skillet, cook ground round, onions, and mushrooms over medium-high heat, stirring often to break up lumps of meat, until beef has lost its pink color, about 5 minutes. Drain off excess fat. Stir in carrots, dill, salt, and pepper.

3. Sprinkle on flour and cook, stirring, 1 minute. Add sour cream and cook, stirring, until thickened, about 1 minute. Remove from heat and let cool until tepid.

4. Preheat oven to 400°. On a lightly floured work surface, roll out two-thirds of pastry to a 12-inch circle, about ⅛ inch thick. Ease pastry circle into a 9-inch pie plate, letting excess hang over sides. Roll out remaining one-third of pastry to a 10-inch circle and set aside.

5. Spoon meat mixture into pastry-lined pie plate. Cover with pastry circle. Press edges of pastry together to seal, fold over to form a seam, and crimp. In a decorative manner, cut four 1-inch slashes in top to allow steam to escape.

6. Brush pastry with some of beaten egg. Place pie plate on a baking sheet and bake until golden brown, about 45 minutes. Let stand at least 20 minutes before cutting into wedges to serve.

309   DIANE'S BEEF PELEMI WITH TOMATO-PEPPER RELISH

Prep: 1 hour   Stand: 30 minutes   Cook: 10 minutes   Serves: 6 to 8

This authentic Russian family recipe is worth every second of the labor it takes. For easy entertaining, the *pelemi* can be formed up to a month in advance and frozen. The actual cooking time is brief.

3 cups flour	2 medium onions, minced
2¼ teaspoons salt	½ teaspoon pepper
1 egg	Tomato-Pepper Relish
1 pound ground round	(recipe follows)
(85% lean)	Sour cream
6 ounces ground pork	

1. In a food processor, pulse flour and 1 teaspoon salt to combine. In a measuring cup, beat egg and 1 cup cold water until blended. With machine on, pour egg mixture through feed tube in a steady stream. Process until dough forms a ball on top of blade. (If dough is too wet or dry, ball will not form. Feel dough, and if sticky and wet, add additional flour, 1 tablespoon at a time, processing after each addition, until dough forms a ball. If dough is crumbly and dry, follow same procedure, adding additional water 1 tablespoon at a time.) Process 45 seconds to knead. Transfer dough to a floured work surface, knead briefly until smooth, and cover with a kitchen towel. Let stand 30 minutes.

2. Meanwhile, in a large bowl, combine ground round, ground pork, onions, remaining 1¼ teaspoons salt, and pepper. Knead together with your hands until well blended.

3. Divide dough into 4 equal parts. Working with 1 piece at a time, keeping remaining dough covered, roll out on a lightly floured work surface into a large sheet, about ¹⁄₁₆ inch thick. Using a 2½-inch round cookie cutter, cut out about 30 rounds. Gather up scraps, knead together into a ball, and place with remaining dough under cloth.

4. Place about ¾ teaspoon meat filling off-center in a round, fold over in a half-moon to enclose filling, and press edges together with a fork to seal. Transfer filled pelemi to a wax paper–lined baking sheet. Continue procedure with remaining dough and meat filling, using balls of dough scraps last. (If desired, freeze pelemi at this point. Freeze pelemi, unwrapped, on baking sheets until frozen. Place frozen pelemi in plastic freezer bags and freeze for up to 1 month.)

5. Bring 2 large pots of salted water to a boil over high heat. Gradually add pelemi, keeping water at a boil, and cook until pelemi are cooked through, 8 to 10 minutes.

6. Using a skimmer, transfer pelemi to individual soup plates. Serve with bowls of Tomato-Pepper Relish and sour cream.

TOMATO-PEPPER RELISH
Makes about 2½ cups

2 pounds plum tomatoes	1 teaspoon salt
2 large green bell peppers	½ teaspoon pepper
¼ cup vodka	

In a food processor, combine all ingredients. Process until finely chopped. Transfer to a bowl, cover, and refrigerate at least 1 hour or up to 1 day.

---

310 HUNGARIAN BEEF AND MUSHROOM STRUDEL
Prep: 30 minutes   Cook: 40 minutes   Serves: 4 to 6

2 pounds ground round (85% lean)	½ teaspoon salt
	¼ teaspoon cayenne
1 large onion, chopped	1 cup beef broth
1 medium green bell pepper, chopped	2 tablespoons sour cream
	2 tablespoons butter
2 garlic cloves, minced	2 tablespoons vegetable oil
2 tablespoons flour	4 filo sheets
2 teaspoons paprika	2 tablespoons dried bread crumbs
1½ teaspoons dried dill	

1. Preheat oven to 375°. In a large skillet, cook ground round, onion, bell pepper, and garlic over medium-high heat, stirring often to break up lumps of meat, until beef loses its pink color, about 7 minutes. Drain off excess fat. Sprinkle on flour, paprika, dill, salt, and cayenne and cook, stirring constantly, 1 minute.

2. Stir in beef broth and ¼ cup water. Bring to a boil, reduce heat to low, and simmer until thickened, about 2 minutes. Remove from heat and stir in sour cream.

3. In a small saucepan, melt butter in oil over heat. Place 1 filo sheet, long side facing you, on a clean kitchen towel. Lightly brush filo sheet with some of butter mixture. Repeat layering and brushing procedure with remaining 3 filo sheets. Sprinkle bread crumbs evenly over top. Spread meat filling over filo sheets in a 3-inch-wide strip, starting 1 inch from bottom and leaving a 1-inch border on both short sides. Fold up bottom of filo, then fold in sides to partially enclose filling. Using towel to help lift, roll up into a cylinder. Transfer strudel, seam side down, onto a large ungreased baking sheet.

4. Bake until golden brown, 25 to 30 minutes. Let cool 10 minutes before cutting into 1-inch slices to serve.

311   CHINESE CURRIED BEEF TURNOVERS
Prep: 30 minutes   Cook: 30 minutes   Makes: 30 turnovers

½ pound ground chuck
  (80% lean)
1 small onion, minced
1 teaspoon minced fresh
  ginger
1 garlic clove, minced
1 tablespoon curry powder
1 tablespoon soy sauce

½ teaspoon sugar
¼ teaspoon salt
1 teaspoon cornstarch
½ cup reduced-sodium
  chicken broth
1 egg, beaten
Flaky Pastry Dough
  (page 228)

1. In a large skillet, cook ground chuck, onion, ginger, and garlic over medium-high heat, stirring often to break up lumps of meat, until beef has lost its pink color, about 5 minutes. Drain off excess fat.

2. Add curry powder, soy sauce, sugar, and salt. Cook, stirring 1 minute.

3. In a small bowl, dissolve cornstarch in chicken broth. Add to meat mixture and cook, stirring, until mixture comes to a boil and thickens, about 1 minute. Remove from heat and cool completely.

4. Preheat oven to 400°. On a lightly floured work surface, roll out half of Flaky Pastry Dough to a 14-inch circle about ½ inch thick. Using a 3¼-inch round cookie cutter, cut out about 12 rounds. Gather up scraps into a flat disc and reserve.

5. Place about 1 teaspoon beef filling in center of each round. Brush edges of round with beaten egg. Fold over to enclose filling and press edges sealed with a fork. Transfer turnovers to a lightly greased baking sheet. Repeat procedure with remaining dough and filling, combining dough scraps and rolling out as last batch.

6. Lightly brush turnovers with beaten egg. Bake until golden brown, 15 to 20 minutes. Serve warm.

312   BEEF AND ONION KNISHES
Prep: 20 minutes   Cook: 1 hour   Serves: 8

3 medium russet potatoes (1 to
  1¼ pounds), peeled
⅔ cup potato starch
1 egg, beaten
1 teaspoon salt

½ teaspoon pepper
½ pound ground chuck
  (85% lean)
1 medium onion, minced

1. In a large saucepan of boiling salted water, cook potatoes until just tender when pierced with tip of a sharp knife, about 25 minutes. Drain well. While still warm, mash until very smooth. Reserve 2 cups mashed potatoes; save remaining potatoes for another use.

2. In a medium bowl, combine 2 cups mashed potatoes with potato starch. Stir in egg, ½ teaspoon salt, and ¼ teaspoon pepper. Cover and set aside.

3. In a large skillet, cook ground chuck and onion over medium-high heat, stirring often to break up lumps of meat, until beef loses its pink color, about 5 minutes. Drain off excess liquid. Season with remaining salt and pepper, remove from heat, and let cool slightly.

4. Preheat oven to 375°. Divide dough into quarters. On a lightly floured surface, roll out a quarter of dough into a 9 x 5-inch rectangle. Using a sharp knife, cut into two 4½ x 5-inch rectangles. Place about 2 tablespoons meat filling in center of each rectangle. Fold top of dough over to meet bottom edge, enclosing filling. Press edges sealed with a fork. Place knishes on a greased baking sheet. Repeat procedure with remaining dough and filling.

5. Bake until knishes are a deep golden brown, about 30 minutes. Serve warm or at room temperature.

---

313   CORNISH PASTIES, MICHIGAN STYLE
Prep: 30 minutes   Cook: 1 hour   Makes: 6 pasties

Hearty enough to make a coal miner's lunch, these huge turnovers are pronounced "PAHS-tees." Chop all the vegetables about ½-inch square—just the right size for baking to tenderness in 1 hour.

1 **pound ground round** (85% lean)	¼ **cup chopped parsley**
1 **large onion, chopped**	1½ **teaspoons salt**
1 **large russet potato, peeled and chopped**	½ **teaspoon pepper**
1 **medium carrot, peeled and chopped**	2 **recipes Flaky Pastry Dough (page 228)**
3 **small turnips (about ½ pound), peeled and chopped**	

1. Preheat oven to 375°. In a large bowl, mix ground round, onion, potato, carrot, turnips, parsley, salt, and pepper until well combined.

2. On a lightly floured work surface, roll out a sixth of dough to an 8-inch circle, about ⅛ inch thick. Place about 1 cup meat mixture in center of dough, making a thick strip that reaches almost to the right and left sides. Bring top and bottom of dough up to meet on top of meat and pinch closed. Fold over excess dough to form a rope and flute. Transfer pastie to a greased baking sheet. Repeat procedure with remaining dough and filling.

3. Bake until pasties are golden brown, about 1 hour. Serve hot or warm.

314 HERBED BAYOU MEAT AND POTATO PIES
Prep: 30 minutes   Cook: 40 minutes   Makes: 10 pies

¼ **pound bacon, chopped**	½ **teaspoon oregano**
1 **medium onion, finely chopped**	¼ **teaspoon crushed hot red pepper**
2 **celery ribs, finely chopped**	¾ **cup beef broth**
¾ **pound ground chuck (80% lean) or ground round (85% lean)**	2 **tablespoons Worcestershire sauce**
1 **large russet potato, scrubbed and grated**	¼ **cup chopped parsley**
2 **garlic cloves, minced**	**Flaky Pastry Dough (recipe follows)**
½ **teaspoon salt**	1 **egg, beaten with 1 teaspoon milk to make a glaze**
1 **teaspoon thyme**	

1. Preheat oven to 400°. In a large skillet, cook bacon over medium heat, stirring often, until crisp, 3 to 5 minutes. With a slotted spoon, transfer bacon to paper towels to drain. Pour off all but 2 tablespoons of fat from skillet.

2. Add onion and celery to skillet and cook, stirring often, until softened, about 5 minutes. Add ground chuck, grated potato, garlic, salt, thyme, oregano, and hot pepper. Cook, stirring often, until beef is no longer pink, about 5 minutes. Stir in beef broth and Worcestershire sauce, scraping up browned bits from bottom of skillet. Cook, stirring often, until grated potato is tender, about 5 minutes. Remove from heat, stir in parsley, and let filling cool completely.

3. On a lightly floured surface, roll out half of dough ⅛ inch thick. Using a 6-inch saucer as a guide, cut out 5 circles, gathering up dough scraps and rerolling as necessary. Place about ⅓ cup cooled filling on lower half of dough circle. Brush edge of dough with some egg glaze and fold dough in half to enclose filling. Press edges together and seal with tines of a fork. Pierce top of dough with fork to allow steam to escape. Repeat with remaining dough and filling.

4. Lightly brush pies with egg glaze. Bake until golden brown, about 20 minutes. Serve hot, warm, or at room temperature.

FLAKY PASTRY DOUGH
Makes enough for 10 pies

2 **cups flour**	⅔ **cup solid vegetable shortening, chilled**
½ **teaspoon salt**	**About ½ cup ice water**

1. In a medium bowl, combine flour and salt. Using a pastry blender or 2 knives, cut shortening into flour until mixture resembles small peas.

2. Tossing mixture with a fork, gradually sprinkle in ice water until dough is moist enough to hold together when pinched between thumb and forefinger. (You may have to add a little more ice water.) Gather dough into a thick, flat disc, wrap in wax paper, and refrigerate at least 1 hour or overnight.

---

315 BEEF EMPANADAS WITH PEACHES
Prep: 20 minutes Cook: 30 minutes Makes: 8 empanadas

1 pound ground round
   (85% lean)
1 medium onion, finely
   chopped
1 medium green bell pepper,
   finely chopped
1 garlic clove, minced
1 (14-ounce) can Italian peeled
   tomatoes, drained and
   chopped

1 (8.5-ounce) can peaches in
   light syrup, drained and
   chopped
1 teaspoon salt
¼ teaspoon oregano
⅛ teaspoon pepper
   Flaky Pastry Dough (page
   228)
1 egg, beaten

1. In a large skillet, cook ground round, onion, bell pepper, and garlic over medium-high heat, stirring often to break up lumps of meat, until beef loses its pink color, about 5 minutes. Drain off excess fat.

2. Add tomatoes, peaches, salt, oregano, and pepper. Cook, stirring often, until excess liquid is evaporated, about 8 minutes.

3. On a lightly floured surface, roll out half of dough to a 12-inch circle about ⅛ inch thick. Using a 6-inch saucer or pot lid as a template, cut out 3 rounds. Gather up dough scraps. Repeat procedure with remaining dough, gathering up scraps. Knead scraps briefly and roll out to cut more rounds to get 8 rounds total.

4. Preheat oven to 400°. Place 1 pastry round on work surface and brush edges of pastry with some of beaten egg. Place about ⅓ cup filling in center of round. Fold dough in half to enclose filling and press edges with a fork to seal. Repeat procedure with remaining dough and filling. Transfer empanadas to a greased baking sheet and brush lightly with beaten egg.

5. Bake until empanadas are golden brown, about 20 minutes.

316   CANADIAN PORK AND APPLE TOURTIERE
Prep: 20 minutes   Cook: 1 hour   Serves: 6 to 8

Tourtiere, a double-crust meat pastry, is a Christmastime tradition on the Canadian holiday buffet table.

1½ **pounds ground pork**	1½ **teaspoons savory**
1 **medium onion, chopped**	1½ **teaspoons salt**
1 **medium Granny Smith**	1 **teaspoon sage**
apple, peeled, cored, and	½ **teaspoon pepper**
sliced	**Flaky Pastry Dough**
1 **medium russet potato,**	**(page 228)**
thinly sliced	⅓ **cup heavy cream**
½ **cup beef broth**	1 **egg, beaten**

1. In a large skillet, cook ground pork, onion, apple, and potato over medium-high heat, stirring often to break up lumps of meat, until pork loses its pink color, about 5 minutes. Drain off excess fat.

2. Add beef broth, savory, salt, sage, and pepper. Bring to a boil and cook, stirring often, until liquid is absorbed, about 3 minutes. Remove from heat and let filling cool completely.

3. Preheat oven to 400°. On a lightly floured work surface, roll out two-thirds of pastry to a 12-inch circle about ⅛ inch thick. Ease pastry circle into a 9-inch pie plate, letting excess hang over sides. Roll out remaining third of pastry to a 10-inch circle and set aside.

4. Spoon cooled meat filling into pastry-lined pie plate. Cover with pastry circle. Press edges of pastry together to seal, fold over to form a seam, and crimp. Cut a ½-inch hole in center of top crust. Pour heavy cream slowly into hole to moisten pie filling.

5. Brush pastry with some of beaten egg. Place pie plate on a baking sheet and bake until golden brown, about 45 minutes. Let stand at least 10 minutes before cutting into wedges to serve. Serve warm or room temperature.

317   CHICKEN PASTRY POCKETS
Prep: 20 minutes   Cook: 25 minutes   Serves: 4; makes 8 pastries

1 **pound ground chicken**	¼ **teaspoon cayenne**
1 **medium onion, chopped**	1 **(6-ounce) can tomato paste**
1 **medium green bell pepper,**	½ **cup reduced-sodium**
chopped	**chicken broth**
2 **garlic cloves, minced**	½ **cup sliced black olives**
1 **teaspoon paprika**	1 **(17¾-ounce) package puff**
¾ **teaspoon salt**	**pastry sheets, thawed**
½ **teaspoon ground cumin**	1 **egg, beaten**

1. In a large skillet, cook ground chicken, onion, bell pepper, and garlic over medium heat, stirring often to break up lumps of meat, until chicken loses its pink color, about 5 minutes. Drain off excess liquid. Add paprika, salt, cumin, and cayenne. Cook, stirring, 1 minute.

2. Add tomato paste and chicken broth and bring to a boil. Cook, stirring often, until liquid is evaporated and mixture is thickened, about 3 minutes. Stir in olives, remove from heat, and let cool slightly.

3. Preheat oven to 400°. On a lightly floured work surface, roll out 1 pastry sheet to a 12-inch square. Using a sharp knife, cut into four 6-inch squares.

4. Brush edges of 1 pastry square with beaten egg. Place about ½ cup filling in center of square. Fold over diagonally to enclose filling. Using a fork, press edges to seal. Pierce top of pastry square with fork to allow steam to escape. Transfer pastry to an ungreased baking sheet. Repeat procedure with remaining pastry and filling, using 2 baking sheets.

5. Brush beaten egg over tops of pastries. Bake until puffed and golden brown, about 15 minutes.

---

318 PORK AND SAUERKRAUT PIROSHKI, DELI STYLE

Prep: 15 minutes   Cook: 30 minutes   Makes: 40 piroshki

While in college, I lunched on piroshki from a deli in San Francisco's Richmond district every day. Try as I might to recreate their dough, I could never get mine to taste the same. Finally, I discovered their secret was the same as many a Russian grandmother's—refrigerated store-bought buttermilk biscuit dough.

1 **pound ground pork**	½ **teaspoon sweet paprika,**
2 **medium onions, chopped**	**preferably Hungarian**
1 **pound sauerkraut, rinsed**	¼ **teaspoon salt**
and squeezed dry	⅛ **teaspoon pepper**
1 **tablespoon tomato paste**	4 **(7½-ounce) cans buttermilk**
1 **teaspoon caraway seeds,**	**biscuits**
crushed	1 **egg, well beaten**

1. In a large skillet, cook ground pork and onions over medium-high heat, stirring often to break up lumps of meat, until pork is no longer pink, about 5 minutes. Drain off excess fat. Stir in sauerkraut, tomato paste, caraway seeds, paprika, salt, pepper, and ½ cup water. Cook, stirring often, until liquid is completely evaporated, about 5 minutes. Remove from heat and let filling cool completely.

2. Preheat oven to 400°. One can at a time, separate biscuits. On a lightly floured surface, roll each biscuit out to a 3-inch circle. Place about 2 teaspoons filling in center of dough. Fold dough over to enclose filling and pinch edges shut. Press edges with a fork to seal closed. Transfer filled piroshki to ungreased baking sheets. Repeat procedure with remaining dough and filling.

3. Just before baking, lightly brush piroshki with beaten egg. Bake, in batches if necessary, until golden brown, 15 to 20 minutes. Serve hot or warm.

319 PORK AND CABBAGE STRUDEL

Prep: 30 minutes   Cook: 45 minutes   Serves: 6 to 8

1 medium head of cabbage (1½ to 2 pounds), shredded	¼ cup plus 2 tablespoons vegetable oil
2¼ teaspoons salt	1 teaspoon paprika
1 pound ground pork	¼ teaspoon pepper
1 garlic clove, minced	⅓ cup sour cream
1 medium onion, finely chopped	4 tablespoons butter
	8 filo sheets
	¼ cup dried bread crumbs

1. Preheat oven to 375°. In a large colander, toss cabbage with 1 teaspoon salt. Let stand 15 minutes. Rinse cabbage well with cold water. One handful at a time, squeeze excess liquid from cabbage.

2. In a large skillet, cook ground pork and garlic over medium-high heat, stirring often to break up lumps of meat, until pork has lost its pink color, about 5 minutes. Using a slotted spoon, transfer meat mixture to a large bowl, leaving behind fat in skillet.

3. Add onion to skillet and cook over medium-high heat, stirring often, until golden, about 4 minutes. Stir into meat mixture.

4. Add 1 tablespoon oil to skillet and heat over medium heat. Add half of cabbage and cook, stirring often, until cabbage is wilted and beginning to brown, about 6 minutes. Stir into meat mixture. Add 1 tablespoon oil to skillet and repeat with remaining cabbage. Add paprika and pepper and stir. Stir sour cream into meat and cabbage mixture.

5. In a small saucepan, melt butter with remaining ¼ cup oil over low heat. Place 1 filo sheet, long side facing you, on a clean kitchen towel. Lightly brush filo sheet with some of butter mixture. Layer on 3 more filo sheets, brushing each sheet with butter mixture. Sprinkle 2 tablespoons bread crumbs evenly over top sheet of buttered filo. Spread half of cabbage filling over filo in a 3-inch-wide strip starting 1 inch from bottom of filo sheet and leaving a 1-inch border on both short sides. Fold up bottom of filo, then fold in sides to partially enclose filling. Using towel to help lift, roll up into cylinder. Transfer strudel, seam side down, onto a large ungreased baking sheet. Repeat procedure with remaining ingredients.

6. Bake until golden brown, 25 to 30 minutes. Let cool 10 minutes before cutting into 1-inch-thick slices to serve.

320   CRUSTY PATE PIE

Prep: 30 minutes   Cook: 1 hour 25 minutes
Chill: Overnight   Serves: 8

1 tablespoon butter	½ teaspoon thyme
1 medium onion, finely chopped	½ teaspoon pepper
1 garlic clove, minced	¼ teaspoon ground allspice
½ cup dry white wine	1¼ pounds ground pork
½ cup fresh bread crumbs	1¼ pounds ground veal
¼ cup heavy cream	¼ pound boiled ham, cut into
3 eggs	¼-inch pieces
¼ cup chopped parsley	¼ cup shelled pistachio nuts
2 teaspoons salt	1 (17½-ounce) package frozen
1 teaspoon tarragon	puff pastry, thawed
	1 tablespoon Dijon mustard

1. Preheat oven to 375°. In a medium skillet, melt butter. Add onion and cook over medium heat, stirring often, until softened, about 4 minutes. Add garlic and cook 1 minute. Add wine, bring to a boil, and cook until liquid is almost completely evaporated, about 5 minutes.

2. In a large bowl, combine onion mixture, bread crumbs, cream, 2 eggs, parsley, salt, tarragon, thyme, pepper, and allspice. Add ground pork and ground veal and mix well. Stir in ham and pistachios.

3. On a lightly floured surface, roll out 1 sheet of puff pastry ⅛ inch thick. Fold into quarters and unfold into a lightly buttered 8-inch springform pan, easing pastry into bottom edges and letting excess hang over sides of pan. Brush mustard on pastry in pan. Pack pâté mixture into pastry-lined pan.

4. Roll out remaining sheet of pastry ⅛ inch thick. Cut into a circle about 10 inches in diameter. Prick dough all over with a fork. Place pastry circle on top of meat mixture. Using scissors or a sharp knife, trim off excess dough to top edge of pan. Press pastry circles together. Roll edges of dough up into a rope, folding down inside of pan, and flute. Cut a 1-inch slash in center of crust to allow steam to escape. In a small bowl, beat remaining egg well. Brush lightly over top of dough.

5. Bake until crust is golden brown and a meat thermometer inserted into center of loaf (through slash) reads 160°, about 1¼ hours. (If pastry starts to brown too darkly, cover loosely with foil.) Let cool completely. Cover with foil and refrigerate overnight. Let come to room temperature before removing sides of pan. Cut into wedges to serve.

321 HERBED LAMB PELEMI WITH SOUR CREAM

Prep: 30 minutes   Cook: 10 minutes   Serves: 4

Prepared gyoza wrappers substitute for homemade dough to speed the preparation of these Russian dumplings. If 2½-inch round gyoza wrappers are unavailable, use a cookie cutter to cut rounds out of square won ton wrappers.

½ pound lean ground lamb
1 medium onion, minced
1 scallion, minced
1 garlic clove, minced
¼ cup chopped parsley
2 tablespoons ice water

½ teaspoon salt
¼ teaspoon pepper
50 gyoza wrappers
Sour cream and chopped cilantro

1. In a medium bowl, combine ground lamb, onion, scallion, garlic, parsley, ice water, salt, and pepper. Knead together until well blended.

2. Place about ¾ teaspoon meat filling off center in middle of a gyoza wrapper. Brush edges of wrapper with cold water. Fold wrapper in a half-moon shape to enclose filling and press edges together with a fork to seal. Moisten 2 corners of wrappers and bring together to form a won ton shape; press to adhere. Place pelemi on a baking sheet. Repeat procedure with remaining meat filling and gyoza wrappers.

3. Bring a large pot of salted water to a boil over high heat. Gradually add pelemi, keeping water at a boil, and cook until pelemi are cooked through, about 8 minutes.

4. Using a skimmer, transfer pelemi to individual soup plates. Garnish with dollops of sour cream and a sprinkling of cilantro.

---

322 SPICY LAMB SAMOSAS

Prep: 45 minutes   Cook: 55 minutes   Serves: 12; about 60 samosas

¾ pound medium red potatoes (about 2 medium)
1 tablespoon vegetable oil
1 large onion, chopped
¾ pound lean ground lamb
2 teaspoons minced fresh ginger
2 garlic cloves, minced
¾ teaspoon salt
½ teaspoon ground coriander
½ teaspoon ground cumin

½ teaspoon curry powder
½ teaspoon crushed fennel seed
¼ teaspoon turmeric
¼ teaspoon crushed hot red pepper
Whole-Wheat Samosa Dough (recipe follows)
Vegetable oil, for deep-frying

1. In a medium saucepan of boiling salted water, cook potatoes until just tender, 15 to 20 minutes. Drain and rinse under cold water until cool enough to handle. Peel, if desired, and cut into ½-inch cubes.

2. In a large skillet, heat oil. Add onion and cook over medium heat, stirring often, until lightly browned, about 6 minutes. Add ground lamb, ginger, and garlic and cook, stirring often to break up meat, until lamb loses its pink color, about 5 minutes. Add potatoes, salt, coriander, cumin, curry powder, fennel seed, turmeric, and hot pepper. Reduce heat to low and cook, stirring often, until liquid has evaporated, about 15 minutes. Remove from heat and let meat mixture cool completely before using.

3. Pinch off about 2 tablespoons dough and roll into a ball about 1¼ inches in diameter. (Keep remaining dough covered with a damp towel.) On a lightly floured work surface, flatten ball with heel of hand and roll out to a circle about 4 inches in diameter. With a sharp knife, cut circle in half crosswise to make 2 semicircles.

4. Moisten straight edge of 1 semicircle with cold water. Lift up ends of straight edge to meet and overlap slightly, forming a cone shape. Press overlapping seam of dough to seal. Place about ¾ teaspoon cooled meat filling into cone. Pinch open top of cone shut, then press with tines of a fork to seal. Place filled samosa on a baking sheet. Repeat procedure with remaining dough and filling. (Samosas can be prepared up to 3 hours ahead, covered with plastic wrap, and refrigerated.)

5. Preheat oven to 200°. In a large deep skillet or flameproof casserole, heat enough oil to reach 1 inch up sides to 375°. (An electric skillet works best.) In batches, without crowding, fry samosas, turning once, until golden brown, 4 to 6 minutes. Transfer samosas to a paper towel–lined baking sheet and keep warm in oven. Serve samosas as soon as possible.

WHOLE-WHEAT SAMOSA DOUGH
Makes enough for 60 samosas

1 cup all-purpose flour
1 cup whole-wheat flour
¾ teaspoon salt

2 tablespoons plus 1 teaspoon
vegetable oil

1. In a food processor, pulse all-purpose flour, whole-wheat flour, and salt to combine. In a measuring cup, combine ¾ cup water and 2 tablespoons vegetable oil. With machine on, pour liquid through feed tube in a steady stream and process until dough forms a ball on top of dough. (If dough is too dry, ball will not form. If necessary, add additional water, 1 tablespoon at a time, processing after each addition.)

2. Transfer dough to a clean work surface and knead briefly until smooth. Brush top of dough lightly with remaining oil. Cover dough with a clean, damp kitchen towel until ready to use. (Dough can be prepared, kept under damp towel at room temperature, up to 3 hours ahead.)

323   JAMAICAN LAMB TURNOVERS
Prep: 30 minutes   Cook: 40 minutes   Serves: 8

Jamaicans would make these with baby goat, but I'm using more easily available lamb. Short of taking a plane, they are the best way I know of to get that Caribbean feeling.

¾ pound lean ground lamb
1 medium onion, chopped
2 garlic cloves, minced
1 jalapeño pepper, seeded and minced, or ⅛ teaspoon cayenne
2 plum tomatoes, seeded and chopped

1 teaspoon curry powder
½ teaspoon thyme
¼ teaspoon ground allspice
¼ teaspoon salt
2 egg yolks
   Flaky Pastry Dough (page 228)
1 whole egg, beaten

1. In a large skillet, cook ground lamb, onion, garlic, and jalapeño pepper over medium-high heat, stirring often to break up lumps of meat, until lamb loses its pink color, about 5 minutes. Drain off excess liquid. Add tomatoes, curry powder, thyme, allspice, and salt. Cook, stirring often, until liquid is almost completely evaporated, about 5 minutes. Remove from heat and let cool slightly.

2. In a medium bowl, beat egg yolks. Gradually stir about 1 cup meat mixture into yolks. Return to remaining meat mixture in skillet, set over low heat, and cook, stirring, until thickened, about 1 minute. (Do not let mixture boil after adding egg yolks.) Transfer meat filling to a medium bowl and let cool completely.

3. Preheat oven to 400°. On a lightly floured surface, roll out dough to a 12 x 14-inch rectangle. Using a sharp knife, cut into eight 6 x 3½-inch rectangles. Place about ¼ cup meat filling in center of each rectangle. Brush edges of rectangles with beaten egg. Fold top of dough over to meet bottom edge, enclosing filling. Press edges sealed with a fork. Transfer turnovers to a greased baking sheet and brush lightly with beaten egg.

4. Bake until golden brown, about 30 minutes. Serve turnovers warm or at room temperature.

324 LAMB, MUSHROOM, AND CILANTRO PIROSHKI WITH SOUR CREAM PASTRY

Prep: 45 minutes   Cook: 35 minutes   Makes: 48 piroshki

4 tablespoons butter
1 pound fresh mushrooms, finely chopped
3 medium onions, chopped
2 garlic cloves, minced
1 pound ground lamb
½ teaspoon salt
¼ teaspoon pepper
½ cup chopped fresh cilantro or parsley
Sour Cream Pastry (recipe follows)
1 egg, well beaten

1. In a large skillet, melt butter. Add mushrooms, onions, and garlic and cook over medium-high heat, stirring often, until mushrooms have given off their liquid and liquid has almost evaporated, about 6 minutes. Add ground lamb, salt, and pepper and cook, stirring often to break up lumps of meat, until lamb is no longer pink, about 5 minutes. Drain off excess fat. Off heat, stir in cilantro and let cool completely.

2. Preheat oven to 400°. On a lightly floured surface, roll out a fourth of pastry dough to ⅛-inch thickness. Using a 3-inch round cookie cutter or top of a glass, cut out about 10 rounds. Place about 1 tablespoon cooled filling in center of each round. Fold circles in half and pinch edges shut. Press edges with fork to seal closed. Place filled piroshki on ungreased baking sheets. Repeat procedure with remaining dough and filling. (Gather up dough scraps, knead together lightly, and reroll as necessary.)

3. Just before baking, lightly brush tops of piroshki with beaten egg. Bake, in batches if necessary, until golden brown, 20 to 25 minutes. Serve hot or warm. (Baked piroshki can be wrapped tightly and frozen for up to 1 month. Defrost and reheat in 350° oven 15 minutes.)

SOUR CREAM PASTRY
Makes enough for 48 piroshki

3 cups flour
¾ teaspoon salt
1½ sticks (6 ounces) cold butter, cut into ½-inch cubes
1½ cups sour cream

In a medium bowl, stir together flour and salt. Using a pastry blender, cut in butter until mixture resembles small peas. Stir in sour cream just until mixture is moistened. Press dough together into a flat disc. (Do not overwork dough.) Wrap disc in plastic wrap and refrigerate at least 1 hour or overnight.

325   MARRAKESH LAMB TURNOVERS

Prep: 40 minutes   Cook: 20 minutes   Makes: 24 turnovers

1 pound lean ground lamb or ground sirloin (90% lean)	⅓ cup chopped parsley
1 small onion, chopped	3 tablespoons grated Parmesan cheese
1 garlic clove, minced	2 hard-boiled eggs, chopped
1 tablespoon lemon juice	12 filo sheets
½ teaspoon salt	¼ cup olive oil or melted butter
⅛ teaspoon pepper	

1. In a large skillet, cook ground lamb, onion, and garlic over medium heat, stirring often, until meat is no longer pink, about 5 minutes. Drain off excess fat. Add lemon juice, salt, and pepper and cook 1 minute. Remove from heat and stir in parsley, Parmesan cheese, and hard-boiled eggs; let filling cool completely.

2. Preheat oven to 400°. Place 1 sheet of filo dough, long side facing you, on a work surface. (Keep remaining dough under a moist, clean kitchen towel.) Lightly brush entire surface of dough with oil. Using a sharp knife or a pastry wheel, cut dough in half from top to bottom, making two 8-inch-wide rectangles. In bottom left corner of each pastry column, place about 1 tablespoon lamb filling. Fold bottom right corner of dough diagonally up so that the bottom edge meets the left-hand edge and encloses filling. Continue folding filling and dough up and over on themselves as if you were folding a flag, finishing with a plump triangle. Transfer triangles to baking sheets in single layers. Repeat procedure with remaining filo sheets and filling.

3. Just before baking, lightly brush tops of triangles with olive oil. Bake, turning once, until golden brown, 12 to 15 minutes. Serve hot or warm.

Chapter 14

Burgers—Indoors and Out

Grilling is America's favorite form of warm-weather cooking, for everyday and for entertaining. With a platter of great grilled burgers, all you need is a favorite potato salad and coleslaw for a feast everybody loves. Indoors, pan-fried meat patties and oven-broiled burgers are the stuff of which delicious, speedy suppers are formed. Scandinavian Beef Patties with Pickled Beets and Capers, Potato Chip Burgers with Grilled Onions, Chicken Fajita Burgers, Stovetop BBQ Turkey Burgers, and Nutty Blue Cheese Burgers are just a few of the over three dozen exciting ideas you'll find in this chapter.

While most cooks are familiar with skillet burgers and broiling, the new ground meats—ground turkey and ground chicken—have some special requirements on the outdoor grill. Here are some tips for grilling success, no matter what kind of ground meat your are using.

Start a charcoal fire in your grill, using about 5 pounds of charcoal briquets for an average-sized kettle grill. Real charcoal chunks are great, but remember they burn hotter than briquets. Let the charcoal burn until it is covered with white ash. The fire is now hot, with the center of the grill being the hottest area, and the outside edges cooler. Before proceeding, quickly grease the grill with an oil-dipped wad of paper towels or a long-handled brush.

It's important to know about the temperature difference between the center and outside edges of the grill, especially when you're grilling poultry burgers. Sear the poultry burgers in the hot center of the grill until lightly browned on the outside, about 2 minutes per side. Then move the burgers to the cooler outside edges to grill at a moderate temperature until completely cooked through. If you have a gas grill, cook the poultry burgers over consistently medium heat by adjusting the control dial. Grilling poultry burgers over moderate heat retains more valuable juices. Beef burgers can be grilled over hot heat for the entire cooking period.

Many of these outdoor recipes can be adapted to the kitchen broiler. Adjust the broiler rack about 4 to 6 inches from the source of heat, and preheat the broiler thoroughly for about 10 minutes. Then cook the burgers, turning once, 8 to 12 minutes for rare to medium-rare.

While the smoky flavor of a charcoal-broiled burger is unsurpassable, stovetop pan-fried burgers are awfully good, too. They are certainly one of the quickest ways to feed a bunch of hungry kids. Some ideas for stovetop burgers are in this chapter, but look in Chapter 9, Dinner Against the Clock, page 179, for especially speedy versions.

Most of the recipes here use ground round or ground chuck, which make especially juicy burgers. If you use other, leaner cuts of meat, be sure to add 2 tablespoons of liquid for each pound of ground meat. Ketchup, barbecue sauce, mustard, or even ice water will add moisture as well as flavor and avoid dried-out burgers.

No matter where you cook them, indoors or out, cook ground poultry or pork burgers until they are well done. You can cut into the center of a patty to take a peek, checking to be sure the juices are clear with no sign of pink. Or lightly press the burger in the center. If the meat is firm and springs back, it is done. In fact, you can use this touch test for all ground meat burgers. If the burger is soft in the center, it is rare. The firmer the burger feels, the more well done it is.

---

326 ABILENE BURGERS WITH MARINATED RED ONIONS

Prep: 15 minutes   Chill: 2 hours   Cook: 8 to 12 minutes   Serves: 4

2 small red onions, thinly sliced into rings	½ teaspoon pepper
2 tablespoons cider vinegar	¾ cup barbecue sauce
1 tablespoon sugar	4 onion or hamburger rolls
1½ teaspoons salt	Optional: Ketchup,
1⅓ pounds ground round (85% lean)	mustard, mayonnaise, tomato slices, shredded lettuce, sliced dill pickles

1. In a large saucepan of boiling salted water, cook red onion rings 30 seconds. Drain, rinse under cold running water, and drain again.

2. In a medium bowl, toss red onion rings with vinegar, sugar, and ¼ teaspoon salt. Cover tightly with plastic wrap and refrigerate at least 2 hours or overnight.

3. Prepare a hot fire in a grill. In a medium bowl, working as quickly and gently as possible, mix ground round with remaining 1¼ teaspoons salt and pepper. Lightly form into 4 patties about 1 inch thick.

4. Place on an oiled grill set 4 to 6 inches from coals. Grill, turning once, until outside is browned, about 4 minutes. Brush with barbecue sauce and grill 2 minutes. Turn, brush with sauce, and grill until outside is glazed but inside is still pink and juicy, about 2 minutes for rare, or longer if desired. (If grilling longer, move to sides of grill to avoid burning glaze.)

5. Meanwhile, split open rolls and toast on sides of grill until warm and lightly browned. Place cooked burgers on rolls and top with marinated onions. Let everyone choose their own fixings.

327   HAMBURGER DELUXE
Prep: 5 minutes   Cook: 8 to 12 minutes   Serves: 4

Ground chuck makes the juiciest, most toothsome burgers you can imagine. Ground round runs a close second. If you prefer to use ground sirloin, see Igloo Burgers, page 245.

1⅓ pounds ground chuck (80% lean)	Optional: Mustard, ketchup, mayonnaise
1½ teaspoons salt	sliced onion, hamburger
½ teaspoon pepper	relish, lettuce leaves,
4 hamburger buns	sliced tomatoes

1. Prepare a hot fire in a grill or preheat a broiler. Set an oiled broiler rack or grill 4 to 6 inches from source of heat. In a medium bowl, working as quickly and gently as possible, mix ground chuck, salt, and pepper. Lightly form into 4 burgers about 1 inch thick.

2. Place burgers on grill or broiler rack and cook, turning once, until outside is well browned but inside is still pink and juicy, about 8 to 12 minutes for rare to medium-rare, or longer if desired.

3. Meanwhile, open buns and toast on sides of grill until warm and lightly browned. Place cooked burgers in buns and let everyone choose their own fixings.

328   CHEESEBURGER DELUXE
Prep: 5 minutes   Cook: 8 to 12 minutes   Serves: 4

1⅓ pounds ground chuck (80% lean)	4 hamburger buns Optional: Mustard,
1½ teaspoons salt	ketchup, mayonnaise
½ teaspoon pepper	sliced onion, hamburger
4 slices of American, Cheddar, Monterey Jack, pepper Jack, Swiss, or blue cheese	relish, lettuce leaves, sliced tomatoes

1. Prepare a hot fire in a grill or preheat a broiler. Set an oiled broiler rack or grill 4 to 6 inches from source of heat. In a medium bowl, working as quickly and gently as possible, mix ground chuck, salt, and pepper. Lightly form into 4 burgers about 1 inch thick.

2. Place burgers on grill or broiler rack. Cook, turning once, until outside is well browned but inside is still pink and juicy, about 8 to 12 minutes for rare to medium-rare, or longer if desired. During last 2 minutes of cooking, top each burger with a slice of cheese and cover grill or tent burgers with foil.

3. Meanwhile, open buns and toast on sides of grill until warm and lightly browned. Place cooked burgers in buns and let everyone choose their own fixings.

329 DANNY'S KEFTEDES
Prep: 10 minutes   Chill: 1 hour   Cook: 4 minutes
Serves: 6 to 8; makes 25

My Greek cousin Danny makes these to offer with cocktails. There's no need to fuss and serve them hot from the skillet; they are just as good at room temperature.

1 medium onion, minced	½ cup flour
2 teaspoons dried mint	3 tablespoons olive oil
1 teaspoon oregano	· Plain low-fat yogurt
1 teaspoon salt	(optional)
¼ teaspoon pepper	
1 pound ground chuck	
(80% lean)	

1. In a medium bowl, combine onion, mint, oregano, salt, and pepper. Add ground chuck and mix well. Cover and refrigerate at least 1 hour or overnight.

2. Using about 1 tablespoon for each, form into 25 small patties about ¾ inch thick. Dredge patties in flour; shake off excess.

3. In a large skillet, heat oil over medium-high heat. Add patties and cook, turning once, until crusty on the outside but still juicy inside, about 4 minutes, or longer if desired. Transfer to paper towels to drain briefly. Serve keftedes hot, warm, or at room temperature, with yogurt for dipping, if desired.

330 INDONESIAN BEEF BURGERS WITH PEANUT SAUCE
Prep: 10 minutes   Cook: 15 minutes   Serves: 4

2 tablespoons butter	1 teaspoon brown sugar
2 medium shallots or	½ teaspoon crushed hot red
scallions, finely chopped	pepper
2 teaspoons minced fresh	½ cup heavy cream
ginger	¼ cup reduced-sodium
1 garlic clove, minced	chicken broth
1½ teaspoons curry powder	1⅓ pounds ground round
½ cup peanut butter,	(85% lean)
preferably salt- and sugar-	¼ cup coarsely chopped dry-
free	roasted peanuts
1 tablespoon soy sauce	½ teaspoon salt
1 teaspoon lime or lemon	· Hot cooked rice
juice	

1. In a small saucepan, heat butter. Add shallots, ginger, garlic, and 1 teaspoon curry powder. Cook over medium heat until softened and fragrant but not browned, about 1 minute. Transfer vegetables to a blender or food processor.

2. Add peanut butter, soy sauce, lime juice, brown sugar, and ¼ teaspoon hot pepper. With machine on, gradually pour in heavy cream and chicken broth; blend until smooth. Return to saucepan and bring to a simmer over low heat, stirring often. Remove from heat and cover to keep warm.

3. Position a broiler rack 6 inches from source of heat and preheat broiler. In a medium bowl, combine ground round, chopped peanuts, salt, and remaining ½ teaspoon curry powder and ¼ teaspoon hot pepper. Working as quickly and gently as possible, mix well. Lightly form into 4 burgers about 1 inch thick.

4. Broil, turning once, until well browned outside but still juicy inside, about 8 minutes for rare, or longer if desired. Serve burgers with hot rice; pass peanut sauce on the side.

---

331 TRUCKSTOP MEATLOAF BURGERS
Prep: 10 minutes   Cook: 10 to 12 minutes   Serves: 5

Because of the pork content of these delicious burgers, cook them until well-done. They will still be juicy and flavorful, due to the ketchup, egg, and bread crumbs.

½ cup fresh bread crumbs	½ pound ground veal
½ cup ketchup	½ pound ground pork
¼ cup minced onion	5 hamburger buns
1 egg	Optional: Crisp cooked
2 tablespoons Worcestershire	bacon slices, ketchup,
sauce	mayonnaise, mustard,
½ teaspoon salt	sliced tomatoes and
¼ teaspoon pepper	onions, shredded lettuce
½ pound ground chuck	

1. Prepare a hot fire in a grill or preheat broiler. In a medium bowl, combine bread crumbs, ketchup, onion, egg, Worcestershire sauce, salt, and pepper; stir until mixed. Add ground meats and working as quickly and gently as possible, mix with seasonings until blended. Lightly form into 5 patties about 3½ inches in diameter and ¾ to 1 inch thick.

2. Place patties on a lightly oiled rack and grill, or broil about 4 inches from heat, turning once, until just cooked through but still juicy, 8 to 10 minutes if grilled, 6 to 8 minutes if broiled.

3. Toast buns on sides of grill or under broiler, 1 to 2 minutes. Place cooked burgers in buns and let everyone choose their own fillings.

332   PIZZERIA BURGERS
Prep: 10 minutes   Cook: 8 to 12 minutes   Serves: 4

¾ **pound ground round (85% lean)**	¾ **teaspoon salt**
½ **pound sweet Italian sausage, casings removed**	¼ **teaspoon pepper**
⅓ **cup sliced black olives**	½ **cup bottled pizza sauce**
1 **teaspoon Italian seasoning**	4 **slices of mozzarella cheese**
	4 **slices of Italian bread**
	1 **tablespoon olive oil**

1. Prepare a hot fire in a grill. In a medium bowl, working as quickly and gently as possible, mix ground round, Italian sausage, olives, Italian seasoning, salt, and pepper. Lightly form into 4 patties about 1 inch thick. Warm pizza sauce in small saucepan on edge of grill.

2. Place patties on an oiled grill set 4 to 6 inches from coals. Grill, turning once, until outside is well browned but inside is still pink and juicy, about 8 to 12 minutes for rare to medium-rare, or longer if desired. About 30 seconds before removing burgers from grill, top each with a slice of mozzarella.

3. Meanwhile, brush each Italian bread slice with olive oil and toast on sides of grill until lightly browned. Top each toasted bread slice with warm pizza sauce, then a burger. Serve at once, with forks and knives.

---

333   NEW AMERICAN BISTRO BURGERS
Prep: 10 minutes   Cook: 8 to 12 minutes   Serves: 4

1⅓ **pounds lean ground lamb or ground sirloin (90% lean)**	8 **slices of French bread, preferably sourdough**
3 **tablespoons pesto**	2 **tablespoons olive oil**
2 **tablespoons grated Parmesan cheese**	**Optional: Arugula leaves, Dijon mustard, tomato slices, red onion slices**
½ **teaspoon salt**	
¼ **teaspoon pepper**	
4 **ounces goat cheese log, cut into 8 thin slices**	

1. Prepare a hot fire in a grill. In a medium bowl, working as quickly and gently as possible, mix ground lamb with pesto, Parmesan cheese, salt, and pepper. Lightly form into 4 patties about 1 inch thick.

2. Place burgers on an oiled grill set 4 to 6 inches from coals. Cook, turning once, until outside is well browned but inside is pink and still juicy, 8 to 12 minutes for rare to medium-rare, or longer if desired. About 30 seconds before moving burgers from grill, top each with 2 overlapping slices of goat cheese.

3. Meanwhile, brush bread slices with oil and toast on sides of grill until warm and lightly browned. Place cooked burgers between bread slices and let everyone choose their own fixings.

334   IGLOO BURGERS
Prep: 10 minutes   Cook: 8 to 12 minutes   Serves: 4

As the ice melts, it bastes the burger from the inside, adding extra moisture while grilling.

1⅓ **pounds ground sirloin**
  (90% lean)
¼ **cup crushed ice**
1½ **teaspoons salt**
½ **teaspoon pepper**
4 **hamburger buns**

Optional: Mustard,
  ketchup, mayonnaise,
  sliced onion, pickles,
  sliced tomatoes, lettuce
  leaves

1. Prepare a hot fire in a grill or preheat a broiler, adjusting broiler rack or grill 4 to 6 inches from source of heat. In a medium bowl, working as quickly and gently as possible, mix ground sirloin with crushed ice, salt, and pepper. Lightly form into 4 burgers about 1 inch thick.

2. Place burgers on an oiled grill or broiler rack. Cook, turning once, until outside is well browned, but inside is still pink and juicy, about 8 to 12 minutes for rare to medium-rare, or longer if desired.

3. Meanwhile, open buns and toast on sides of grill until warm and lightly browned. Place cooked burgers in buns and let everyone choose their own fixings.

335   SPICY GRILLED ONION BURGERS
Prep: 10 minutes   Cook: 13 to 19 minutes   Serves: 4

1⅓ **pounds ground chuck**
  (80% lean)
2 **tablespoons steak sauce**
1 **teaspoon garlic salt**
¼ **teaspoon crushed hot red**
  pepper
1 **large onion, thickly sliced**

1 **tablespoon olive oil**
4 **slices of Cheddar cheese**
4 **hamburger buns**
  Optional: Ketchup,
  mustard, mayonnaise,
  sliced tomatoes, shredded
  lettuce

1. Prepare a hot fire in a grill. In a medium bowl, working as quickly and gently as possible, mix ground chuck with steak sauce, garlic salt, and hot pepper. Lightly form into 4 patties about 1 inch thick.

2. Brush onion slices with olive oil and place on an oiled grill set 4 to 6 inches from coals. Grill, turning once, until lightly browned and tender, 5 to 7 minutes. As onions cook, move them to sides of grill.

3. Place burgers on grill and cook, turning once, until outside is well browned but inside is still pink and juicy, about 8 to 12 minutes for rare to medium-rare, or longer if desired. About 30 seconds before removing burgers from grill, top each with a slice of Cheddar cheese.

4. Meanwhile, split open buns and toast on sides of grill until warm and lightly browned. Place cooked burgers in buns and top with grilled onions. Let everyone choose their own fixings.

336 POTATO CHIP BURGERS WITH GRILLED ONIONS

Prep: 10 minutes   Cook: 20 minutes   Serves: 4

1⅓ pounds ground round
     (85% lean)
  1 cup crushed no-salt potato
     chips (about 4 ounces)
  1 teaspoon salt
  ¼ teaspoon pepper
  2 large onions, sliced
     ½ inch thick

  2 tablespoons olive oil
  4 hamburger buns or kaiser
     rolls
     Optional: Mayonnaise,
     ketchup, mustard, tomato
     slices, shredded lettuce

1. Prepare a hot fire in a grill or adjust a broiler rack about 4 inches from source of heat and preheat broiler. In a medium bowl, working as quickly and gently as possible, mix ground round with crushed potato chips, salt, and pepper. Lightly form into 4 burgers about 1 inch thick.

2. Brush onion slices with olive oil and place on an oiled grill set 4 to 6 inches from coals or place in broiler. Cook, turning once, until lightly browned and tender, 5 to 7 minutes. As onions cook, transfer to a plate and cover with foil to keep warm.

3. Place burgers on grill or broiler and cook, turning once, until outside is well browned but inside is still pink and juicy, about 8 to 12 minutes for rare to medium-rare, or longer if desired.

4. Meanwhile, split open buns and toast on sides of grill or under broiler until warm and lightly browned, about 1 minute. Place cooked burgers in buns and top with grilled onions. Let everyone choose their own fixings.

337 FLORENTINE BEEF PATTIES

Prep: 10 minutes   Cook: 8 to 12 minutes   Serves: 4

  1 pound ground round
     (85% lean)
  1 small onion, finely chopped
  1 garlic clove, minced
  1 (10-ounce) package frozen
     chopped spinach, thawed
     and squeezed dry
  ¼ cup Italian-seasoned dried
     bread crumbs

  ¼ cup grated Parmesan cheese
  3 tablespoons pine nuts
  1 egg
1¼ teaspoons salt
  1 teaspoon basil
  ¼ teaspoon pepper
  1 tablespoon olive oil
  1 (14-ounce) jar marinara
     sauce

1. In a medium bowl, working as quickly and gently as possible, mix ground round, onion, garlic, spinach, bread crumbs, cheese, pine nuts, egg, salt, basil, and pepper. Lightly form into 4 patties about 1 inch thick.

2. In a large skillet, heat olive oil. Add patties and cook over medium-high heat, turning once, until browned outside but still juicy and pink inside, 8 to 12 minutes for rare to medium-rare, or longer if desired. Transfer to a plate and cover with foil to keep warm.

3. Pour off any fat from skillet. Add marinara sauce and cook, scraping up browned bits from bottom of pan, until heated through. Pour hot marinara sauce over patties and serve.

---

338 BEEF BURGERS WITH SMOTHERED ONIONS

Prep: 15 minutes   Chill: 30 minutes   Cook: 40 minutes   Serves: 4

1 large russet potato (about 8 ounces), peeled and cut into 1-inch chunks	1¼ teaspoons salt
	⅜ teaspoon pepper
	3 tablespoons butter
1 pound ground sirloin (90% lean)	½ teaspoon sugar
	1 egg
4 large onions, sliced, plus 1 small onion, finely chopped	½ cup flour
	2 tablespoons vegetable oil
2 tablespoons chopped parsley	

1. In a medium saucepan of boiling salted water, cook potato until tender, about 15 minutes. Drain and mash until smooth.

2. In a medium bowl, combine ground sirloin, mashed potato, chopped onion, parsley, 1 teaspoon salt, and ¼ teaspoon pepper. Mix well. Cover and place in freezer until well chilled, about 30 minutes.

3. Meanwhile, in a large skillet or flameproof casserole, melt 2 tablespoons butter. Add sliced onions and sugar. Cover and cook over medium heat, stirring occasionally, until onions are soft, about 6 minutes. Uncover and cook, stirring often, until onions are golden brown, about 6 minutes longer. Transfer to a plate and set aside.

4. Form chilled meat mixture into 4 burgers about 1 inch thick. In a small bowl, beat egg well. Place flour on a plate. Dip each burger in egg, then dredge in flour, shaking off excess.

5. In a large skillet, melt remaining 1 tablespoon butter in oil over medium-high heat. Add burgers and cook, turning once, until browned on both sides and cooked to medium doneness, about 10 minutes. (Adjust heat to prevent crust from burning.) Transfer burgers to a warm serving platter and cover with foil to keep warm.

6. Return onions to skillet, increase heat to high, and cook, stirring, until reheated, about 2 minutes. Cover burgers with browned onions and serve.

339 STUFFED SURPRISE BURGERS

Prep: 15 minutes   Cook: 14 minutes   Serves: 6

2 eggs
2 pounds ground round (85% lean)
2 tablespoons Worcestershire sauce
1 teaspoon salt
½ teaspoon pepper
2 tablespoons prepared mustard
1 large tomato, cut into 6 slices

1 small red onion, cut into thin slices
6 thin slices of Cheddar cheese
2 tablespoons hamburger relish
4 hamburger buns
Optional: Ketchup, mayonnaise, lettuce leaves

1. Prepare a hot fire in a grill. In a large bowl, beat eggs with a fork. Working as quickly and gently as possible, add ground round, Worcestershire sauce, salt, and pepper and mix well. Form into 8 patties about ½ inch thick. Spread mustard over 4 patties, then layer on tomato, onion, and Cheddar cheese slices, trimmed to fit, if necessary. Spread relish over cheese. Place remaining patties on filled patties and pinch edges together to enclose filling and create 4 stuffed burgers.

2. Place patties on an oiled grill set 4 to 6 inches from coals. Grill, turning once, until well browned outside but still pink and juicy inside, about 14 minutes for medium, or shorter or longer if desired. (They should be cooked long enough to melt cheese. The stuffing will keep burgers flavorful and juicy.)

3. Meanwhile, open buns and toast on sides of grill until warm and lightly browned. Place cooked burgers in buns and let everyone choose their own fixings.

340 BROILED ORANGY BEEF BURGERS

Prep: 10 minutes   Cook: 8 to 12 minutes   Serves: 4

If you like sweet-and-sour flavor, here's the broiled burger for you.

½ cup orange marmalade
1 tablespoon soy sauce
1 tablespoon rice vinegar
½ teaspoon ground ginger
1⅓ pounds ground round (85% lean)
½ cup water chestnuts, finely chopped

¼ cup finely chopped green bell pepper
Grated zest of 1 medium orange
1 teaspoon salt
¼ teaspoon pepper

1. In a small nonreactive saucepan, combine marmalade, soy sauce, rice vinegar, and ginger. Bring to a simmer over low heat, stirring constantly. Set orange glaze aside.

2. Position a broiler rack about 4 inches from source of heat and preheat broiler. In a medium bowl, working as quickly and gently as possible, mix ground round with water chestnuts, bell pepper, orange zest, salt, and pepper. Lightly form into 4 patties about 1 inch thick.

3. Broil burgers, turning once, until browned, about 4 minutes. Brush with glaze and broil 2 minutes. Turn, brush with glaze, and cook 2 minutes for rare, or longer if desired.

---

341   SCANDINAVIAN BEEF PATTIES WITH PICKLED BEETS AND CAPERS

Prep: 30 minutes   Chill: 1 hour   Cook: 30 minutes   Serves: 4

1 medium russet potato (about 6 ounces)	1 pound ground sirloin (90% lean)
2 tablespoons heavy cream	1 egg yolk
1¼ teaspoons salt	½ cup finely chopped pickled beets
¼ teaspoon pepper	
Pinch of ground cloves	1 tablespoon capers
2 tablespoons butter	½ cup flour
1 small onion, minced	1 tablespoon vegetable oil

1. In a large saucepan of boiling salted water, cook potato until tender when pierced with tip of a sharp knife, about 20 minutes. Drain, peel, and mash with heavy cream, salt, pepper, and cloves.

2. In a small skillet, melt 1 tablespoon butter over medium heat. Add onion and cook, stirring often, until softened, about 3 minutes. Stir into mashed potato.

3. Add ground sirloin and egg yolk to potato and mix well. Stir in pickled beets and capers. Form mixture into 4 patties about 1 inch thick. Transfer patties to a wax paper–lined baking sheet, cover with plastic wrap, and refrigerate 1 hour.

4. Dredge patties in flour; shake off excess. In a large skillet, melt remaining 1 tablespoon butter in oil over medium-high heat. Add patties and cook until bottoms are browned, about 4 minutes. Turn and cook until desired doneness, about 5 minutes for medium.

342   CHICKEN TERIYAKI BURGERS

Prep: 5 minutes   Cook: 8 to 12 minutes   Serves: 4

1¼ pounds ground chicken
¼ cup thick teriyaki baste and glaze
1 scallion, minced
¼ teaspoon salt
¼ teaspoon ground pepper
4 soft onion rolls or sesame hamburger buns

Optional: Pickled ginger slices, thin cucumber slices, hot Chinese mustard, onion slices, watercress

1. Prepare a medium-hot fire or preheat broiler. In a medium bowl, mix ground chicken with 1 tablespoon teriyaki glaze, minced scallion, salt, and pepper. Working as quickly and gently as possible, lightly form into four 4-inch round patties about ½ inch thick.

2. Place chicken burgers on an oiled rack and grill, or broil about 6 inches from heat, turning once and brushing occasionally with remaining 3 tablespoons teriyaki glaze, until just cooked through but still juicy, 8 to 10 minutes if grilled, 6 to 8 minutes if broiled.

3. Toast rolls on sides of grill or under broiler, 1 to 2 minutes. Place cooked burgers in rolls and let everyone choose their own fillings.

343   CHICKEN POJARSKI WITH HORSERADISH CREAM

*Prep: 15 minutes   Chill: 15 minutes   Stand: 20 to 30 minutes
Cook: 10 minutes   Serves: 6*

3 cups fresh bread crumbs
½ cup heavy cream
1 teaspoon salt
¼ teaspoon pepper
¼ teaspoon grated nutmeg
1 pound ground chicken
1 egg
½ cup sour cream

1 scallion, chopped
2 tablespoons prepared horseradish
1½ teaspoons lemon juice
2 tablespoons butter
2 tablespoons vegetable oil
Lemon wedges

1. In a medium bowl, mix 1 cup bread crumbs, cream, salt, pepper, and nutmeg. Add ground chicken and mix well. With wet hands, form into 6 ovals about 1 inch thick.

2. In a medium bowl, beat egg with 1 tablespoon water. Place remaining 2 cups bread crumbs on a plate. Dip chicken "cutlets" into egg mixture, then coat with bread crumbs. Refrigerate cutlets 15 minutes to set coating.

3. Make horseradish cream: In a small bowl, combine sour cream, scallion, horseradish, and lemon juice. Let stand at room temperature 20 to 30 minutes to allow flavors to blend.

4. In a 12-inch skillet, melt butter in oil over medium heat. Add cutlets and cook, turning once, until golden brown on both sides and cooked medium well-done, about 5 minutes per side. (Adjust heat as necessary to avoid burning crust.) Drain cutlets on paper towels. Serve with horseradish cream and lemon wedges

---

344 CHICKEN BURGERS WITH CUCUMBER-PEANUT RELISH

Prep: 10 minutes   Chill: 2 hours   Cook: 12 to 15 minutes   Serves: 4

1 tablespoon plus
   2 teaspoons Asian fish
   sauce (see Note)
1 tablespoon rice vinegar
1 tablespoon vegetable oil
¾ teaspoon sugar
½ teaspoon crushed hot red
   pepper
2 Kirby cucumbers, thinly
   sliced (about ½ pound)
1 shallot, chopped, or
   1 tablespoon chopped
   red onion

1¼ pounds ground chicken
   Grated zest of 1 small lemon
1 garlic clove, minced
¼ teaspoon salt
4 hamburger buns, split
2 tablespoons chopped
   cilantro
2 tablespoons chopped
   unsalted roasted
   peanuts

1. In a small bowl, whisk together 2 teaspoons fish sauce, rice vinegar, oil, sugar, and ¼ teaspoon hot pepper. Add cucumbers and shallot to toss to combine. Cover relish and refrigerate at least 2 and up to 8 hours.

2. Prepare a hot fire in a grill. In a medium bowl, mix together ground chicken, remaining 1 tablespoon fish sauce and ¼ teaspoon hot pepper, lemon zest, garlic, and salt. With wet hands, form into 4 patties about 3½ inches in diameter.

3. Place chicken burgers in center of fire on an oiled grill set 4 to 6 inches from coals. Grill, turning once, until browned on both sides, about 2 to 3 minutes per side. Transfer to outer edges of grill and cook, turning once again, until burgers are cooked through with no trace of pink in center, about 8 to 10 minutes.

4. Warm hamburger buns on side of grill until hot and lightly browned. Stir cilantro and peanuts into cucumber mixture. Serve each burger in a bun, topped with cucumber-peanut relish.

    NOTE: *Fish sauce is available in Asian markets and in many supermarkets. It is called* nuoc mam *in Vietnam,* nam pla *in Thailand, and* pastis *in Indonesia. If unavailable, substitute a mixture of equal parts soy sauce, Worcestershire sauce, and water.*

345   CHICKEN FAJITA BURGERS

Prep: 20 minutes   Cook: 20 minutes   Serves: 4

1 tablespoon olive oil	1 tablespoon lime juice
1 small red onion, chopped	1 teaspoon chili powder
1 small red bell pepper, chopped	1 teaspoon salt
1 garlic clove, minced	4 flour tortillas
1¼ pounds ground chicken	1 cup tomato salsa
	Guacamole (recipe follows)

1. Prepare a hot fire in a grill. In a large skillet, heat oil. Add onion and red pepper and cook over medium heat, stirring often, until vegetables are lightly browned, about 4 minutes. Add garlic and cook 1 minute. Remove from heat and let cool slightly.

2. In a medium bowl, combine cooked vegetables, ground chicken, lime juice, chili powder, and salt. Using wet hands, form into 4 ovals about 2 inches wide and 4½ inches long.

3. Place patties in center of an oiled grill set 4 to 6 inches from coals. Cook, turning once, until browned, about 4 minutes. Transfer burgers to outside edge of grill and continue grilling, turning once, until burgers are cooked through and meat springs back when pressed lightly with a finger, 8 to 10 minutes.

4. Meanwhile, wrap tortillas in aluminum foil and place on sides of grill to heat through.

5. Place warm tortillas and bowls of salsa and guacamole on table. Let each guest place a burger on a tortilla, top with salsa and guacamole, roll up, and enjoy.

GUACAMOLE
Makes about 1½ cups

2 ripe avocados, chopped	⅛ teaspoon cayenne
1 medium ripe tomato, chopped	1 garlic clove, minced
2 tablespoons chopped onion	1 tablespoon lime juice
	1 teaspoon salt

In a small bowl, using a fork, mash together all ingredients until chunky. If not using immediately, press plastic wrap directly on surface and refrigerate up to 1 day.

346 TURKEY BURGERS WITH ONION CONFIT
Prep: 15 minutes   Cook: 30 minutes   Serves: 4

Balsamic vinegar, with its complex, mellow flavor, is now available in many supermarkets and specialty food stores. Don't substitute other vinegars here; they're too tart.

2 tablespoons butter	1 egg
2 medium onions, sliced	¼ teaspoon salt
¼ cup balsamic vinegar	¼ teaspoon pepper
1 teaspoon sugar	1 pound ground turkey
¾ cup grated Parmesan cheese	1 tablespoon olive oil
¼ cup fresh bread crumbs	

1. In a medium nonreactive saucepan, melt butter over medium heat. Add onions and cook, partially covered, stirring often, until onions are golden brown, 8 to 10 minutes. Add balsamic vinegar and sugar and cook, uncovered, stirring occasionally, until liquid is evaporated to a glaze, 4 to 5 minutes. Remove from heat and cover onion confit to keep warm.

2. In a medium bowl, mix together Parmesan cheese, bread crumbs, egg, salt, and pepper until blended. Add ground turkey and mix well. With wet hands, form into 4 patties about 1 inch thick.

3. In a large skillet, heat olive oil over medium-high heat. Add patties and cook, turning once, until outsides are browned, about 1 minute on each side. Reduce heat to medium and cook, turning once, until well done, about 5 minutes longer per side. Transfer to paper towels to drain briefly. Serve patties topped with warm onion confit.

347 TURKEY BURGERS DIJON
Prep: 10 minutes   Cook: 14 to 16 minutes   Serves: 4

1½ pounds ground turkey	¼ teaspoon pepper
1 scallion, chopped	4 French or Italian rolls
2 tablespoons Dijon mustard	Optional: Mayonnaise,
1 teaspoon tarragon	sliced tomatoes, shredded
1 teaspoon salt	romaine lettuce

1. Prepare a hot fire in a grill. In a medium bowl, mix ground turkey with scallion, mustard, tarragon, salt, and pepper. Using wet hands, lightly form into 4 rectangular patties about 1 inch thick, shaped to fit into French rolls.

2. Place patties in center of an oiled grill set 4 to 6 inches from coals. Cook, turning once, until browned, about 4 minutes. Transfer burgers to sides of grill and continue to cook, turning once, until burgers are cooked through and meat springs back when pressed lightly with a finger, 10 to 12 minutes.

3. Meanwhile, split open rolls and toast on sides of grill until warm and lightly browned. Place cooked burgers in rolls and let everyone choose their own fixings.

348 STOVETOP BBQ TURKEY BURGERS
Prep: 15 minutes   Cook: 20 minutes   Serves: 4

1¼ pounds ground turkey
¾ cup plus 2 tablespoons chili
   sauce
1 medium onion, chopped
1 teaspoon garlic salt
¼ teaspoon pepper

2 tablespoons vegetable oil
1 tablespoon brown sugar
1 tablespoon prepared
   mustard
1 tablespoon lemon juice
2 teaspoons Worcestershire
   sauce

1. In a medium bowl, combine ground turkey, 2 tablespoons chili sauce, half of chopped onion, garlic salt, and pepper. Using wet hands, form into 4 burgers about 1 inch thick.

2. In a large skillet, heat oil. Add turkey burgers and cook over medium heat, until bottoms are just browned, about 2 minutes. Turn and sprinkle remaining chopped onion around patties. Cook, stirring onions occasionally, until second side of patties is just browned and onions are softened, about 2 minutes.

3. Add remaining ¾ cup chili sauce, brown sugar, mustard, lemon juice, Worcestershire sauce, and 2 tablespoons water. Bring to a simmer, reduce heat to low, cover, and cook until sauce is thickened and burgers are cooked through with no trace of pink in center (meat should spring back when lightly pressed with a finger), about 15 minutes.

349 PECAN-COATED TURKEY BURGERS WITH SOUR CREAM-TARRAGON SAUCE
Prep: 10 minutes   Cook: 20 minutes   Serves: 4

1⅓ pounds ground turkey
2 tablespoons Dijon mustard
1 teaspoon salt
¼ teaspoon pepper
1½ cups finely chopped pecans
   (6 ounces)

2 tablespoons vegetable oil
⅓ cup sour cream
1 scallion, chopped
½ teaspoon tarragon

1. Preheat oven to 350°. In a medium bowl, combine ground turkey, 1 tablespoon mustard, salt, and pepper. Using wet hands, form into 4 burgers about 1 inch thick.

2. Place chopped pecans on a plate. Place turkey burgers on pecans and turn to coat both sides, patting pecans lightly to adhere.

3. In a large skillet, heat oil. Add burgers and cook over medium-high heat, turning once, until pecan crust is lightly browned, about 2 minutes on each side. Transfer burgers to a baking sheet.

4. Bake burgers until cooked through with no trace of pink in center, about 15 minutes.

5. Meanwhile, in a small bowl, combine sour cream, remaining 1 tablespoon mustard, scallion, and tarragon. Serve burgers with a dollop of sour cream sauce.

---

350 SALSA TURKEY CHEESEBURGERS
Prep: 10 minutes   Cook: 8 to 12 minutes   Serves: 4

1⅓ pounds ground turkey
1 cup tomato salsa, well drained
1 tablespoon chopped cilantro
½ teaspoon salt
¾ cup shredded Cheddar cheese

4 hamburger buns
Optional: Mayonnaise, shredded lettuce, avocado slices, red onion slices, additional salsa

1. Prepare a hot fire in a grill. In a medium bowl, combine ground turkey, salsa, cilantro, and salt. Using wet hands, form into 4 patties about 1 inch thick.

2. Place patties in center of an oiled grill set 4 to 6 inches from coals. Grill, turning once, until browned on both sides, about 4 minutes. Transfer burgers to outside edge of grill and continue to grill until burgers are cooked through and meat springs back when pressed lightly with a finger, 10 to 12 minutes. Just before removing burgers from grill, sprinkle cheese over tops of burgers, cover grill, and cook until cheese melts, about 1 minute. (Never cook turkey burgers less than mediumwell- done.)

3. Meanwhile, open buns and toast on sides of grill until warm and lightly browned. Place cooked burgers in buns and let everyone choose their own fixings.

---

351 TURKEY BURGERS PARMESAN
Prep: 10 minutes   Cook: 12 minutes   Serves: 4

1¼ pounds ground turkey
¼ cup olive oil
1 teaspoon salt
¼ teaspoon pepper

1 egg
⅓ cup fresh bread crumbs
⅓ cup grated Parmesan cheese
1 lemon, quartered

1. In a medium bowl, combine ground turkey, 1 tablespoon olive oil, salt, and pepper. Using wet hands, form into 4 patties about 1 inch thick.

2. In a small bowl, beat egg well. In a plate, combine bread crumbs and Parmesan cheese. Dip patties in egg, then dredge in Parmesan crumbs, patting gently to adhere.

3. In a large skillet, heat remaining 3 tablespoons olive oil. Add patties and cook over medium-high heat, turning once, until browned outside and cooked through with no trace of pink in center, about 12 minutes. Adjust heat, if necessary, to avoid burning. Transfer to paper towels to drain briefly, then serve with lemon wedges.

352 PLYMOUTH ROCK BURGERS
Prep: 15 minutes   Cook: 20 minutes   Serves: 6

1 tablespoon butter
1 small onion, finely chopped
1 small celery rib, finely chopped
⅓ cup reduced-sodium chicken broth
¾ cup herb-seasoned stuffing mix
¾ teaspoon salt

½ teaspoon poultry seasoning
¼ teaspoon pepper
1½ pounds ground turkey
4 onion rolls
Optional: Cranberry sauce, mayonnaise, ketchup, mustard, tomato slices, lettuce leaves

1. In a small skillet, heat butter. Add onion and celery and cook over medium heat, stirring often, until softened, about 4 minutes. Add broth and bring to a boil. Remove from heat and stir in stuffing, salt, poultry seasoning, and pepper; let cool completely.

2. Prepare a hot fire in a grill. In a large bowl, combine ground turkey with stuffing mixture. Form into 6 burgers about 1 inch thick.

3. Place burgers on center of an oiled grill set 4 to 6 inches above coals. Grill, turning once, until lightly browned on both sides, about 4 minutes. Move patties to cooler outer edges of grill. Continue grilling, turning once, until burgers are cooked through with no trace of pink in center, about 12 minutes.

4. Meanwhile, split onion rolls and toast on sides of grill until warm and lightly browned, 1 to 2 minutes. Place cooked burgers in rolls and let everyone choose their own fixings.

353 FRENCH WHITE SAUSAGE
Prep: 15 minutes   Chill: 30 minutes   Cook: 20 minutes   Serves: 6

1 tablespoon butter
1 small onion, minced
½ cup heavy cream
3 cups fresh bread crumbs
4 eggs
2 teaspoons salt
½ teaspoon white pepper
¼ teaspoon ground allspice

¼ teaspoon ground coriander
¼ teaspoon ground ginger
⅛ teaspoon grated nutmeg
1 pound ground chicken
1 pound ground pork
1 cup flour
3 tablespoons vegetable oil

1. In a medium skillet, melt butter. Add onion and cook over medium heat, stirring often, until just softened, about 2 minutes. Do not brown onion.

2. Add cream and 1 cup bread crumbs to skillet. Bring to a boil and cook, stirring constantly, until thickened into a paste, about 2 minutes. Transfer to a medium bowl and let cool slightly.

3. Add 1 egg, salt, white pepper, allspice, coriander, ginger, and nutmeg. Mix to blend. Add ground chicken and ground pork and mix well. Form into 6 patties about 1 inch thick.

4. Place flour on a plate. In a medium bowl, beat remaining 3 eggs well. Place remaining 2 cups bread crumbs on a plate. Dredge each patty in flour, shaking off excess, dip into eggs, and coat with bread crumbs, patting crumbs gently to adhere. Place patties on a wax paper–lined baking sheet and refrigerate 30 minutes.

5. In a large skillet, heat oil. Add patties and cook over medium heat, turning once, until browned outside and meat springs back when pressed in center, about 15 minutes. (Be sure to cook meat well done, and adjust heat to prevent burning.)

---

354 HERO VEAL BURGERS WITH SWEET PEPPERS

Prep: 20 minutes   Cook: 5 minutes   Serves: 4

The fire will burn down to medium-hot after roasting the peppers, so grill the hero burgers on a covered grill so you can retain the remaining heat.

3 large bell peppers, preferably 2 red, 1 yellow	1 pound ground veal
1 garlic clove, minced	¾ pound sweet Italian sausage, casings removed, sausage crumbled
2 tablespoons olive oil	
1 tablespoon red wine vinegar	4 individual Italian hero rolls
¾ teaspoon salt	
¼ teaspoon crushed hot red pepper	

1. Prepare a hot fire in a grill or preheat a broiler with broiler rack adjusted about 6 inches from source of heat. Grill or broil whole peppers, turning frequently, until skin is black all over, about 10 minutes. Remove from grill and enclose in a bag. Set aside about 5 minutes, until cool enough to handle. Remove peppers from bag and peel off blackened skin under cold running water. Discard stems and seeds. Slice peppers into ½-inch-wide strips.

2. In a medium bowl, toss pepper strips, garlic, olive oil, vinegar, ¼ teaspoon salt, and ⅛ teaspoon hot pepper. Set aside.

3. In another medium bowl, combine ground veal, Italian sausage, and remaining ½ teaspoon salt and ⅛ teaspoon hot pepper. Divide into 4 even parts and shape into ovals about 1 inch thick to fit rolls.

4. Place burgers on an oiled grill or preheated broiler. Cover and grill, or broil, turning once, until outside is browned and meat springs back when pressed in center, about 15 minutes. Be sure to cook burgers until well done but still juicy.

5. Meanwhile, split open rolls and toast on sides of grill until warm and lightly browned. Place cooked burgers on rolls and top with roasted pepper slices.

355 DANISH PAN-FRIED BURGERS

Prep: 5 minutes   Chill: 20 minutes   Cook: 10 minutes   Serves: 4

Club soda is the secret ingredient here. It gives these burgers a particularly tender texture.

½ pound ground veal	¾ teaspoon salt
½ pound ground pork	¼ teaspoon pepper
1 medium onion, finely chopped	½ cup club soda
	1 tablespoon butter
1 egg	1 tablespoon vegetable oil
¼ cup flour	

1. In a large bowl, mix ground veal, ground pork, onion, egg, flour, salt, and pepper until well blended. Gradually beat in club soda. Cover and freeze until well chilled and easier to handle, 20 to 30 minutes. Form mixture into 4 patties about 1 inch thick.

2. In a large skillet, melt butter in oil over medium-high heat. Add patties and cook, turning once, about 10 minutes for medium well-done; meat should be juicy but with no trace of pink. (Do not undercook. If you insist on rare meat, substitute ground beef for pork.)

356 NUTTY BLUE CHEESE BURGERS

Prep: 10 minutes   Cook: 14 minutes   Serves: 4

1⅓ pounds ground veal	2 medium apples, cored and cut into ½-inch rings
⅓ cup crumbled blue cheese	
⅓ cup chopped walnuts	1 tablespoon butter, melted
2 tablespoons heavy cream	4 hamburger buns, preferably whole wheat
¾ teaspoon salt	
¼ teaspoon pepper	⅓ cup honey-flavored mustard

1. In a medium bowl, working as quickly and gently as possible, mix ground veal with blue cheese, walnuts, cream, salt, and pepper. With wet hands, form into 4 patties about 1 inch thick.

2. Place patties on an oiled grill set 4 to 6 inches from coals. Grill, turning once, until outside is lightly charred but inside is juicy, about 14 minutes for medium, or longer if desired. During last 4 minutes of cooking, brush apples with butter and cook, turning once, until lightly browned.

3. Meanwhile, open buns and place on sides of grill until warm and lightly browned. Spread buns with mustard. Place cooked burgers in buns. Top each burger with apple slices and serve at once.

357 CALICO VEAL BURGERS
Prep: 10 minutes   Cook: 12 to 15 minutes   Serves: 4

1 scallion, chopped
1 small red bell pepper, finely chopped
1 garlic clove, minced
2 teaspoons tomato paste
½ teaspoon Italian seasoning
¼ teaspoon salt
¼ teaspoon pepper
1⅓ pounds ground veal
Lemon wedges

1. Position a lightly oiled broiler rack 6 inches from source of heat and preheat broiler. In a medium bowl, combine scallion, bell pepper, garlic, tomato paste, Italian seasoning, salt, and pepper. Working as quickly and gently as possible, add ground veal and mix until blended. Lightly form into 4 patties about 1 inch thick.

2. Broil veal burgers, turning once, until well browned outside but still juicy inside, about 12 minutes for medium well-done, or longer if desired. Serve with lemon wedges to squeeze over burgers.

358 NORMANDY PATTIES WITH APPLE AND CREAM
Prep: 15 minutes   Cook: 15 minutes   Serves: 4

1 medium Granny Smith apple
½ pound ground pork
½ pound ground veal
1 tablespoon applejack or brandy
¾ teaspoon salt
¼ teaspoon ground ginger
¼ teaspoon ground allspice
¼ teaspoon pepper
⅛ teaspoon grated nutmeg
2 tablespoons butter
1 tablespoon vegetable oil
¼ cup beef broth
¾ cup heavy cream

1. Peel, quarter, and core apple, then chop finely. In a medium bowl, combine ground pork, ground veal, ¾ cup chopped apple, applejack, salt, ginger, allspice, pepper, and nutmeg. (Reserve remaining apple for sauce.) Mix to blend well. Form into 4 patties about 1 inch thick.

2. In a large skillet, melt 1 tablespoon butter in oil over medium-high heat. Add patties and cook, turning once, until browned outside and cooked through with no trace of pink in center, about 12 minutes. Transfer patties to a serving platter and cover with foil to keep warm.

3. Pour off fat from skillet. Add remaining 1 tablespoon butter and melt. Add remaining chopped apple and cook over medium-high heat, stirring often, until apple is lightly browned, about 2 minutes. Add beef broth and cream, bring to a boil, and cook until evaporated to about ½ cup, 2 to 3 minutes. Season sauce with additional salt and pepper to taste and pour over patties.

359   PORK BURGERS, CHARCUTERIE STYLE
Prep: 10 minutes   Cook: 15 minutes   Serves: 4

1½ pounds lean ground pork
¼ cup chopped parsley
1 teaspoon salt
½ teaspoon tarragon
¼ teaspoon pepper
⅓ cup flour
3 tablespoons cold butter
1 tablespoon vegetable oil

1 shallot, minced, or
    1 tablespoon minced red
    onion
1 cup beef broth
2 tablespoons chopped sour
    pickles, preferably
    cornichons
2 tablespoons capers

1. In a medium bowl, combine ground pork, 2 tablespoons parsley, salt, tarragon, and pepper. Form into 4 patties about 1 inch thick. Dredge patties in flour.

2. In a large skillet, melt 1 tablespoon butter in oil over medium-high heat. Add patties and cook, turning once, until well done but still juicy inside, about 5 minutes per side. (Adjust heat as necessary to avoid burning.) Transfer patties to paper towels to drain briefly. Place patties on a serving platter and cover with aluminum foil to keep warm.

3. Drain off all but 1 tablespoon fat from skillet. Add shallots and cook until softened, about 30 seconds. Add beef broth, pickles, and capers. Bring to a boil, scraping up browned bits from bottom of pan with a wooden spoon. Boil until sauce is evaporated by half, 1 to 2 minutes. Remove from heat and whisk in remaining cold butter, 1 tablespoon at a time. Whisk in remaining parsley. Pour sauce over patties and serve.

360   SPANISH PORK PATTIES WITH SHERRY SAUCE
Prep: 10 minutes   Cook: 15 minutes   Serves: 4

1⅓ pounds ground pork
1 tablespoon minced onion
1 garlic clove, minced
1 jalapeño pepper, seeded and
    minced, or ⅛ teaspoon
    cayenne
1 tablespoon sweet vermouth

1 teaspoon chili powder
1 teaspoon paprika
¾ teaspoon salt
¼ teaspoon pepper
1½ tablespoons olive oil
¾ cup dry sherry

1. In a medium bowl, combine ground pork, onion, garlic, jalapeño, vermouth, chili powder, paprika, salt, and pepper. Form into 4 patties about 1 inch thick.

2. In a large skillet, heat olive oil. Add patties and cook over medium-high heat, turning once, until browned outside and cooked through with no trace of pink in center, about 12 minutes. Transfer patties to paper towels to drain. Drain off all fat from skillet.

3. Pour sherry into skillet and bring to a boil, scraping up browned bits from bottom of pan with a wooden spoon. Cook until evaporated to about ⅓ cup, 2 to 3 minutes. Transfer patties to a serving platter, pour on sherry sauce, and serve.

---

361 PORK PLUM BURGERS WITH CHINESE CABBAGE SLAW

Prep: 20 minutes   Cook: 15 minutes   Chill: 1 hour   Serves: 4

1⅓ pounds ground pork	1 teaspoon minced fresh ginger
1 scallion, chopped	½ teaspoon salt
1 garlic clove, minced	¼ teaspoon pepper
2 tablespoons Chinese plum sauce, chopped (see Note)	4 hamburger buns Chinese Cabbage Slaw (recipe follows)
1 tablespoon soy sauce	

1. Prepare a hot fire in a grill. In a medium bowl, working as quickly and gently as possible, mix ground pork, scallion, garlic, plum sauce, soy sauce, ginger, salt, and pepper. Lightly form into 4 patties about 1 inch thick.

2. Place patties on an oiled grill set 4 to 6 inches from coals. Grill, turning once, until outside is well browned, burger is cooked through with no trace of pink in center, and meat springs back when pressed lightly with a finger, 12 to 15 minutes.

3. Meanwhile, open buns and toast on sides of grill until warm and lightly browned. Place cooked burgers in buns and pass Chinese Cabbage Slaw to top burgers on the side.

NOTE: *Chinese plum sauce is available in Chinese markets and in the Asian foods section of many supermarkets.*

CHINESE CABBAGE SLAW
Makes about 2 cups

2 tablespoons rice vinegar	½ medium head of Chinese (napa) cabbage (about 1 pound), shredded
½ teaspoon salt	
¼ teaspoon sugar	2 scallions, minced
¼ teaspoon pepper	1 medium carrot, grated
¼ cup vegetable oil	
1 tablespoon Asian sesame oil	

In a medium bowl, whisk together vinegar, salt, sugar, and pepper. Gradually whisk in vegetable oil and sesame oil. Add Chinese cabbage, scallions, and carrot and toss well. Cover with plastic wrap and refrigerate at least 1 hour, or overnight.

362 CAPONATA LAMB BURGERS
Prep: 5 minutes   Cook: 8 to 10 minutes   Serves: 4

1 (7½-ounce) can eggplant
   appetizer (caponata)
2 tablespoons Italian-
   seasoned dried bread
   crumbs
½ teaspoon salt
¼ teaspoon pepper

1 pound lean ground lamb
4 crusty French or Italian rolls
   Optional: Store-bought
   pesto, Dijon mustard,
   ketchup, mayonnaise,
   sliced tomatoes, shredded
   romaine lettuce

1. Prepare a hot fire in a grill or preheat broiler. In a medium bowl, combine caponata, bread crumbs, salt, and pepper. Add ground lamb and mix, working as quickly and gently as possible. Divide into quarters and lightly form into four 4-inch round patties, about ¾ inch thick.

2. Place burgers on an oiled rack and grill, or broil 4 inches from heat, turning once, until outside is well browned but inside is still pink and juicy, about 8 to 12 minutes if grilled 5 to 6 minutes if broiled, for rare to medium-rare, or longer if desired.

3. Meanwhile, split open rolls and toast on sides of grill or under broiler until warm and lightly browned, 1 to 2 minutes. Place cooked burgers in rolls and let everyone choose their own fillings.

363 BROILED KOFTAS
Prep: 10 minutes   Cook: 8 to 12 minutes   Serves: 4

1 small onion, minced
2 garlic cloves, minced
2 teaspoons minced fresh
   ginger
2 tablespoons tomato paste
1 tablespoon lemon juice
1 teaspoon salt
1 teaspoon curry powder

½ teaspoon ground cumin
½ teaspoon ground coriander
¼ teaspoon cayenne
1½ pounds ground round
   (85% lean) or lean
   ground lamb
¼ cup plain low-fat yogurt

1. Position a broiler rack 6 inches from source of heat and preheat broiler. In a medium bowl, combine onion, garlic, ginger, tomato paste, lemon juice, salt, curry powder, cumin, coriander, and cayenne. Working as quickly and gently as possible, add ground round and mix. Lightly form into 4 patties about 1 inch thick.

2. Broil koftas, turning once, until well browned outside but still pink and juicy inside, about 8 minutes for rare, or longer if desired. Top each kofte with a dollop of yogurt.

364 BACKYARD GYROS
Prep: 15 minutes   Chill: 2 hours   Cook: 8 to 12 minutes   Serves: 4

A gyro is a Greek pita sandwich filled with meat sliced from a huge meatloaf that turns on a spit in front of a grill. These burgers, stuffed with Mediterranean vegetable salad and drizzled with yogurt, are inspired by this popular street food.

¾ pound lean ground lamb
½ pound ground round
  (85% lean)
1 cup fresh bread crumbs
1 medium onion, minced,
  plus 1 small onion, sliced
1 garlic clove, crushed
  through a press
½ teaspoon ground allspice
½ teaspoon ground coriander
  seed
½ teaspoon ground cumin
1¼ teaspoons salt

⅜ teaspoon pepper
2 tablespoons red wine
  vinegar
½ teaspoon oregano
⅓ cup olive oil
4 plum tomatoes, chopped
1 small Kirby cucumber,
  seeded and chopped
½ head romaine lettuce,
  shredded
1 cup plain low-fat yogurt
4 pita breads

1. In a large bowl, combine ground lamb, ground round, bread crumbs, minced onion, garlic, allspice, coriander, cumin, 1 teaspoon salt, and ¼ teaspoon pepper. Knead with your hands until well mixed. Form into 4 patties about 1 inch thick. Cover and refrigerate at least 2 hours and up to 8 hours.

2. In a medium bowl, whisk together vinegar, oregano, and remaining ¼ teaspoon salt and ⅛ teaspoon pepper. Gradually whisk in olive oil until well blended. Add tomatoes and cucumber; toss to coat. Cover and refrigerate salad at least 2 hours and up to 8 hours. Place lettuce and yogurt in bowls.

3. Prepare a hot fire in a grill. Place patties on an oiled rack and grill, turning once, until outside is well browned but inside is still juicy, about 8 to 12 minutes for rare to medium-rare, or longer if desired.

4. Meanwhile, slit sides of pita breads to form pockets. Warm pita breads on side of grill until heated through and lightly browned. Fill each pita with a burger. Let each guest fill their pita with tomato salad, lettuce, and yogurt as desired.

365 DIANA'S LAMB BURGERS

Prep: 10 minutes   Freeze: 30 minutes   Cook: 10 minutes   Serves: 4

1½ cups fresh bread crumbs	1 teaspoon salt
¾ cup heavy cream	¼ teaspoon paprika
Grated zest of 1 small lemon	⅛ teaspoon grated nutmeg
1 tablespoon chopped parsley	1 pound lean ground lamb
1 teaspoon basil	1 tablespoon vegetable oil

1. In a medium bowl, mix bread crumbs, cream, lemon zest, parsley, basil, salt, paprika, and nutmeg. Add ground lamb and mix until well blended. With wet hands, form into 4 patties about 1 inch thick. Transfer patties to a plate, cover, and freeze 30 minutes to make them easier to handle.

2. In a large skillet, heat oil over medium-high heat. Carefully add patties and cook, turning once, until medium well-done, about 5 minutes per side. (These burgers are best at medium-well done so bread crumbs can cook until firm.)

Index

Acknowledgments

To Diane Kniss, deepest gratitude and admiration for her invaluable help with this project. Special thanks to Perdue Farms, Inc., particularly Chris Whaley and Nancy Plumaker, who generously provided products for recipe testing. The National Livestock Board and the Beef Industry Council supplied helpful printed information. Cuzin's Meat Market and Elk Market kept me well supplied with ground meats and good humor. Most of all, I want to express my appreciation to the many friends across the country who donated recipes from their collections for use in this book.

About the Author

Rick Rodgers, food writer and media personality, is author of *The Turkey Cookbook* (HarperCollins) and *Best-Ever Brownies* (Contemporary).